Studying Language

English in Action

Urszula Clark

First published 2007 by
PALGRAVE MACMILLAN
Houndmills, Basingstoke, Hampshire RG21 6XS and
175 Fifth Avenue, New York, N.Y. 10010
Companies and representatives throughout the world

PALGRAVE MACMILLAN is the global academic imprint of the Palgrave Macmillan division of St. Martin's Press, LLC and of Palgrave Macmillan Ltd. Macmillan® is a registered trademark in the United States, United Kingdom and other countries. Palgrave is a registered trademark in the European Union and other countries.

ISBN-13: 978–1–4039–2207–6   hardback
ISBN-10: 1–4039–2207–1   hardback
ISBN-13: 978–1–4039–2208–3   paperback
ISBN-10: 1–4039–2208–X   paperback

This book is printed on paper suitable for recycling and made from fully managed and sustained forest sources.

A catalogue record for this book is available from the British Library.

Library of Congress Cataloging-in-Publication Data
Clark, Urszula.
     Studying language : English in action / Urszula Clark.
         p. cm. – (Perspectives on the English language)
     Includes bibliographical references and index.
     ISBN-13: 978-1-4039-2207-6 (cloth)
     ISBN-10: 1-4039-2207-1 (cloth)
     ISBN-13: 978-1-4039-2208-3 (paper)
     ISBN-10: 1-4039-2208-X (paper)
         1. English language–Rhetoric. 2. Sociolinguistics. 3. English language–Discourse analysis. 4. English language–Variation. I. Title.

PE1408.C5224 2007
420.72–dc22   2006047164

10   9   8   7   6   5   4   3   2   1
16 15 14 13 12 11 10 09 08 07

Printed and bound in China

Studying Language

PERSPECTIVES ON THE ENGLISH LANGUAGE
Series Editor: Lesley Jeffries

Siobhan Chapman   Thinking About Language: Theories of English
Urszula Clark   Studying Language: English in Action
Lesley Jeffries   Discovering Language: The Structure of Modern English

Perspectives on the English Language Series
Series Standing Order
ISBN 0-333-96146-3 hardback
ISBN 0-333-96147-1 paperback
(*outside North America only*)

You can receive future titles in this series as they are published by placing a stand-ing order. Please contact your bookseller or, in the case of difficulty, write to us at the address below with your name and address, the title of the series and one of the ISBNs quoted above.

Customer Services Department, Macmillan Distribution Ltd,
Houndmills, Basingstoke, Hampshire RG21 6XS, England

Contents

List of Figures and Tables

Figures

Tables

Series Preface

This series has been a twinkle in my eye for a number of years. I am delighted to be able to launch it with the three 'core' books, *Discovering Language*, *Studying Language* and *Thinking about Language*, which together make a broad introduction to language study in general and the study of English in particular. An explanation of why I felt these books were needed is probably useful here, and it will also serve as an explanation of the series as a whole.

The first thing to note is that English language study is growing in Britain and elsewhere, to some extent at the expense of general linguistics. As a linguistics graduate myself I both regret this and also celebrate the numbers of students wanting to study English language. These students may be studying English language as part of a more general degree course, or as a single subject. All such students need tools of analysis. They need to be able to say what is going on in a text, whether that be a literary or non-literary text, spoken or written. *Discovering Language: The Structure of Modern English* aims to provide just these tools at the level required by undergraduates and their teachers.

Whilst there are many other introductory books on the market, and some of them are very good in different ways, none of them does exactly what *I* want as a teacher of English language undergraduates. I want to be able to teach them the tools of analysis and gain expertise in using them separately from the question of where they come from and whether the theory behind them is consistent or eclectic. We have therefore separated out the contextual and theoretical issues, making sure that all the basic tools are in one volume, *Discovering Language: The Structure of Modern English*, while the issues of context are collected together in *Studying Language: English in Action*, and the basic theories of language which inform all of these approaches are discussed in *Thinking about Language: Theories of English*.

The aim of the second volume, then, *Studying Language: English in Action*, is to put into practice some of the analytical techniques learnt in *Discovering Language*, and to add to these skills by learning about the techniques and problems of studying real language data, either spoken or written, from different points of view, whether social, geographical or even historical. The third book, *Thinking about Language: Theories of English*, enables the student to take a step back from the detail of description and research in order to consider what the underlying views of human language may be. It is likely that students will use these three books at different points in their studies, depending on the kind of course they are taking and the uses their tutors wish to make of them.

The first three books in the series have a logical relationship (description, research and theory), but they can be used in flexible and inventive ways by tutors who find that the individual books do not fit exactly into the modules or course structures they are working to. The series will be developed from here with a 'second wave' of higher-level textbooks, each of which will cover the kind of topic that might be introduced in final-year optional modules or on Masters' courses. These books are currently being commissioned, and the list is not final, but we hope to have titles on English Pragmatics, Conversation Analysis, Critical Discourse Analysis, Literary Stylistics and History of English. They will build upon the core texts by emphasising the three strands of these books: descriptive tools, underlying theories and the methodological issues relating to each topic. They will be written by scholars at the cutting edge of research, and will include both an overview and the latest developments in the field concerned.

LESLEY JEFFRIES

Acknowledgements

In the course of writing this book, I have been helped in many ways by colleagues, students, friends and family. I give my thanks to them all, and especially to those mentioned below.

Lesley Jeffries, as the series editor, has given valuable guidance and support at every stage, as has Kate Wallis at Palgrave Macmillan. I would like to thank all those colleagues who commented on preliminary and final drafts. Most of their suggestions have been acted upon and have resulted in a greatly improved book. In particular, I wish to thank Dan McIntyre for his invaluable comments on Chapter 1, Derek Bousfield, Sue Garton, Carol Marley, Debbie Orpin and Gertrude Reershemius on Chapter 2, Sonia Zyngier on Chapter 3 and Christina Scaeffner on Chapter 4. Any defects and errors are of course my own.

URSZULA CLARK

The author and publishers wish to thank the following for permission to use copyright material: Pearson Education Ltd, for the figures on pp. 155 and 160, from Norman Fairclough, *Language and Power*, 2nd edn (2001); London Management on behalf of the author for material from Peter Shaffer, *Equus* (1975). Every effort has been made to trace all the copyright-holders, but if any have been inadvertently overlooked the publishers will be pleased to make the necessary arrangement at the first opportunity.

Introduction

Studying Language: English in Action is one of three companion books in the series *Perspectives on the English Language*. The other two are *Discovering Language: The Structure of Modern English* (Jeffries, 2006) and *Thinking about Language: Theories of English* (Chapman, 2006). Together these three books provide the student of English with the foundation in descriptive apparatus, theoretical background and research skills that are needed at the undergraduate level.

The current volume aims to provide students with guidance on studying 'real' language data, setting aside (to the other volumes) tools of analysis (*Discovering Language*) and the theories underpinning these tools (*Thinking about Language*).

As the title of this volume suggests, it introduces ideas and debates about the English language as it is actually used in social and cultural contexts. It also provides guidance and practical suggestions on how to conduct research into each of the topics covered. Its primary concern is how language is used in everyday life. As such it addresses the use of descriptive and theoretical frameworks to researching and analysing data, both written and spoken. Consequently it differs from more traditional textbooks that focus either on speech or on writing.

The book is divided into four chapters, each of which provides an overview of the topic in question and examines the current issues, debates and research methods in the field. Every chapter ends with a section that provides students with guidance on conducting their own research on the topic. There are also suggestions for further reading.

Chapters 1 and 2 deal with spoken language. Chapter 1 considers key areas of sociolinguistics, with particular reference to accents, dialects, linguistic variability and factors that change the way we speak. Chapter 2 examines the growing field of pragmatics and discourse; that is, the interactive nature of language and how communication involves more than the words that are actually spoken. English in action manifests itself not only in speech but also in writing. Chapter 3 therefore, considers language in written texts, and in particular the application of linguistics to the study of literature. It also describes the frameworks and methods currently used to analyse written texts. Finally, Chapter 4 considers critical discourse analysis (CDA), which examines the relationship between the use of language and the possession/exercise of power. As such CDA goes beyond linguistics to examine the structures of discourse in both speech and writing. The chapter provides a theoretical framework that draws on the methods of analysis presented in the previous chapters, and offers practical guidance on applying the framework to a chosen area of study.

Variation and Change in English

1.1 Introduction

Linguistics is concerned with the study of language, including theories of language and the ways in which a language is structured and patterned. Language can be theorised and described in a general and abstract way, or a particular language can be categorised and described. However when we look at how language is actually used in everyday life it becomes clear that, far from being spoken and written in exactly the same way by everybody, it is in fact tremendously varied. This chapter considers different spoken varieties of English and the extent to which the society and communities in which we live affect the ways in which we speak and write.

Section 1.2 begins by defining 'language', 'dialect', 'accent', 'variety' and 'standard' English, and then considers people's attitudes towards variations in language use. Section 1.3 outlines the history of the standardisation of English in order to illustrate why dialectal variations persist in England and the United Kingdom as a whole. This section also traces the origins of prejudice against variations that continues to this day. In the United States the processes of standardisation have been very different from those in England. The resultant variations are fewer than in the United Kingdom and there is less prejudice against them. Our investigation of these two examples shows that linguistic variations depend a great deal on specific social, economic, political, geographic and historical variables.

Section 1.4 discusses two methodological approaches to research into variation, the first of which focuses on linguistic variables and the second on social variables and social networks. Investigation of variations in phonology, morphology and syntax is the realm of traditional dialectology and can be found in regional studies such as *The Survey of English Dialects* (Orton, 1962)

3

and *A Handbook of Varieties of English* (Kortmann and Schneider, 2004). Studies of social variables are the focus of sociolinguistic dialectology, which considers the effect of social factors such as race, class and gender on linguistic variation. Examples of studies in this field are Labov (1966, 1972a, 1979) and Trudgill (1974, 1978). More recently, Milroy (1987) and Milroy and Gordon (2003) have examined the influence of social networks on language. They argue that, in addition to linguistic and social variables, attention should be paid to the communities and contexts within which speech occurs. Finally, Section 1.5 provides students with guidance on conducting their own studies of variation and change, and Section 1.6 offers suggestions for further reading.

1.2   Language, dialect, accent and variety

1.2.1   Language

Let us consider the meaning of the term 'language' and to what it refers. In the first of the companion volumes in this series Jeffries (2006) distinguishes between language as a system and language use. A language system is an idealised form of the language in question, which differs from the way in which it is actually used. In the second companion volume Chapman (2006) considers language from three theoretical perspectives: as a type of behaviour, as a state of mind and as a form of communication. The sociolinguistic approach to the study of language considers language as behaviour. It takes into account the regional and social situations in which language occurs, as well as the social and linguistic factors that affect how speakers relate to one another. Thus the sociolinguistic approach to language, rather than being concerned with language in a general or abstract sense, asks questions such as 'What is a language?' and 'What is language for?' Hence language is not just about communication but also about identity, a factor that is paramount in sociolinguistics.

Deciding which criteria to adopt when defining a language, is far from straightforward. Take English for example. Who are the speakers of English? Are they solely the people who live in the country, England, that gives its name to the language? We generally assume that all the people who live in a geographically defined country speak the language associated with it: French in France, German in Germany and so on. However it is not always the case that all the people who live in a country speak the same language, or that the language is the exclusive property of that country. This is certainly not the case with English, which is spoken as the first language not only in the countries that make up the United Kingdom, but also in many other countries around the world, including the United States and Australia. Moreover it is widely used by speakers of other languages throughout the world as the language of business, diplomacy, medicine and the internet.

We should also take account of the fact that there are many countries that are not monolingual: that is, they have more than one official language. For example in Switzerland there are three official languages: German, French and Italian. Switzerland recognises itself as a multilingual society whereas most of us would agree that Britain (with the exception of Wales and some parts of Scotland) is thought of as a monolingual society in which everyone speaks English all the time. The same could be said of the United States. However if we look at the actual languages spoken there are many others besides English. So far from being monolingual, these countries are actually multilingual, with many inhabitants speaking languages other than English.

One of the countries that makes up Great Britain, the principality of Wales, has two official languages – Welsh and English – and in some areas most of the inhabitants are bilingual and school children receive a bilingual education. This situation is similar to that in the province of Quebec in Canada, where people are bilingual in French and English. In the United States there is no official language and legislation to impose one is forbidden by the constitution, although to all intents and purposes English functions as the national language through its use in education, business, the law and so on. What these examples illustrate then is that language depends not only on geography but also on history, politics and economics.

The association between language and nationhood or nationality is a very strong and powerful one, as is the association between language and identity of all kinds: regional and social as well as national. The language, languages or dialects of a language that we speak are an integral part of who we are, and attempts to impose one language or a variation of it are often bound up with the exercise of power and ideology. The reasons why a language becomes associated with a particular nation are many and varied, and they result from a combination of historical and social developments. Throughout history one of the first things an invading force has imposed on the conquered people is its language, particularly in respect of political, economic and educational institutions and the like. Examples are the Norman Conquest of England in 1066, the Roman colonisation of numerous countries from the first century BC and the combining of a vast swathe of national territories into the Soviet Union from 1922. What counts as the language of a country at any particular moment in time, therefore, is not as simple and straightforward as it seems. The term language is also very difficult if not impossible to define linguistically, as the example in the following section illustrates.

1.2.2   The Ebonics debate

In December 1996 the Oakland School District Board in the US State of California passed a resolution that gave official recognition to Ebonics, a language that was viewed as distinct from English. Ebonics is a compound word made up of from the words 'Ebony', meaning black, and 'phonics' meaning sound. Thereafter schools in the Oakland district were required to provide black pupils with a bilingual education in Ebonics, and English. The impetus for this resolution came from the persistently low educational achievements of black students, who made up over 50 per cent of the school population in the district. The issue quickly became national news and provoked a fierce debate across the United States. Amongst the topics raised was whether or not black English could be shown to be a linguistically separate language. This brought to the fore the broader, more politically sensitive question of the relationship between language and ethnicity, and between African Americans and Anglo-Americans in contemporary American society. Hence the debate moved away from the matter of Ebonics *per se* and on to the issue of equality: the right to equal educational provision for all young Americans regardless of ethnicity and, by extension, full participatory status in American life regardless of class, ethnicity and gender (Clark, 2001, pp. 237–52).

According to Tatalovich (1995, p. 1) whenever an opportunity arises in the United States to debate matters of language, 'ordinary people rise to defend the English language against those who speak other tongues'. He points out that the Oakland resolution, in common with similar episodes throughout the history of the United States, 'is symptomatic of the debate over whether the United States should reflect a dominant English-speaking majoritarianism or encourage a multilingual culture' (ibid., p. 2). Thus for Tatalovich, controversies over language are not only linguistic conflicts but also moral ones. As noted in the previous section, although English is by far the most common language in the United States and is used in most areas of public life, the constitution prevents it from being enshrined as the official language. Therefore, unlike in many of the other major English-speaking countries in the world, the US federal government has not been able to assert the dominance of English or legislate any national language policy. Despite this immigrants who wish to acquire US citizenship are required to take a test in English.

Not surprisingly the Ebonics debate found its way onto the agenda of the Linguistics Society of America. In 1997 the society passed a resolution calling for Ebonics, alongside African American Vernacular English (AAVE) and Vernacular Black English, to be recognised as a systematic language governed by linguistic rules. However the society refused to be drawn on the issue of classification, on the ground that the distinction between 'languages' and 'dialects' or 'varieties' was usually made more on social and political grounds than on purely linguistic ones. It argued that what was important from a linguistic and educational perspective was not whether Ebonics and AAVE could be called languages but that they, in common with other speech varieties, be recognised as systematic and governed by linguistic rules. At the heart of the debate, then, was not what counted as a language but the social and political issues that surrounded the establishment and maintenance of language hierarchies.

If linguistics cannot help us to define the term language, another approach is to think of language in terms of subdivisions or as a collection of mutually intelligible dialects, such as the south-west dialect of France, the Black Country dialect of English, the Bavarian dialect of German and so on. So English as a language consists not only of what is known as standard English (see Section 1.3), but also of all other dialects that exist within the geographical boundaries of England and elsewhere. Mutual intelligibility is not an important criterion, since different languages as well as dialects can be mutually intelligible. For example Norwegian, Swedish and Danish, though accepted as different languages, can each be understood by speakers of the other languages. Other factors relating to intelligibility do have to be taken into account, however, such as an individual's degree of exposure to a language, her or his educational background and willingness to understand.

1.2.3   Dialect, accent and variety

One way of defining a language is as a group of dialects and accents that have certain forms and structures in common. Put simply, dialect refers to words and syntactic structure, whereas accent refers to the sounds that speakers produce and the intonations and pitches that accompany these sounds. The two often go hand in hand. For example if people speak in a regional dialect of English, such as Scouse in the North West or Black Country in the Midlands, then their pronunciation will be particular to that area. If you were to walk north from Land's End in Cornwall to John O'Groats in the very north of Scotland you would hear a progressive range of accents and dialects. This a known as a dialect continuum or a chain of mutual intelligibility; that is, there is no distinct or complete break from one dialect and accent to another, and speakers of geographically adjacent dialects can understand one another. However the cumulative effect is such that the greater the geographical separation, the greater the difficulty of understanding what people say. Europe has many dialect continua, one example of which is Romance, which stretches across the Iberian peninsula through France and parts of Belgium down to the southern tip of Italy.

There is also a social dimension to accents and dialects. As Chambers and Trudgill (1980, p. 3) point out, dialects are commonly viewed as:

substandard, low status, often rustic forms of language, generally associated with the peasantry, the working class, or other groups lacking in prestige. DIALECT is also a term which is often applied to other forms of language, particularly those spoken in more isolated parts of the world, which have no written form. And dialects are often regarded as some kind of (often erroneous) deviation from a norm – as aberrations of a correct or standard form of language.

According to Trudgill and Chambers people who speak with rural accents are sometimes typified as dim-witted but trusting, whereas people with some urban accents may be stereotyped as quick-witted but untrustworthy. By contrast speakers of standard English with a Received Pronunciation accent (see Section 1.3.1) are often portrayed as more intelligent than speakers of other dialects as well as morally and socially superior.

Linguists prefer to use the term 'variety' when describing variations in language as this has none of the negative connotations associated with the terms dialect and accent, and fits in with the idea of descriptive linguistics; that is, basing descriptions of language upon actual use. It can also be applied across a wider range of language features. For example we can talk of linguistic variation, historical variation, social variation, geographic variation, stylistic variation and so on.

Language operates across two dimensions simultaneously: the horizontal dimension of space, called the 'diachronic' axis, and the vertical dimension of time, called the 'synchronic axis'. In addition there is a social dimension, which takes account of variations between social classes and cuts across both. The reason why there is so much geographic variation in language in England and so little in the United States is historical, as is the prejudice commonly held against linguistic variations. Consequently in order to comprehend variations in English and the attitudes towards them it is necessary to consider the social history of English.

1.3 Standards of English

1.3.1 What is standard English?

The term standard English (SE) is the one most commonly applied to the language 'English'. It is the variety of English used in public life, for example in education, the law, medicine and government. Nowadays it has no geographical boundary and is used throughout the United Kingdom and other English-speaking countries. In England it has an associated accent, known as Received Pronunciation, or RP for short. Because of their origins and history, SE and RP are closely associated with the middle and upper classes and are known variously as 'the Queen's English' or 'BBC English'. The concept of RP is a peculiarly English one and it has no equivalent in any other part of the English-speaking world. Some linguists argue that SE is best defined as the written form of English, because it is not a matter of pronunciation and is therefore not tied to any particular accent (see: Crystal, 1995; Trudgill, 1999). Rather it is a matter of grammar, vocabulary and orthography (spelling). However Stubbs (1986) argues that accent is involved in the notion of standard since people have an idea of what is and what is not standard in pronunciation. That is, RP is widely regarded as the standard accent of British English, just as standard English is widely regarded as the standard written form of English.

There is also disagreement amongst linguists as to whether SE can be classed as a dialect. Some, such as Chambers and Trudgill (1980) and Milroy (1987) insist that it is, pointing out that all speakers speak at least one dialect and that standard English is as much a dialect as any other form of English. Thus some speakers may have no other variety than SE whilst others may have a regional variety and SE. Other linguists disagree, on the ground that SE differs from dialects in a number of ways, especially in respect of it having its own writing system. Because of this they argue that the study of dialect should concentrate upon speech. This, however, ignores the fact that many non-standard English dialects in England, such as the Black Country dialect in the West Midlands and Geordie in the North East, have an established form of writing. Also, if standard English is not a dialect it is difficult to see what else it could be.

Whilst regional accents and dialects go hand in hand, standard English can be spoken in any accent. So it is possible (but not very likely) that someone may speak the Geordie dialect with an RP accent, but it is both possible and probable that someone will speak standard English with a Geordie accent. Indeed the BBC, once the bastion of standard English and RP, has in recent years adopted a much more liberal policy towards employing presenters with regional accents. When the BBC was founded in the 1930s all broadcasters spoke standard English with a uniform RP accent, but nowadays a range of regional accents can be heard. Indeed the attitude towards the use of regional dialects and accents in public life has altered so significantly since the 1930s that in 2005 the BBC launched a national campaign, called *Voices*, to celebrate and promote regional linguistic diversity. In addition to television and radio programmes on the subject the BBC, working together with dialectologists at the universities of Leeds and Cardiff, is conducting a comprehensive survey of contemporary English dialects and accents via the internet and phone-ins. The BBC takes issue with the correlation between RP and BBC English, and is fighting hard to dissociate itself from any gate-keeping role in language use and accusations of holding back the tide of language change. It argues that the fact that news broadcasters spoke RP in the early days was more the product of the restricted group from which employees were drawn than part of a deliberate policy. (Nonetheless employees from outside that group were given elocution lessons to ensure their use of RP.) However if you call the accent normally used in BBC news broadcasts BBC English, and accept that it is an example of RP, then by definition BBC news broadcasters are RP speakers. This circularity in defining BBC English in relation to RP and RP in relation to BBC English renders both concepts meaningless. It is also ironic that this is happening at a time when the relationship between RP and so-called BBC English is being viewed as a thing of the past.

Nevertheless, and initiatives such as *Voices* aside, there is still a strong correlation in Britain between dialect, accent and social class. There still is a hierarchy of English dialects and accents, with SE and RP being held as the most prestigious, and those of speakers from some large urban conurbations being viewed as the least prestigious. Speakers of the most marked form of RP appear at the top of the pyramid and tend to be accorded the highest status, whereas speakers with a marked regional pronunciation are accorded the lowest. Even in London, which is the historical centre of standard English, there are geographically bound accents and dialects that are given less prestige and made subject to ridicule. No wonder that the playwright George Bernard Shaw wrote in 1916 that 'it is impossible for an Englishman to open his mouth without making some other Englishman despise him.' Such prejudices go back centuries to the time when the process of standarising English began, as discussed in the following subsection.

1.3.2   A brief history of the standardisation of English in England

On any day of any week we can open English newspapers and find articles on or letters about the degeneration and corruption of the English language. We might be tempted to think of this as a modern concern, but in fact it dates back to at least the fifteenth century. The need for a unified language arose during the late middle ages and the beginning of the Renaissance period for political and economic reasons. Politically, it was becoming necessary for the holders of power to be able to communicate in a common language with their counterparts far away, and economically a common language was a necessity for trade. This concept of a national language also began to be linked to the notion of national identity, and as a result the nation states of modern-day Europe began to take shape.

Haugen (1972) divides the process of standardisation into four stages:

1. Selection: an existing dialect is selected to be standardised. In the case of English, this was the East Midlands dialect of the Middle English period.

2. Elaboration: the chosen dialect is expanded and elaborated so that it can fulfil the variety of functions it is intended to serve. That is, the vocabulary is extended and/or the grammatical structure is elaborated. In the case of English, the East Midland vocabulary was supplemented by words from French and Latin and its grammatical structure was elaborated by the adoption of Latinate constructions.

3. Codification: the full vocabulary and new grammar is written down. Once codified in writing, the language became an object of consciousness in that it can be seen as well as heard, and is thus 'fixed' or 'pinned down'. Changes to the language then become subject to regulation and control by its community of users, especially those in the more powerful sections of society.

4. Implementation: the chosen variety is implemented throughout a community, usually by becoming the language of instruction in education and being adopted by public institutions such as the law, government and the media.

The evolution of the English language can be divided into four periods: Old English (400–1100 AD); Middle English (ca.1100–1500 AD); Early Modern English (ca.1500–1800 AD) and Modern English (1800 to the present). By the end of the Middle English period, England had five main dialects, each with its own history. The Old English Northumbrian dialect had separated into Scots and Northern English, the Mercian dialect had become the West Midland and East Midland dialects, the Southern dialect was spoken south of the Rivers Thames and Severn and Kentish was the dialect of the far South East.

People of all social backgrounds, from very rich to very poor, spoke in the dialect of the region in which they lived. Moreover Medieval writers wrote in the language of their birthplace, so all the English dialects had a written equivalent. Even after English was standardised and codified in writing, people continued to speak and write in their local dialect. Indeed many of today's regional dialects, such as that of the Black Country, can be traced back to the Middle English period and syntactic forms, vocabulary and pronunciation have remained much the same.

Although English had yet to be standardised Renaissance writers often referred to a variety of English called the 'common dialecte' or 'common language'. Common, that is, in the sense of a shared usage and understanding. Identifying, elaborating, and codifying this language took place in the Early Modern English period, (ca. 1500–1800). Not without contestation, the East Midland dialect had been selected for the purpose. This was largely due to the fact that the region had come to exert tremendous power – intellectually, economically and politically.

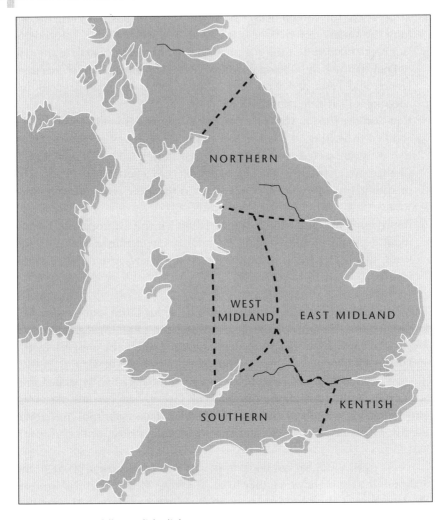

Figure 1.1   Middle English dialect map

Unlike in other European nation states that were forming at that time, in England the standardisation of language did not happen in a planned or systematic way. For example, whilst the Tudors were keen to establish a standard language in the interest of national unity, they did not appoint a body of people to plan and regulate the process. During the Renaissance (1400–1700) two important factors affected the course of standardisation: the invention of printing and the increased mobility of the aristocracy, both of which helped to promote the selected dialect over the others. Another notable feature of the construction of the language was the borrowing of words from Latin, Greek, Italian and Spanish. This was the result of the diffusion of classical learning across Europe, with Latin and Greek becoming the languages of 'civilised' and educated people. Between 1500 and 1650 more than 10,000 new words were incorporated into the emerging language. Newly invented words such as *allurement, allusion* and *atmosphere*, were added to those borrowed from other languages, for instance *bombast, chocolate, genteel*, and *shock*.

There was also a change in the pronunciation of vowels to sounds that are more or less recognisable today. For example Chaucer's pronunciation of 'name', /nɑːm/, became Shakespeare's /neːm/, or /neɪm/ in today's RP accent. This became known as the great vowel shift. No one knows precisely why it happened, but one suggestion is that it was to do with speakers' sense of their own prestige (see for example Baugh and Cable, 2002). At a time of growing urbanisation in London and the formation of the modern class system, sensitivity had been growing to accents that betrayed people's origins. During the sixteenth century people from East Anglia and the Midlands who moved to London did not want to sound like 'country bumpkins' and therefore tried to emulate the local accent. As often happens when people do this they hypercorrected their pronunciation; that is, they over emphasised the sound they wished to make, for instance by putting an 'h' before vowels, as in *whonder* and *whay*. These hypercorrected pronunciations gradually became an indicator of rising wealth and were emulated by others. Thus what was originally an accidental innovation became prestigious and spread. Similar vowel shifts did not occur in all regional dialects, and this accounts for some of the variations that continue to this day.

This new variety of English rapidly became dissociated from its East Midland origins. Indeed it was viewed more in terms of a foreign language, designed to function as a lingua franca (a language used internationally in trade or business) in the same way as Ancient Greek and Latin had done. During this period prescriptivism took a firm hold on the standardisation of English, especially in the case of establishing a grammatical structure. This was based on the notion that the description of a language should abide by the set of rules prescribed for it, rather than, as is the case with modern grammar, describing how it actually works. In England, then, the codification of English was marked by the theoretical foundations of prescriptivism, which inextricably linked language to social class and moral values (see Chapman, 2006, section 4.1). Throughout Renaissance Europe questions of language were tied to questions of literary language, and linguistics – as it existed then – was the study of language in general, particularly poetic language. A distinction was made between literary, including poetic, language and the form of language used for transactional purposes. In England, by contrast, writings on literary language doubled as texts on English usage, as though the two styles of language were or should be the same. This written, literary form of standard English entrenched even further the link between standard English and social class, since its use demanded a degree of literacy that was not possessed by the vast majority of the population. Education thus played an important part in the standardisation process and it continues to be important in its reproduction and maintenance.

The next step in the process was to codify the new standard English in dictionaries and grammars. The first of these were written with the purpose of disseminating the 'best' forms of English. The idea that the 'best' English was that spoken by the 'best' people, as personified by the nobility, gave rise to the notion that everything else was not only linguistically but also morally and socially inferior. All the other dialects – Northern, Southern, West Midland and Kentish – were treated as second class and ignored, unless written as poetry. However they did not fossilise but continued to be used by the inhabitants of those regions.

Towards the end of the Early Modern English period there was talk of establishing a language academy of the kind set up in France (1635) and Italy (1582). However this idea found little public sympathy, and it was pointed out that the French tended to change their language despite having an academy. In England language was perceived as an embodiment of the spirit of individual liberty and resistance to central regulation. Nevertheless this did not prevent people from trying to fix the language by means of dictionaries and grammars. Samuel Johnson saw his dictionary as a means 'by which the pronunciation of our language may be fixed and its attainment facilitated; by which its purity may be preserved, its use ascertained and its duration lengthened' (Johnson, 1755). It may seem odd to us that there was ever a time when words did not have a standard spelling, but before Johnson's dictionary this was the case. Words were spelt in several ways without much thought or anxiety. For instance Shakespeare used five different spellings of his own name during the course of his life.

Johnson's dictionary was by no means exhaustive and he excluded all terms to do with manufacturing, law, medicine and the physical sciences on the grounds that 'I could not visit caverns to learn the miner's language, nor take a voyage to perfect my skill in the dialect of navigation, nor visit the warehouses of merchants, and shops of artificers, to gain the names of wares, tools and operations, of which no mention is found in books' (ibid.). Johnson's principal sources of spelling and definition were literary texts.

By the beginning of the Modern English period (1800), England had been divided geographically by regional dialect and accent, and socially by the fact that standard English had become the language not only of government and administration but also of the cultural elite. Thus contrary to what had originally been intended, standard English served to divide rather than unite. This situation subsequently changed and the use of standard English spread throughout the country to all social classes, especially after 1870 when compulsory education was introduced in England (1872 in Scotland). Spoken and written standard English was held up as a model of refinement and, with the expansion of the British Empire, a carrier of political power world-wide.

During the nineteenth century, language, as with science and other disciplines, became to be an object of study. For Max Muller, the first professor of philology at Oxford, the object of study was language in general rather than any specific aspects of its use. The academic study of language as a science resulted in deviations from standard English being viewed not only as improper speech but also as improper behaviour. Thus speaking the 'superior', 'refined' language demonstrated that one belonged to a superior class, and speaking a 'vulgar' language correspondingly meant that one belonged to a vulgar class. As Smith (1984, pp. 2–3) puts it:

> The study of universal grammar at that time stipulated that languages were fundamentally alike in that they represented the mind, and fundamentally different in the quality of mind and civilisation that they represented . . . By dividing the population into two extremes, ideas about language firmly distinguished those who were within the civilised world from those who were entirely outside it.

The grammar books and dictionaries used in schools during the first half of the twentieth century continued to be prescriptive. Grammar was thought of as a universally applicable concept and if a language did not fit the grammatical prescription it was deemed imperfect and full of errors. This concept remained unchallenged until the 1950s when the first modern grammars were written. These were based on description rather than prescription and represented a seismic shift in linguistic grammatical theory.

In the 1920s the influential phonetician Wyld (1927, p. 606) argued that RP was 'superior, from the character of its vowel sounds, to any other form of English, in beauty and clarity'. Appealing to aesthetics, however, is hardly a scientific basis for arguing the case for superiority. Wyld tried to prove scientifically that there was a hierarchy of pronunciation, with RP ranking as the most superior accent. His ideas were very influential in the English curricula in elementary schools and the teacher training institutions and this persisted long afterwards. For example when a national curriculum was reintroduced into English schools in the late 1980s, and revised shortly afterwards in the early 1990s, one of the most controversial issues was around the teaching of standard English and RP in the speaking and listening curriculum (see Clark, 2001).

Although RP is not exclusive to any social class, throughout its history it has been associated with the upper and upper-middle classes, whilst regional accents have been associated with the lower-middle and working classes. In recent evaluations of speakers whose speech differs solely in terms of accent, the speakers of RP are always rated as sounding more pleasant, having greater prestige, being more ambitious and competent, and being better suited for higher-status jobs than speakers with regional accents. In some earlier studies, however, RP speakers were rated as less sincere, trustworthy, friendly, generous and kind than speakers with other accents. The prestige associated with RP is therefore a social rather than a linguistic phenomenon and can change.

Another important point to note here is that made by Aitchison (1981, 2001), namely that changes in language are neither degenerative nor progressive: they simply happen and no amount of 'fixing' can prevent this from occurring. There is no way of predicting what the English language will be like in another five centuries, but it will be different from today's English. The fact that English has not remained constant over time is due to its being a living language, and change is an integral aspect of this. This has implications for the ways in which language variations and change are studied, and especially for the methods used to reconstruct our linguistic past.

Dialects and accents also continue to change, as do our attitudes towards them. Although it could be said that accents and dialects have to some extent converged and and are now more mutually intelligible than they were, say, two centuries ago, there is still a great deal of variation. The factors that bring about changes in dialects and accents are difficult to determine, but like the great vowel shift they are likely to have a social origin rather than simply being a linguistic change (see Section 1.4).

This section has described how the English language became standardised in England, explained why regional varieties persist to this day and noted where notions such as 'correctness' and 'purity' of language come from. The next section considers the process of standardisation in a different national context and illustrates how, although the process may have been similar the result has been very different.

1.3.3 A brief history of the standardisation of English in the United States

American English now dominates the world. Standard American English is taught to foreign learners around the globe and it is not unusual for people from the Pacific, the Far East and even Europe to speak English with an American accent and to use American idioms. From the 1940s onwards American English consolidated its position through the US dominance of the entertainment industry and later of information technology and the internet. American English, like British standard English, owes a great deal to its social and cultural history.

The main contrasts between American English and British English lie in lexical variation and variations in pronunciation. There is very little syntactic variation. Many words, such as *moccasin, jazz, zucchini, bagel*, and *kosher* have been borrowed from the languages of indigenous peoples and non-English speaking immigrants. Some recognisably British words have developed variant meanings, for example *mad* can mean *angry*; *Are you through?* means Are you finished?; and *bad* or *wicked* can mean *good*. There is also a good deal of cross-over between the two varieties of English in that American technical innovations have imported into British English words such as *program, telephone* and *typewriter*. Other words reflect cultural and environmental differences between the two countries, including *lynch, blizzard, joy-ride, bayou, levy* and *prairie*. In British English you drive a *car*, fill up with *petrol*, wipe your *windscreen*, check your *bonnet* and *boot* are shut, drive down the *dual carriageway* or *motorway* and overtake *lorries*. In American English you drive an *automobile*, fill up with *gas*, wipe your *windshield*, check that your *hood* and *trunk* are shut, drive down the *divided highway* or *freeway* and overtake *trucks*. In England people *queue* whilst in America they *stand in line*. Phonetic variations also exist in the United States, but given its relative youth as a country these are not as pronounced as the regional variations in England and tend to be related to divisions between urban and rural areas and between different ethnic groups.

American English dates back to the seventeenth century and the colonisation of the 'New World' by a number of European nations. When the Pilgrim Fathers and subsequent colonists landed in America from 1620 they brought with them the newly developed standard English and this became the common language in the various English colonies. Hence American English was founded on the pre-existing grammars and syntactic structure of British standard English and the association between linguistic variation and social class that was so prevalent in British English was absent. In terms of standardisation, then, American English followed a very different course from that in England and the differences between British English and American English arose during the subsequent processes of elaboration and codification. In order to survive, the early colonists enlisted the aid of native Indians and drew on their local knowledge. During the course of this process, Indian words such as *moose, wigwam* and *naiack* (meaning a point or corner and the origin of the expression *that neck of the woods*) became part of the vocabulary. Dillard (1976) estimates that some 17,000 of these borrowed words are still in use today.

As intimated above, the English were not the only new inhabitants of the continent. Dutch traders landed shortly after the first pilgrims and established colonies on Manhattan island and along the Hudson River. Meanwhile Germans formed colonies near Philadelphia. As time went on some colonists expanded their horizons beyond the East coast. A number of pioneers moved westwards while others travelled to the south, encountering colonies of French and Spanish settlers as they went. As unfamiliar terrains and wildlife were encountered, names were needed for them. The French settlers had already named most of the geographical features and natural flora and fauna around the Saint Lawrence and Mississippi Rivers, and words such as *chowder*, *bayou*, *voyager* and *brave* were absorbed into the English pioneers' lexicon. From Spanish, which had moved north to the Gulf of Mexico from the Caribbean islands and South and Central America, came words such as *alfalfa*, *pumpkin*, *canyon*, *chaparral*, *corral*, *apache*, *fiesta* and *stampede*. In 1804 the explorers, Lewis and Clark led an exploration of the unknown territories west of the Mississippi. As they journeyed they named everything that passed before them. Thus a new vocabulary, distinct from that in Britain, was constructed to cater to all the new aspects of life in the colonies.

Although numerous languages existed in America in the seventeenth and early eighteenth centuries, and despite the anti-British sentiments that prevailed during the War of Independence (1775–83), English became the lingua franca for communication between speakers of different languages. In Jefferson's Declaration of Independence no official language was named as this was seen as contrary both to the spirit of freedom and pluralism of the time and to a constitution that espoused egalitarianism. Instituting a national language was seen as redolent of the monarchical policies that the migrants to the New World had left behind. Nevertheless, while the constitution proscribed English from being recognised as the official language of the United States, in practice it was and still is the only language spoken in most areas of public life, including government, the media and education.

The alternative to a national language, it was proposed, was a distinct form of English that would reflect the American cultural and national identity. in this regard Noah Webster was arguably one of the most important men in the development of the American language. He not only compiled the first American English dictionary incorporating words and phrases from the many peoples who inhabited the country, but was also aware of the need for a culturally independent society, not one that was still influenced by Britain. The printed word was the most powerful medium of communication at the time, and in order to disseminate and propagate a new national culture a national book trade was required (Simpson, 1986, p. 58). As a fervent nationalist Webster envisaged a purely American set of manners, morals, politics and culture. He proclaimed the need to establish a national language as well as a national government: as an independent nation its honour requires a system of its own, in language as well as in government (quoted in Mencken, 1921, p. 12).

To make cultural distinctions between America and Britain, Webster initially devised a completely new system of spelling, but he later settled on modification rather than wholesale change, realising the impossibility of implementing such a system. He deplored the pronunciations and spellings in the written English of the time, believing that the British system of spelling was class-ridden and created divisions in society as it demanded an educated knowledge of the language and was therefore inaccessible not only to the lower classes but also to foreign nationals. Webster resolved to construct spellings that were more uniform in their sounds than those proposed by Johnson. For example he excised the 'u' in the suffix '-our', so *honour* became *honor* and so on; reversed the final letters of words ending with -re to form *theater* and *center*; changed the 'c' to 's' in words such as *defense*, and the suffix -ise to -ize; and dropped the doubling of consonants in words such as *traveling* and *program*, as well as the silent 'e' in the latter.

Webster claimed that simplifying spelling in this way would make it easier for the primarily agrarian population to learn to write, and that this would assist the development of a uniquely American culture. It would also make the language easier for newcomers to learn. Moreover he saw his modifications as challenging British people's assumption that the English language belonged to them and that any change to it was solely their prerogative.

By the mid nineteenth century, cultural divergence and isolation, coupled with Webster's influence, had resulted in a form of English that was noticeably different from that used in Britain. However arguments continued on both sides of the Atlantic about the nature and purpose of this new form of English. In Britain 'Americanism' became a pejorative term, and in 1842 Charles Dickens wrote in his *American Notes* that he was at a loss when asked by a waiter if he wanted his food 'right away': 'I need not tell you that the prevailing grammar [in America] is more than doubtful, and that the oddest idioms are received idioms' (Dickens, 2000, p. 14). However what were sometimes thought of as aberrations were actually forms of English that had fallen out of use in Britain but were continuing to be used in America. For example the word *sick* (meaning to be unwell) had been widely used in Shakespeare's time and was still in use in America, but in Britain it had changed to *ill*. The past participle *gotten* had also been in use in Elizabethan times. Other terms that were common in Elizabethan England were *fall* for *autumn*, *progress* as a verb, *mean* for *unpleasant*; and *deck of cards* for *pack of cards*.

By the end of the nineteenth century there was also a literary canon of American English with writers such as James Fennimore Cooper and Mark Twain encapsulating the essence of frontier America in their works. The poet Ralph Emerson had declared that now America was free from the literary constraints of English romantic poetry, an American poet was needed to represent the nation's poetic aspirations. Walt Whitman established himself as that poet with works such as *Leaves of Grass* (1855, see Whitman, 2005). Literary achievements may seem trivial in the context of the development of a language, but the establishment of a literary canon is an indication of linguistic recognition.

During the twentieth century, the dissemination of American English throughout the world – via the entertainment media and later the internet – transformed it into a global language. There was also a reverse flow between the two varieties of English, with British people adopting terms such as *okay* and *hi*. Other examples are shown in Table 1.1.

There have been numerous analyses of the lexical differences between the two varieties of English, spawning a large dictionary industry. A distinct characteristic of the differentiation of early American English from British English was the formation of new words by means of **back formation** and **word blends**. One of the consequences of this is known as **tall talk**.

Back formation is the creation of new terms, usually verbs, by removing affixes from an existing word. American English had many nouns with the suffix *-ion*. When related verbs did not exist they were created by deleting the suffix and adding an 'e'. Early examples of this were the formation of *locate* from *location* in 1652, *donate* from *donation* (1795), *commute* from *commutation* (1865) and *electrocute* from *electrocution* (1889). More recent derivations that have removed different suffixes are *housekeep*, *burgle*, *shoplift* and *babysit*.

Word blends refers to the blending of phonological elements of existing words to form a new term. This practice has always had a place in the evolution of English but it is especially prevalent in American English. Examples are:

Cablegram	(from cable and telegram)
Travelog	(from travel and monologue)
Newscast	(from news and broadcast)
Telecast	(from television and broadcast)
Motel	(from motor and hotel)
Brunch	(from breakfast and lunch)

Most of these American terms have now been assimilated into British English.

Tall talk refers to the imagery and vivid expressions that have been central to American linguistic development, created by processes similar to back formation and word blending. During the frontier times the nation was a rough and ready one, but frontiersmen, desiring to make the ordinary seem grander than it actually was, elaborated and exaggerated their descriptions to spawn a host of bizarre lexical creations, including *ripsnitious*, *absquatulate*, *flusticated*, *elegantiferously* and *teetotacuiously*. Tall talk also exists in contemporary American English, such as *discombobulating*, *rambunctious*, *fantabulous* and *bodacious*.

Table 1.1 American words and idioms that have been absorbed into British English

Terms			Idioms
french-fries	truck	movie	fly off the handle
snoop	bar (pub)	has-been (adjective)	give me the bottom line
teenager	fan(sports)	burger	pass the buck
soap opera	parking ticket	download	it's a walk in the park
commute	gameshow	phoney	it comes with the territory
babysitter	downsize	gimmick	take the bull by the horns
gridlock	hospitalize	hopefully	let the cat out of the bag

By far the greatest variation between British English and American English lies in the phonological distinctions of accent. Although American accents are more homogeneous than British ones there are differences in accent across the United States: Labov (1997) identifies eight. Nonetheless American accents are far more uniform than those in Britain, and this is one of the reasons why American English is so much more appealing to foreign learners. The greatest difference is the number of vowel phonemes. Both British English and American English have the same number of consonant phonemes (24) but RP has 20 vowel phonemes while General American (GA) has 16. This is probably due to the fact that many American English accents are rhotic (see Jeffries, 2006, sections 1.4, 2.3.4). This means that the phoneme /r/ is pronounced after vowels, whereas British speakers may omit an orthographic 'r'. Another distinguishing feature is intervocality, where the alveolar plosives /t/ and /d/ are, through a process of voicing, merged together and words such as *ladder* and *latter* sound identical.

In the United States, unlike in Britain, the majority of regional dialects are largely free from social stigma and prejudice, but there is one notable exception: African American English (AAE). The latter is an umbrella term for African American Vernacular English (AAVE), Black English (BE), Inner City English (ICE) and Ebonics (see Section 1.2.2). It is spoken by many in the large population of Americans of African descent, and is a consequence of the historical discrimination against African Americans that isolated them both socially and from mainstream American speech. There are some who equate AAVE with inferior intelligence and cultural backwardness because, they claim, it is a deficient or incomplete language. Others believe that different races inherently speak differently. The former view has no linguistic foundation and it is as unscientific in reference to AAVE as it would be to standard American English, Russian or Chinese. Equally a child's race plays no part in the language it learns: a white child raised in an AAVE environment will learn to speak AAVE just as a black child raised by a white middle-class American family will speak standard American English. The position accorded to AAVE and its speakers in the United States, and to a lesser extent the speakers of regional dialects in the United Kingdom, illustrate just how deeply entrenched attitudes towards and prejudices against certain types of language use are, and the social and cultural thinking that forms the basis of these attitudes and prejudices.

1.4   Studies in variation and change

1.4.1   Linguistic variation

Early twentieth century research into dialects and accents tended to concentrate on descriptions of linguistic variation, particularly lexis and phonology, and linguistic atlases were compiled to show the distribution of different dialect forms. The purpose of this research was to counter the mainstream view in linguistics that without exception all sound change was regular. Dialectologists aimed to show that linguistic change, far from being regular, was in fact the opposite and that not all sounds and/or words were affected equally. They were particularly interested in lexical variation, and how different words were used to refer to the same thing in different places. They investigated this by going out and collecting examples of speech (known as **data**) from people (**informants**) in the regions in which they were interested, a process known as **fieldwork**.

One such study was the *Survey of English Dialects* (Orton, 1962). The impetus for Orton's survey, in addition to the reasons cited above, was his fear that as agriculture was rapidly becoming mechanized the lexical items associated with rural life would die out, and he wanted to capture them before they did so. The fieldwork was conducted during the 1950s and 1960s in over 300 rural communities throughout England. About 1,000 men were interviewed. The selection criteria were that the informants should be aged 60 or over, have little or no formal education, and had remained in the area in which they had been born. Such people were most likely to be still speaking dialects that had escaped the influence of standardisation and thus still bore a resemblance to the Middle English dialects described in Section 1.3.2 above. In this regard Orton's survey was intended to serve as a resource for linguistic historians to investigate the phonology, lexis and syntax of Medieval English. It has since been drawn upon to reconstruct the English spoken at the times of Shakespeare, Chaucer and even earlier.

However the ways in which data was collected provoked severe criticism in terms of the methodology and the **sampling**; that is, factors such as the age, social class, geographical location, gender and ethnicity of the informants from whom the data was gathered. The main data-gathering method was a long questionnaire, usually with one-word answers to questions such as 'You sweeten your tea with . . . ?'. The answers were then transcribed phonetically by the survey worker. Critics argued that one-word answers were too divorced from everyday use to provide an accurate account of how people actually used language. They also took issue with the sampling, arguing that dialectology should not restrict itself to people who were old, rural and male, but should also consider young men and women, and people from urban as well as rural areas. As a result traditional dialectologists changed both their methods and their samples accordingly.

The invention firstly of sound recording and portable tape recorders, and more recently video recorders, digitisation and computer technology, has revolutionised research into dialectology. Most books now published on the topic are accompanied by a CD or references to websites and electronic databases. One survey that has benefited from the more interactive techniques of data gathering is the Survey of Regional English, based at the University of Leeds. This also became part of a large web-based project called *Voices*, sponsored by the BBC (see Section 1.3.1 above). Data collected as part of the *Voices* project revealed ten alternatives to the term 'to play truant': *skive, bunk off, wag, skip, mitch, dog, hookey, twag, sag* and *nick off.* Although most of these terms can be found across the United Kingdom, *twag* is specific to Hull and Doncaster in the North East of England, *cap* to Derby and Nottingham in the Midlands, and *skidge* to Paisley in Northern Ireland.

In addition to lexical variation, dialectologists are also concerned with phonological variation. The methods of data collection and sampling used for this are the same as for lexical variation, but the focus of analysis is sounds rather than words. The basic conceptual tool here is the **linguistic variable**, meaning a linguistic item that has identifiable variants. There are at least two kinds of variation. The first is where the variation results in the use of a distinct phoneme of the language. For example words such as *laughing* and *going* can be pronounced as *laughin'* and *goin'*. The final sound of these two words is the linguistic variable 'ng' the two variants being [ŋ] in *laughing* and [n] in *goin'*. Another example is provided by the words *car* and *farm*, which can be be given r-less pronunciations: [kɑː] and [fɑːm]. Here the linguistic variable 'r' has the variants [r] as in *car* and ø (i.e. not pronounced) as in *fahm* (see also Section 1.4.2 below). The second kind of variation is more subtle, for example involving the nasalisation of vowels. For example the vowel in *bend* is sometimes nasalized and sometimes not. The degree of nasalisation can vary greatly (see also Section 1.5; and Jeffries, 2006, ch. 3).

Linguistic variables have also been used when studying grammatical variation. For example the presence or absence of 's' in the third person singular, as in *she goes* or *she go*; the form of the verb *be* in sentences such as *she's glad*, *she be glad* and *she glad*; and multiple negation, such as *he don't mean to hurt nobody* and *I done nothing* (see Section 1.4.3 below).

In sociolinguistic research that focuses on phonology, one sound is selected as the linguistic variable; that is, the sound against which other sounds are measured. Other variables, such as social class, age, gender, region and ethnic group, are the social variables; that is, the variant is compared for each of these variables. This enables comparison of the speech of older informants and younger ones, men and women, lower class and upper class, and so on.

Sound recording has made it possible to investigate patterns of stress and tone, known as **prosodic features**, in addition to those of sound when study-ing speech. English accents vary tremendously in this respect. As Wells (1999) points out, in many Northern English dialects vowels tend not to be reduced in unstressed Latinate prefixes (for example *con-* and *ex-*), unlike in RP and other Southern-based varieties. Although relatively little research has been conducted on dialect intonation, Wells notes that certain British accents – including those of Birmingham, Liverpool, Newcastle and Glasgow – tend to have rising tones where most other accents have falling ones. According to Biddulph (1986) West Midland speech characteristically has terminal rises in statements, and negative verbs (such as <wor> – *wasn't/weren't*) have a markedly high tone. Wells (1999) also points out that West Midlands work-ing-class accents (as well as those of Liverpool and some in New York) have a **velarised** voice quality; that is, articulation takes place further back and higher on the tongue than is the case with other accents.

1.4.2   Social variation

During the latter half of the twentieth century linguists turned their attention to the relationship between language and social class, particularly in respect of accent variation. One of the first to do so was the American linguist William Labov (1966) who used linguistic variables to investigate differences between accents. One very noticeable linguistic variable is rhoticity. This refers to the pronunciation of 'r' when it occurs after a vowel – as in *bar, sort, churn* – and is usually known as the 'postvocalic r'. How 'r' is pronounced after vowels differs across the English-speaking world. For example RP is 'r-less' or non-rhotic, whilst Scots English and Cornish are 'r-ful' or rhotic. In the British Isles rhotic-ity differentiates Scottish, Irish, Cornish, West Country, rural East Anglian and Northumbrian accents from most Midland and southern accents. It is regarded as a low-prestige feature and is associated with 'backward' rural areas, whereas in most of the United States, rhoticity is prestigious and its absence is stigmatised.

Labov's (1966) study was based on the hypothesis that if speakers were ranked according to social class, then they could also be ranked in the same order by differences in the use of certain linguistic variables. One of these was the variable 'r' after vowels in words such as *lark* and *bar*. Labov wished to demonstrate that variations in New York accents centred on the use of the postvocalic 'r'. Before embarking on a large-scale survey Labov conducted a pilot study; that is, a much smaller survey to test the reliability of his research methods. He selected three department stores in Manhattan where the sales assistants' accents were likely to reflect those of their typical customers. This, he believed, could be extrapolated to categorise patterns of variation across the city. The three stores were Saks's Fifth Avenue, an expensive high-status store, Macy's, which was regarded as middle-class and middle-priced, and Klein's, which sold cheaper items and catered to poorer customers. Pretending to be a customer, Labov checked what items were for sale on the fourth floor of each store and then asked sales assistants on other floors for the whereabouts of the selected items. He chose that particular floor because 'fourth floor' contained two instances or 'tokens' of postvocalic [r]. Having asked his question, for example 'Excuse me, where are the women's shoes?', he listened to the answer and then pretended to be hard of hearing, uttering a further 'Excuse me?'. In this way he obtained two more tokens presented in a careful, stressed way as the sales person repeated 'fourth floor'. Next he repeated the exercise on the fourth floor itself by saying to sales assistants, 'Excuse me, which floor is this?'

Once Labov had received his answers he quickly moved out of sight and wrote down the pronunciation and details such as the gender, race and approximate age of the assistant. As all three department stores were very large he was able to gather data from 264 unsuspecting subjects. Multiplied by four tokens per informant, this gave a total of over 1000 tokens. Analysis of the data confirmed Labov's hypothesis and showed that use of the postvocalic 'r' varied according to the speech style, social class and linguistic context associated with each store. Sixty-two per cent of the subjects at Saks, 51 per cent at Macy's and 20 per cent at Klein's pronounced [r] in at least one of the four tokens. All groups increased their use of [r] in the more deliberate repetition, and interestingly it was the employees at Macy's, the middle-class store, who exhibited the greatest increase. As Labov (1972, p. 52) later commented: 'It would seem that *r*-pronunciation is the norm at which a majority of Macy's employees aim, yet not the one they use most often.' On the quieter and often more expensive upper floors of Saks, the highest-ranking store, the percentage of pronounced [r] was much greater than on the much busier ground floor.

Labov's pilot study showed that 'r' could be studied systematically. In the large survey that followed a more representative sample of informants was used and the sampling procedure was similar to that employed in sociological surveys. He divided his informants into six groups, principally on the basis of age and socioeconomic class. His findings confirmed those of the pilot study in that the upper-class informants pronounced the postvocalic 'r' most consistently and lower-class informants pronounced it least. In New York the postvocalic 'r' was associated with high status and prestige. He argued that his findings showed that a language change was in progress, in that pronunciation of the postvocalic 'r' was spreading. According to Labov it was lower-class women who were responsible for diffusing of the [r] pronunciation in the community as they were particularly conscious of its prestige value.

Meanwhile lower middle-class speakers, when speaking more formally, exhibited the phenomenon known as hypercorrection (see Section 1.3.2). These speakers' pronunciation of [r] went beyond that of the high-status group, and this could be attributed to their wish to distance themselves from the working class and to become more like the upper class.

Trudgill (1974) replicated Labov's methodology when conducting a study of non-standard variants in the city of Norwich in the East of England. Like Labov, Trudgill aimed to ascertain the norms in the city by means of detailed interviews with a representative sample of the population, in this case 50 adults and 10 schoolchildren. He analysed several linguistic variables of grammar and accent. For example in Norwich, as in other parts of England, there are two alternative forms of the third person singular in the present tense: the standard English *she runs*, *walks*, *skips* and so on, and the local dialect form without the *-s* inflection: *she run*, *walk*, *skip* and so on. Trudgill found that there was a correlation between social class and the use of this variable. His findings for all variables confirmed those of Labov, in that members of the lower working class used them the most often and that the lower middle class produced relatively more of the prestigious forms than did the members of the social group immediately above them on the social scale.

Like Labov, Trudgill distinguished between **overt** and **covert prestige**. The issue of prestige is an important but complicated one in sociolinguistics. **Overt prestige** refers to the positive or negative assessment of variants or a speech variety in accordance with the dominant norms of educational institutions, public media and upper middle-class speech. In Labov's New York study the informants who exhibited the greatest use of stigmatised forms had the greatest tendency to stigmatise others for their use of the same form. However the working-class informants did not adopt middle-class norms, and this calls for explanations other than those associated with prestige. **Covert prestige** refers to the set of opposing values implicit in lower- and working-class lifestyles that do not appear in conventional subject-reaction tests. Working-class speech is thus seen as a mechanism for signalling adherences to local norms and values, whereas middle-class speech reveals a concern for social status and is therefore a mechanism for class solidarity.

Trudgill investigated gender as well as age and social class, and found that gender was a significant factor in the use of variant forms. In each social group the female informants consistently used fewer of the non-standard variations than men. They also had a tendency to over-report their use of prestige forms whilst male informants were more likely to under-report them. Women in Norwich seemed to be more influenced by the overt prestige of the standard variety, while men seemed to be more influenced by the covert prestige of the localised Norwich variety. Thus whilst Labov's study revealed clear social stratification by status in New York in respect of the variable (r), Trudgill's study highlighted the difference that gender made in adherence to a local variant. The covert prestige of the vernacular therefore counterbalanced the overt prestige of the standard variety. However, account has to be taken of the fact that Trudgill categorised women by their husband's social class, for which he has rightly been criticised. He concluded that the differences in attitude in the two countries reflected differences in class consciousness at the time, particularly the lack of any militant class-consciousness in the United States, unlike in the United Kingdom, and the relative lack of 'embourgeoisement' of the British working class.

1.4.3 Variation and social networks

In the late twentieth century the studies of urban dialectology by linguists such as Labov and Trudgill were challenged by L. and J. Milroy (Milroy, 1987; Milroy, 1992), who took issue with the notion of linguistic variables and variation theory in general. A study they conducted in Belfast led them to conclude that the relationship between linguistic and social structures was not necessarily best examined by exploring only social variables such as age and class. Instead they based their research on the notion of **social networks**. Rather than grouping speakers into predetermined categories such as social class, they situated individuals within the sum of their relationships, both formal and informal: relationships with family, friends and work colleagues, neighbourhood relationships and relationships based on ethnicity. They found that particular kinds of network would either inhibit or advance linguistic variation in a community.

For example men in the Ballymacarett district of Belfast who worked in the local shipyard and had dense social networks bound by strong ties were likely to conform to the prevailing linguistic norms and were less likely to tolerate or encourage change. This differed from the women of the district who often had jobs outside the area and had fewer local ties. This led the Milroys to conclude that dense networks acted as brakes on linguistic innovation, whilst weak ties between individuals facilitated the spread of linguistic innovations – such as new pronunciations and new words – from network to network.

They argued that peripheral members of a community who had ties with other communities (through work, education or friends) carried innovations into a community. Their conclusions complemented Labov's argument about change, but provided far more information about the site and possible explanations of change.

Virtually all of the work undertaken in social and urban dialectology until that point had concentrated on variations in phonology.'Milroy and Milroy (1993) sought to redress this. The aim of their book was to raise the status of English regional dialects and draw attention to their syntactic and morphological characteristics. To give a morphological example, in standard English the past tense forms of *break* and *knew* have been codified as *broke* and *know*. Verb forms such as *breaked* and *knowed* were part of the English language for centuries and are still present in regional dialects today, but since they were not chosen for standard English they are no longer used in writing or 'educated speech'. A syntactic example is multiple negation: *she never said nothing*. This was outlawed by nineteenth-century prescriptive grammarians but was common in the Middle English of Chaucer's time, was used by Shakespeare and continues to be used by native speakers of English today as it remains a grammatical feature of some dialects.

In some English dialects *thee*, *thy* and *thou* are still used instead of *you*. Other dialects retain forms of the verb *be* that differ from those in standard English, including the Black Country dialect in the Midlands towns of Wolverhampton, Dudley and Walsall. For example in the affirmative present tense there are:

I am (am)	I am (am)
you/thou am (y'am)	you are
s/he is	s/he is
we am	we are
you am (Y'am)	you are

Such variations, because of their considerable divergence from standard English grammar, have been interpreted as signs of ignorance and lack of intelligence, and viewed as a bastardised form of English.This attitude can be attributed to the way in which British English was standardised, as summarized in Section 1.3.2 above. However the Black Country dialect, far from being a bastardised form of English, has a pedigree that dates back to the West Midland dialect in the Middle English period. The Black Country dialect is also noted for its highly contracted negative modal forms, including *ain't* (*am not/isn't/aren't, hasn't/haven't*) and *doe/doh/dow* (*doesn' t/don't*) (see Clark, 2004).

An on-going investigation of the Black Country variety (Clark, forthcoming) has revealed that the syntactic forms discussed above are all still widely used by men and women from all social backgrounds and age groups, particularly when talking to friends and relatives. This is the case even for people with a higher education. On the whole, however, Black Country grammatical forms are most prevalent amongst people aged 50 and over. Younger people, especially adolescents and those 20–30, tend to use them less, and then mostly the verb 'be' in its various tenses and its negative form. The use of dialect amongst adolescents has been the focus of a number of studies, including Eckert (1988, 1989) and Kerswill and Williams (2000, 2002). Eckert suggests that American adolescents are linguistically the most innovative of all generations, and that through their peer groups they establish new norms that may diffuse into the wider community.

Kerswill and Williams investigated the role of adolescents in **dialect levelling** in three English towns: two in the south (Reading and Milton Keynes) and one in the north (Hull). Dialect levelling is a term used to describe changes in dialects that make them considerably more like standard English in terms of phonology, grammar and vocabulary. Kerswill and Williams examined phonological and grammatical variables and compared males and females, teenage and elderly subjects, in the middle and working classes. In the case of phonological features they found convergence between the two southern towns, but convergence between the southern towns and the northern one was limited to some consonantal features (see also Section 1.4.1 above). They also tested the Milroys' claim (Milroy, 1987; Milroy, 1992) that network characteristics rather than class accounted for the more levelled, standard speech of the middle classes compared with the working class. They found that, whilst the working-class speakers in Milton Keynes were more linguistically levelled than their Reading counterparts, they remained strongly non-standard and non-RP in terms of grammar and pronunciation. This was ascribed to a lack of social (as opposed to geographical) mobility and to the maintenance of class-based cultural differences concerning relationships with schools, attitudes to literacy, the authorities and employers.

In the same study Kerswill and Williams also investigated adolescents' attitudes towards language and social groups. They found that when discussing aspects of teenage culture, questions about language evoked the strongest response. The adolescents expressed a strong allegiance to their own peer group, framed in terms of in-group and out-group, and usually with reference to a hierarchical class structure. There was often a discrepancy between what adolescents said about the way they spoke and how they actually spoke. This led Kerswill and Williams to conclude that the adolescents were partly but not fully aware of the process of language change. However there was uniformity in attitudes towards language issues in both northern and southern schools, suggesting that part of the mechanism of levelling lay in these subjective parameters.

What all the studies summarised in this section show is that variation in language use and the process of language change are inextricably bound up with class, gender, age and culture. The study of variation and change, then, involves not only linguistic description but also consideration of social and cultural factors.

1.5   Studying variation in English

The earlier sections of this chapter introduced the issues involved in studying variation and change in the English language. As they have shown, research into linguistic variation focuses on differences in the production of language in terms of pronunciation, accent, vocabulary and grammar. Research into language change is normally cross-generational. An associated area of research is attitudes towards variation.

A purely linguistic description of variations does not explain why variations occur. To investigate why they do it is necessary to consider non-linguistic variables that derive from the social context or networks within which linguistic variations take place. A **variable** is a feature that has a number of possible values, or in the case of linguistic variables we might say that they have a number of potential 'realisations'. Thus the phoneme /t/ can be said to have a number of possible variants (or allophones), including [t], [tʰ], [t̪] and [ʔ] (glottal stop). (See Jeffries, 2006, ch. 2 for further information on phonological variation.) Any investigation of the variable 't', therefore, will involve collecting examples of different /t/ phonemes and looking for patterns in the occurrence of variants, perhaps in relation to syllable structure, word structure or, in the case of glottal stop, the formality of the setting or the class of the speaker. In the case of non-linguistic or social variables, the variants will be related to the social class to which the informants belong, their age, geographical origins and so on. Thus the variable will be known by its generic name, such as 'social class' and the variants will be lower-middle class, upper-working class and so on. Much of the discussion and advice that follows will refer to linguistic and non-linguistic variables in the sense just defined.

1.5.1   Selecting a topic for research

The first thing to decide is the topic you wish to address in your research. For example you may wish to investigate variation:

- In a particular geographical area.
- in a particular ethnic group.

- Between two neighbouring areas.
- Across different age groups.
- Across social classes.
- Across different ethnic groups.
- About the same person in different social settings.
- About attitudes towards variation.

The next thing to decide is the focus of your research.

- Investigating variations in a particular geographical area will require you to select the area for your study, decide upon the linguistic variables you wish to investigate, and select the non-linguistic variables for your sample of informants (see Section 1.5.2 below).
- Investigating variations between neighbouring areas will require you to do the same as above but two areas are chosen instead of one. These could be two neighbouring villages or two neighbouring urban suburbs.
- Investigating variations in an ethnic group will require you to select the group you wish to study. If you want to add a social dimension you will need to choose a setting, for example a domestic household or a workplace. You could then investigate the impact that location has on language use.
- Investigating variations across age groups, genders, social classes and/or ethnic groups will require you to decide how to restrict the non-linguistic variables to make the project manageable and the results clear. Investigating variations across age groups, particularly if the ages range from the very old to the very young, will enable you to identify language change over the span of half a century or more.
- Investigating attitudes towards variation should not be confused with investigating linguistic variation itself, since how people think they speak and how they actually speak can be very different. Such studies are best undertaken by means of a questionnaire that includes dialect recognition as part of its design, or as a separate element (see Sections 1.4 3 and 1.5.3).

For all the above examples except the last, and for any study of linguistic variation, once you have decided on the topic and its focus and scope, the next step is to decide which linguistic and non-linguistic variables to investigate.

If you choose to investigate phonological or grammatical variations you will have to decide whether to choose specific variables in advance or select variables that emerge naturally from the data you collect later. Investigating lexical variations will require questions on topics that are most likely to reveal such variations, for example food and drink, or word lists.

Non-linguistic variables include geographical origin, age, gender, social class, ethnicity and so on. Here you have to give thought to the extent to which to control for the chosen variable. For example choosing informants who are of a similar age, live in the same geographical location or are the same gender means that these variables are held constant, allowing you to focus on whichever variable you are investigating. The extent to which you control for the non-linguistic variables will also depend on the scope of your study. If your study is restricted to just one age it will be difficult to identify what is specific to that age group because there will be nothing to compare the results with, so it is best to have informants of different ages. From a practical point of view, however, it is not sensible to investigate variations across age groups if you do not know sufficient people from one of the age groups in question. Equally, if you select gender as one of your non-linguistic variables then you must know enough people of both genders who would be willing to act as informants. If your study relates to a geographical area you need to decide on the extent of that area, its boundaries and ease of access to it. Undertaking fieldwork is fraught enough with pitfalls, you do not need the added complication of setting yourself unrealistic or overambitious parameters (see the discussion on sampling in Section 1.5.2 below). For this reason, and to avoid having to carry out overly complex statistical tests, the topics suggested below involve just one or two non-linguistic variables.

The next step is to design your project and collect the data required for your analysis.

1.5.2   Project design and sampling

Your project should be carefully designed to reflect your research question and will be either a quantitative or a qualitative study. The former is aimed at quantifying the number of variants of a linguistic variable, and sometimes the results are plotted against those for non-linguistic variables. A qualitative study considers the nature of linguistic features in context, and normally explores a text or set of texts in more depth, often considering a range of variables rather than restricting the study to a narrow selection.

For example a quantitative study could be an investigation of h-dropping by different generations of Londoners, with data being obtained from a roughly equal number of informants within a set of predetermined age ranges, those shown in Table 1.2.

We shall look a little later at the tasks involved in analysing the data obtained for a project such as this. First we shall consider a typical qualitative research project in order for the distinction between the two to be made clear. Whilst the h-dropping project focuses on a single variable, in this case the pronunciation (or dropping) of the glottal fricative /h/, a qualitative project

Table 1.2 Suggested age ranges and sample size for a quantitative study

	18–27	35–44	52–60	70+
Number of informants:	20	18	22	16

could be to look more broadly at the phonology of speakers who share a similar background, such as geographical or ethnic origin. This will require more extensive data than that gathered to examine a single variable, as in the case of the h-dropping study.

The precise nature of the data collected is not entirely determined by whether the study is quantitative or qualitative, though it is common to use different methods of data collection to produce statistical or contextual results. We shall consider this in the next section. Here we shall examine the principles of choosing informants for a study, and their geographical location.

Choosing informants is known as **sampling**. there are three kinds of sampling: **random, structured** and **opportunistic**. If you wish to identify the pattern of linguistic usage by a particular group, for example the morphology of New Yorkers' speech, you may decide to use random sampling to acquire your set of informants. Here the term 'random' is a very precise and technical and does not relate to the colloquial use of the word to indicate an accidental set of occurrences or items. The random sample in this more technical sense refers to a set of informants who have been chosen from a well-defined population by means of random number tables or computer-generated random numbers. For the above project, then, the population would be the entire population of the city of New York. In order to be sure that your sample was representative you would need to choose people from the electoral register, the phone book or some other comprehensive list, using random numbers based on the total population to make sure that all the variations in speech are likely to be represented in the sample. You will appreciate that this is not an easy route to take, and you also have to build in factors such as the reluctance of some people to take part in surveys and interviews. If you decide on a much smaller population – such as all students in the first year of a university course – you will have to take care not to skew the results in favour of people who you know, because it is unlikely that they will be representative of the whole population.

Although random sampling is the most reliable method of obtaining a representative sample, there is another kind of sampling technique that is suitable for studies of variation, particularly when you wish to compare linguistic usage by informants of different ages, social classes or ethnic or geograph-

Table 1.3   Suggested age ranges and sample size for a quantitative study with two variables

	18–27	35–44	52–60	70+
Number of male informants	20	18	22	16
Number of female informants	22	16	20	18

ical origins. This is known as structured sampling, and it is used to create a balanced sample by using non-linguistic variables to define the different groups of informants. Thus you may decide to investigate dialect words for small types of bread. Among the many possible variants in British English are *bap*, *roll*, *breadcake*, *teacake* and *barmcake*. In order to establish whether there are regional differences you might decide to examine samples of people in cities located in each of the regions of England – for example Bristol, London, Leicester, Wolverhampton, Newcastle and Manchester. Whilst in an ideal world the informants will be chosen by random sampling, the enormity of the task often precludes this. The easier option is structured sampling. With this it is essential to ensure that the different categories of informant are able to be compared, which requires there to be at least five informants, and preferably more, in each group. To return to the h-dropping project discussed earlier, there is a minimum of 16 in each of the categories and the results are therefore comparable. If we were to add another social variable, for example gender, to see whether h-dropping is more marked in men than in women, this would double the number of informants required (Table 1.3).

An issue that arises when more than one variable is considered is the difficulty of analysing the results. For quantitative projects you would have to perform some fairly sophisticated (multivariate) statistical tests on the data, so it is recommended that you read up on some of the basic principles (for example Woods *et al.*, 1986; see also Section 1.6 below).

The final form of sampling is opportunistic sampling, which involves collecting data from friends, relatives and others with whom you are in contact. This method is fine as long as you are not going to make generalised claims for your findings, as you would with quantitative research.

1.5.3   Methods of data collection

A very common way of collecting quantitative data is to conduct a survey by means of a questionnaire, copies of which can be sent to a large number of people. Making tape recordings of interviews and transcribing them according to pre-established dependent variables is a particularly good quantitative method if you are investigating phonological variables. For example in the study by Kerswill and Williams (2002) summarised in Section 1.5.3 above, 100 adolescents at two secondary schools in each of the three towns in question were tape recorded. The resultant data were compared with those from recordings of four to six elderly working-class participants in each area who had lived in that area since birth, plus data from the SED (see 1.4.2 above).

Qualitative studies are more in-depth and data are normally gathered from a small sample. The most usual means of data collection are interviews, usually taped. In Clark's (2004) study of phonology in the West Midlands of England, five informants were tape recorded and the resultant data were compared with previously published findings, including those by Wells (1999) and Biddulph (1986). Comparisons of this kind add a limited quantitative dimension to a study.

Whereas questionnaires can be sent out to a large number of people, by their very nature interviews are time-consuming and most researchers do not have the time or the resources to conduct a large number of interviews. However talking to people face to face allows a flexibility that is not possible with questionnaires. Therefore it is often useful to send a questionnaire to say, ten informants and then follow this up by interviewing five of them. Both of these methods are qualitative in this case.

As indicated above, the choice of whether to conduct a quantitative or a qualitative study depends very much on your aim. If your aim is to investigate phonological variations between towns (as in Kerswill, 2004) or across the British Isles (Widdowson and Upton, 2006), or grammatical variations across the British Isles (Cheshire, 1993), then a quantitative method is probably best. Equally if the study involves attitudes towards variation then the more informants the better and a questionnaire is appropriate. For example one of my students undertook a study of employers' attitudes towards local accents. She sent questionnaires to the personnel departments of ten national call centres to find out what account was taken of regional accents when engaging employees.

If the aim is to undertake an in-depth study of linguistic variations in a specific geographical location, then a qualitative method is appropriate. Kortmann and Schneider's (2004) study looks at linguistic variations across the world, but each chapter investigates a specific locality and in most cases the methods used were qualitative. For example a local brewery requested that research be undertaken into lexical variations of words to do with beer and drinking that could be used in an advertising campaign targeted at men. The people in charge of the campaign wanted to be sure that the dialect words and phrases they used were not only authentic but also conformed to dialect spelling. This project involved students interviewing and recording men in local pubs about their drinking habits.

The methods of data collection you choose, then, will depend on your research question and the focus of your study. Structured sampling can be used in qualitative studies, although the size and range of the sample may not be sufficient to obtain worthwhile statistical results. For example in one qualitative study of phonological variations between different ethnic groups for both genders in a specific geographical location there were only five informants in total, which is normally the minimum number required for each category for the purposes of comparison. Here, there were two non-linguistic variables: gender and ethnicity. It is sensible to restrict the non-linguistic variables in a qualitative study of this kind to a maximum of two since this makes the focus of the study clear. When there is a small range of informants too many non-linguistic variables would make it impossible to draw any worthwhile conclusions.

Whether the sample is random or structured it is important to bear in mind that just a few interviews will not provide enough data from which to draw general conclusions about social variability. Any conclusions that were drawn would have to be backed up by a larger study in order for them to be considered valid. In the study of dialect words and phrases for beer and drinking mentioned earlier the students interviewed the informants in pairs, and each pair of students interviewed five informants. The data so obtained provided information on lexis, grammar and pronunciation, but the data gathered by each individual pair was not sufficient to draw conclusions about social networks or social class. However the combined data gathered by the 10 pairs of students, involving 10 interviews and 50 informants analysed and conclusions about social variability to be drawn. In another study a doctoral research student investigating variations in register, in which social variation was also a factor, recorded 40 children aged 8–12 in six primary schools. The data collection for this study took 18 months, whereas that by the pairs of students took two weeks. Time factors such as this should also be considered when designing your study.

It is important to obtain biographical details of each of the informants as these details are crucial sources of contextual information. This information should include not only standard items such as name, age and address but also factors that may have a bearing on language use, for example level of education, length of time spent in the locality, and the birth place of parents or even grandparents. The best way of obtaining this information is to draw up a biographical questionnaire covering all the items you wish to be informed about and ask the informants to complete it at the beginning or end of the interview. The advantage of this is that you have a written record to which you can easily refer. The alternative is to ask for the information at the start of the interview by way of an ice-breaker, although this will involve you in additional transcription after the event. Note that the storage of personal details of this kind is subject to the Data Protection Act in Britain.

Once you have established your variables and chosen your sample, then you need to collect your data, as discussed below.

1.5.3.1 Questionnaires

Sufficient questionnaires should be issued to ensure an adequate return that is going to be of any use. As a rough guide, expect a fifty percent return. People do not return questionnaires they are sent for a number of reasons, including lack of time or lack of interest. This means that to obtain ten completed questionnaires, you will need to send out twenty.

A written questionnaire can be used as the main means of data collection when investigating grammar, lexis or attitudes towards language use, though it should be remembered that written English tends to be more formal than spoken English, and therefore a questionnaire may be of limited use if you are trying to obtain information on spoken grammar or informal lexis. When designing a questionnaire, make sure that you are clear about the kinds of questions you want to ask. **Closed questions** require just a yes or no answer; semi-open or **multiple choice questions** allow informants to choose from a restricted list of options; and **open questions** invite informants to give their own answers. For example an investigation of grammatical variation may include a question such as *Do you ever say 'I don't know nothing'?* This question invites a *yes* or *no* answer, and is therefore a closed question. A drawback with this is that while a 'yes' answer will provide information on informants who use this expression, a 'no' answer does not allow for identification of other non-standard negative constructions such as '*I know nothing*'. Therefore a multiple choice question would be more useful for discovering usage in this area. The question could be *Tick the following expressions you are most likely to use*, followed by a list of negative constructions. Also include a final category of 'Other' to capture anything you have not thought of. An open question would invite informants to give their own categories and descriptions such as: *How do you say 'no' to something?* It is important to avoid leading questions that invite a specific response. For example asking '*Do you think the Queen speaks good English?*' is more likely than not to be answered 'yes'. Note that non-standard grammatical constructions may be avoided by respondents who are anxious to be on their 'best' linguistic behaviour.

It is a good idea to have a mixture of all three kinds of questions since it is very difficult if not impossible to predict all possible answers to a closed or multiple-choice question. The amount of time it will take to process the questionnaire should also be taken into account. Although closed questions limit the number of answers they are the quickest to process since all they require is adding up the responses to each option. Open questions require more time as every answer might be different.

Once you have designed your questionnaire you should conduct a pilot survey before distributing it. That is, try it out on a few people to make sure that the questions are clear and elicit the information you want. Any questions that are regularly misunderstood, do not produce the required information or lead the informants more than expected should be redesigned and piloted again.

1.5.3.2 Recordings

If you are investigating spoken language you may wish to use recorded voices as your main form of data. This choice, unless you have a great deal of money and many research assistants to help, will make your project qualitative in nature. If sufficient resources are available it is possible to record a large number of informants in the way described below.

To generate sufficient data for analysis you need to record each informant for up to one hour, depending on the focus of your research. The recording can be of:

- The informant reading word lists or passages aloud.
- An interview between you and the informant.
- A conversation between informants.
- A conversation about written questions or another form of written data such as a spidergram (see Section 1.5.4 below).

The reading aloud method restricts you to identifying phonological variables, and the more formal nature of written passages may alter the informants natural speech. Even so the reading of a passage allows you to test, for example, the pronunciation of /t/ in different contexts, including syllable-final glottal stops. If the data obtained in this way are compared with readings from a word list, which is more formal still, this can give an idea of variations according to social context. Usually reading aloud is accompanied by another method of data collection that produces more naturally occurring speech, such as recorded interviews.

Interviews fall into one of three categories: structured, semistructured and unstructured or open. In **structured interviews** a list of questions is prepared in advance and all the informants are asked the same questions in the same order. No additional or supplementary questions are asked. In **semistructured interviews** most of the preprepared questions are the same and asked in the same order, but additional or supplementary questions are added. In **unstructured interviews** no questions are set in advance and the interview becomes a conversation that can go in any direction. A **structured** interview may have, say, five questions. For example the study undertaken on behalf of the local brewery discussed above consisted of structured interviews. All the informants were asked the following questions in the same order. *Is this your local? What beer do you drink? How does x beer compare with others? What words or phrases do you associate with drinking beer? With drinking x?* The advantage of this method, particularly if you are interviewing a large number of informants, is that comparing the data during the analysis is straightforward. The disadvantage is that it does not allow for any interesting answers to be developed or pursued.

A **semistructured interview** will have say, three main questions plus supplementary questions to draw out further information. For example the main questions could be *Do you go to the cinema often? What was the last film you saw? What is your favourite film?* Each of these questions could be followed by ones such as *Do you go locally or elsewhere?, Do you enjoy films by that director?,* and so on. The advantage of this kind of interview is that it allows a discussion to develop, but it does make the data analysis more time-consuming.

Because **unstructured interviews** have no predetermined questions the discussion can be more free-flowing and the repondents' speech may be more natural. However should the conversation dry up the interviewer may have no resources to turn to and the data generated might not have sufficiently similar items or topics to enable comparison. For occasions of this kind, it is a good idea to have some questions ready such as *when did you last go on holiday?*

For the purposes of sociolinguistic research, and depending on your research question, a semi-structured interview is preferable. It enables you to ensure that the variables you are investigating, particularly phonological ones, are covered by your questions and that the answers will be comparable. The supplementary questions will enable you to cover ground that the informants do not volunteer, and to ensure that all the informants discuss roughly the same topic. Whatever method of data collection you choose, that choice should always be justified in the write-up.

Recording and talking about speech tends to make people conscious of what they are saying and how they are saying it, thus giving rise to a phenomenon called **the observer's paradox** (Labov, 1966). This refers to the fact that it is impossible to observe someone 'behaving naturally' without affecting what they do or how they do it. Informants' speech can be affected in two ways. First, an interview situation brings with it a certain degree of formality and this affects speakers' use of language. Second, if the topic of conversation is the informants' speech they are even more likely to formalise what they say. For this reason you need to think very carefully about the questions you are going to ask. Questions that take their attention away from speech and on to other topics is always a good idea, such as Labov's (1972) 'danger of death' question: *Were you ever in a situation where you thought you were in serious danger?* Another way of minimising the observer's paradox is to interview informants in pairs. This may take the focus of attention away from you as the interviewer and allow for a more varied dialogue.

People's attitudes towards language use is a particularly problematic topic to study, not least because people's perception of how they or others speak is often at odds with the actual speech (see Kerswill and Williams 2002). Hence it is difficult to assess the reliability of a person's judgement without recourse to other evidence, such as a dialect recognition experiment (ibid.). This involves playing taped samples of speech and asking the informants to identify their own community dialect. An experiment of this kind can also be written rather than spoken. A study of attitudes works best if it has a clear focus, such as employers' attitude towards employing workers with a regional accent, as in the call centre example discussed earlier. In the interest of reliability, **triangulation** is often employed in data collection: that is, more than one method of data collection is used and the results are cross-referenced. Thus usage reported by informants can be compared with naturally occurring conversation (perhaps in response to the 'danger of death' question) so that the accuracy of self-reporting can be checked.

A final issue that must be considered before you begin to collect your data, especially tape recordings, is **ethics**. This includes the ways in which the data are collected and obtaining the informants' consent. If your main method of data collection is a questionnaire survey, then completing and returning a questionnaire means that the informant is happy for you to use the information provided. The situation is more complex when it comes to tape recording, which can be done in an **overt** or **covert** way. With **overt** recording the presence of the recorder is obvious, the informants are in no doubt that they are being recorded and have given their permission for it. If no permission is given, then no recording takes place. They are also fully aware of the reasons why they are being recorded and that the topic of the interview or conversation is the subject of the research.

Covert recording is when informants are recorded without their realising it or a reason other than the real one is given as to why the data are being collected. If you record informants without their knowledge you must obtain their permission afterwards if you are to use the data. One way to get around the problem and obtain permission is to give a false reason for the recording. For example you may wish to record the informants' speech in order to study phonological variation and its relation to social class or regional identity, but you tell them that you are conducting a survey of eating habits. Making the focus of the interview something other than the informants' use of language gives you a better chance of obtaining more naturally occurring data than would otherwise be the case. However the informant's ignorance of the real reason why they are being recorded remains an ethical consideration, so you should tell them after the recording has been completed and ask for their permission again. For full guidelines on good practice, see http://www.baal.org.uk/goodprac.pdf

1.5.4   Sound and video recording equipment

The equipment you use to record informants' speech could be a standard audio cassette recoder, an MP3 player, a camcorder, a laptop or a digital audio tape. When researching variations in English, and especially accents, sound recording is by far the most reliable source of data as it captures sounds as they actually are. Video recording gives an extra dimension since it captures the context in which naturally occurring language is used. However because the focus of research is usually the language itself and not, for example, body language or facial expression it is customary to use a sound recorder as the main method of data collection.

The kind of microphone you use is also important. Many cassette players have built-in microphones but the sound quality of the recording can be very poor, and for this reason it is best to have a separate, omni-directional microphone; that is, one that captures sound from all directions. Since an interview can take up to an hour it is best to place the microphone between you and the informant rather than to hold it, since holding a microphone can be not only obtrusive but also tiring. It should be positioned a little below the mouth level and be equidistant from roughly 30 centimetres either way – if it is too close the sound will be distorted. It is vital that you establish beforehand how the microphone works and if it is working properly, for example you should check whether you have plugged it into the correct socket on the tape recorder. You should also check for any peripheral noise, such as a fridge humming in the background, that might affect the recording.

Some recorders allow you to set a recording level to avoid distortion. There will be a meter that shows the level, plus a dial to adjust it. To set the level, ask your informants some simple questions such as *'What did you have for breakfast?'*, or *'Where did you go on holiday?'* whilst you adjust the setting. Some recorders offer level options such as 'high' or 'low'. Here you can ask your questions and then play back the tape to ascertain the right setting.

Another important factor to take into account is the location in which the recording is to take place. As the aim of the exercise is to record speech that is as close as possible to that used by the informants when the recorder is not there it must be a setting where they feel comfortable. For example it could be their own homes, a social setting such as a café, bar or pub, or, if you are investigating the speech of children, a playground at school or close to their homes. If you are investigating lexical variations of words to do with beer and drinking, the most logical setting is a pub. However you need to record at a time when the pub is not too noisy, or arrange with the landlord to have exclusive use of a room. Similarly if you wish to investigate phonological variations between people of different ages, then a family gathering or a social occasion such as a birthday party would be appropriate. It would need to be a small enough event to record individual conversations, but large enough to generate suitable data. You should also let your informants know how long the interview or recording will take, and agree a starting and ending time.

Depending on the focus of your study, your recording could be of a discussion of a document such as a spidergram. Here the informant is given a sheet of paper and asked to list alternative vocabulary items for certain groups of words. This can be given to each informant in advance to complete, with a subsequently recorded discussion of the items listed, or it can be completed as part of the interview. This technique would be a good one to use when interviewing people about drinking habits and beer. (For more information on this technique see www.bbc.co.uk/voices.)

For playing back and transcribing the recorded speech it is important to have a recorder that does the job you want it to do. One with a built-in counter and speed control is especially useful. The counter will let you pinpoint sections of speech, and a speed control will let you vary the playback speed of the recording, which is particularly useful when it comes to transcribing. The development of digital recording has allowed electronic resources such as sound files to be compiled. For example the Newcastle electronic corpus of Tyneside English (see: www.ncl.ac.uk/necte). includes sound files, orthographic and phonetic transcriptions and tagging.

When you are ready to start recording, then note the date, time and location of the recording on the tape itself and on a sheet of paper. Make sure your questions and any other material you may need are to hand, including follow-up questions in case the informant dries up or something unexpected happens. You should also bear in mind that conversation, and the circumstances in which it takes place, can be unpredictable. You have to be prepared to record more than once and for a longer time than you may have thought necessary in order to obtain sufficient data for analysis. It is always far better to have too much than too little.

1.5.5   Transcribing data

Once you have completed your recordings your next task is transcription. This is very time-consuming, and is best done with a playback device that lets you slow down the pace of the speech, as discussed above.

There are two types of transcription: **phonetic transcription** and **orthographic transcription**. Which one you use will depend on your research question. For example if you are conducting a phonological study you will need to transcribe phonetically using the international phonetic alphabet

(IPA – see Jeffries, 2006, ch. 1). The reason for using the IPA is that covers more sounds than the alphabet does, and can be used consistently to represent the same sounds, unlike the alphabet.

There are two types of phonetic transcription: **narrow transcription** and **broad transcription**. Narrow transcription gives precise details of sound and encodes information on the phonetic variations of specific allophones in an utterance. Broad transcription gives a basic idea of the sound and is usually a transcription of the phonemes of an utterance. Broad transcription is generally used in dialectology. For example:

Erm in about (. . .) erm twenty seven weeks I go away to Cuba
ɜːm ən əbæut ɜːm twenti sevən wiːks ə gəʊ əweɪ tə kjuːbə

for two weeks er 'nd four days in Havana and ten days in a holiday
fə tuː wiːks ɜːnd fɔː deɪz ən həvænə ən ten deɪz ən æ hɒlɪdiː

Resort erm it's cost about two thousand pounds for the two of us
rɪzɔːt ɜːm ɪts kɒst əbæut tuː θaʊsənd paʊndz fə ðe tuː əv ʌs

The above transcription was taken from a recording of an informant speaking in a Black Country accent (see Section 1.4.3 above). One of the characteristics of this accent is the presence of dipthongs such as [æʊ] (Mathison, 1999; Clark, 2004), and as Wells (1982) points out there is quite a degree of phonetic variation. These findings are represented in the transcript by æ in əbæut and the variation aʊ in θaʊsənd and paʊndz.

It is important to listen to a passage several times before beginning your transcription. This is because you must be absolutely sure that you know exactly what the speaker has said in order to transcribe it faithfully since you cannot, as in a written text, rely on a variety of interpretations.

For **orthographic** transcriptions the standard alphabet is used and what is said is written down verbatim (see Section 2.8.3). This is usually set out like a play script, with the speakers' names on the left-hand side and the text of what they say next to their names. It is conventional not to use capital letters or punctuation in such transcriptions. It is important to transcribe all that you hear, including utterances not normally found in writing, such as *um*, *er* and so on, and to resist the temptation to turn what is said into grammatical and punctuated standard English.

Once you have decided which form of transcription to use you should select the parts you wish to transcribe. Bearing in mind that phonetic transcription takes longer than orthographic transcription – as a rule of thumb it takes between seven and ten hours to transcribe one hour of recording – it is practical to transcribe only the sections that are pertinent to your study. In this regard it is a good idea to have a list of related criteria when you make your selection. For example if you are analysing accent differences in a particular geographical area you should select the sections in which your informants are most at ease and are speaking naturally, which is likely to be when the interview or conversation has settled in, probably about ten minutes into the recording. If the focus of your study is lexis and/or grammar you may only need to transcribe short sections in which the relevant structures or lexical items are used.

1.5.6 Analysing data

Once you have transcribed your recordings the next step is to analyse them. The focus of your analysis will depend on the nature of your study, but it will almost certainly be on identifying regular differences in accent, vocabulary or grammar. If you have chosen to investigate grammar, vocabulary or attitudes towards language use then you may have other data to analyse, such as questionnaires.

Patterns of linguistic variation can be identified by comparing your data with standard English and RP. Here you will also have to take account of any non-linguistic variables you have included in your study – such as age, gender, social class or ethnicity – that may account for variations. Any conclusion you draw here will of necessity be tentative, since you cannot define which variable is responsible for a linguistic variation unless you are in a position to perform statistical tests on large amounts of quantitative data.

The following transcript is taken from a study of the Black Country dialect. The five (three female, two male) were white, British, informants aged between 40 and 50, had left school at the age of 15–16 and had no formal qualifications. The following features of non-standard grammar were identified:

> J: *yeah, he got me a job 'cos I <u>wor</u>...well, I was working, but I changed jobs 'cos it was nearer, <u>worn</u> it?*
>
> K: *and <u>her</u> came back Sunday*
>
> M: *that's got to be our jodhpurs <u>**wot**</u> we make*
>
> K: *and then <u>her come</u> back Sunday*
>
> K: *<u>them</u> chickens*
>
> J: *<u>Never</u> touched it*
>
> K: *and the zip was <u>broke</u> so he says*
>
> K: *was that one <u>yorn</u>?*

Table 1.4   Example of a transcript table

Feature	Example	Transcript and line
1. Dialect use of preterite <to be> <was> affirmative <were> negative	<was> <worn>	1.3, 1.4
2. Non-standard use of <her> would be <she> in SE	<her>	3.2, 3.3
3. <wot> for SE <that> (relative pronoun)	<what>	2.7
4. Preterite identical to present tense	<come>	3.3, 5.5
5. <them> for demonstrative <those>	<them>	4.1
6. <never> as past tense negator	<never>	5.10, 5.12
7. (adjectival) past participle identical to preterite: <broke> for SE <broken>	<broke>	2.6 (2.8)
8. <yorn> for SE <yours> (2nd person possessive pronoun	<yorn>	2.9

Once you have completed this part of the analysis the grammatical forms you have identified should be presented in a table like the one above. The first column describes the features identified in the Black Country tapes in grammatical terms, the second gives examples, and the third gives the first occurrence of each feature in the transcripts, with subsequent occurrences listed.

The next step is to identify grammatical features that are specific to a particular dialect and those which are present in non-standard dialects. For example the use of *yorn* the second person possessive pronoun (number 8 in the table) is a distinctive feature of the Black Country dialect, while the use of never (number 6) as a past tense negator and *broke* (number 7) as a past participle identical to a preterite can be found in several non-standard dialects.

Having analysed your data and drawn some conclusions you should look at some previously published studies of the same topic to see whether your data confirms or contradicts the findings in them.

If your study is of attitudes towards language use your analysis will focus on identifying these attitudes and perhaps where they came from. As discussed in Sections 1.3.1 and 1.3.2, people's attitude towards language use, including prejudices against certain types of use, can be traced back to a time when people held very different beliefs about language from the ones linguists hold today, but which still persist. You may also wish to investigate the extent to which individuals choose a certain variety of English not only to express ideas but also to establish their own identity and distinguish themselves from other groups of people.

Your analysis of questionnaire data, if any, is likely to involve the production of numerical results if closed or multiple choice questions have been used. There are some simple statistical texts, such as the χ^2 test, that can quite quickly show whether raw scores and/or percentage scores are significantly different from each other.

1.5.7   Writing your report

The overall structure of your report will be different from that of a conventional essay. It should include the following elements:

- Presentation of your hypothesis or hypotheses. This will include a description of the issue(s) in question; the topics to be addressed; what your hypothesis is and why it matters; what type of data will be presented (phonological, lexical, syntactic or people's opinions); if appropriate, which variable(s) and variants of them have been used in the research; a description of the speech community examined; what type of analysis will be presented and, briefly, what conclusions you expect to draw. You should also locate this discussion in the context of previously published studies. This will allow you to set your hypothesis against the work of others and provide a context for it.

- Description of your methodology. Methodologies are normally drawn from certain methodological and analytical frameworks, and when applying them researchers make assumptions about theoretical issues. The description of your methodology should be detailed enough for others to be able to replicate your study, and it should include information about the following: the informants and investigators, and how many there were of each; an explanation of the methods used to locate informants and persuading them to participate; any criteria used for sampling; how the data were collected (for example questionnaires and/or recordings) and transcribed; how many questions were asked or items were elicited; when and where the study took place; and how the results were analysed, including whether any statistical analysis was involved. Your report should include a copy of any research instruments you used, such as interview questions, questionnaires, dialect recognition experiments and completed biographical data sheets.

- Presentation of the data. This is the place to describe the variant(s) or the attitudes you are investigating. You should define the range of variation for the dependent variable(s) you are investigating, plus any other variables that may affect the dependent variable, for example social variables (age, gender, ethnicity), stylistic variables (a casual conversation or the reading of a passage by the informants) or linguistic variables (the position of a variable in a clause, the height of vowel). You will also need to define and discuss all the social factors that are relevant to your project, and provide a table or list of all the relevant linguistic variables and their possible variants, with examples from your data or a summary of your questionnaire responses. Your report should include a copy of the transcript from which you have taken your examples, or a copy of the questionnaire. As mentioned earlier, quantitative studies must be statistically tested for significance.

- Discussion of your findings. Here you should analyse your data (see Section 1.5.5 above), discuss any patterns you have found and comment on how these correspond to your hypothesis. Discuss each independent variable individually, commenting on how it correlates with each dependent variable or each question of your questionnaire, and what it reveals.

- Your results. This section should address questions such as whether your results support your hypothesis, and if not, why not. Make sure you refer to everything you raised in the introduction. Were there any surprises? How do your findings compare with those of others researchers? How might your study be improved? What does your investigation suggest for future research?

1.5.8 Sample projects

Project 1: An analysis of a local accent.
- Choose a geographical area and conduct an analysis of the local accent using your own choice of linguistic variable(s) and two non-linguistic variables. You should have a sample of at least five informants for each combination of variables (eg. each age group × each class × linguistic variable).

The best methods of data collection here would be taped interviews or conversations. As suggested in the previous section, in your report you should outline the scope of your study, state why you chose this particular topic and justify your research methods. You should also provide biographical information about the informants and transcribe selections of your recordings into IPA, using a narrow or broad system of transcription depending on the focus of your study. Your analysis of the transcription would then identify occurrences of the linguistic variable(s) and trace any patterns of variant in relation to the non-linguistic variables or linguistic context. A comparison can also be made with other published studies on the locality, to see whether or not they confirm what has already been found or show something different in drawing your conclusions. Your transcripts will form an appendix to your report and should be referred to in it.

Project 2: Lexical change in (place) circa 1950 to the present day.
- Conduct a study of lexical differences between three generations of the same family, all of whom are still living in the area in which they were born. The sample should consist of at least three informants, one of whom can be yourself. Identify the extent of any lexical changes and the reasons for them.

The method of data collection could be taped interviews based on a written questionnaire or a spidergram. The collection of biographical information is essential, particularly with regard to education, since it could enable you to identify possible reasons for any lexical changes. For this project you could transcribe the selected sections of your recordings orthographically rather than into IPA. Compare your findings with those in published studies on the topic in the same locality, or with data from electronic resources. Do they confirm what was previously found? If not, how do they differ? In your report, outline the scope of your study, explain why you chose this particular one and describe and justify your research methods. Your transcripts should be presented as an appendix to the report, which should refer to it.

Project 3: Grammatical variations in a locality.
The data for this project could be collected by means of a questionnaire or gathered from contemporary writings in the local dialect, for example newspaper articles, poems and short stories. Write down instances of grammatical variation in orthographic notation. Having analysed your data, compare your findings with those from previous research on grammatical variations in the locality in question.

Project 4: Your peer group's attitude towards variations in language use.
Your data for this project should come from a questionnaire survey, possibly followed up by interviews and/or dialect recognition experiments. The success of your project will depend very much upon the design of the questionnaire and the kinds of question you ask in the dialect recognition experiment. The questionnaire should be general enough to elicit a large range of views but also sufficiently focused to obtain the reasons why the informants hold the views that they do. In this regard, biographical questions are essential. The questions you ask as part of your dialect recognition experiment should also allow for elaborated answers rather than merely 'Yes' or 'No'.

1.6   Further reading

Leith (1997) and Beal (2006) are good places to start for sociohistorical accounts of English. Views on standardisation, grammaticality and correctness can be found in Clark (2001), Crowley (1991, 1996), Honey (1989) and Milroy and Milroy (1993). Labov (1978) and Wolfram and Schilling-Estes (2006) cover social and geographical variations in English in the United States, and Milroy (1987) covers those in the United Kingdom. Wells (1999), Hughes *et al.* (2005) and Widdowson and Upton (2006) provide accounts of geographical variations in English in the United Kingdom, while Schneider, Burridge *et al.* (2004) do so for countries across the world. Trudgill (2002) and Kerswill and Williams (2002) discuss aspects of sociolinguistic variation and change. Montgomery (1995) and Wardhaugh (2006) are good introductory books on sociolinguistics in general. Woods *et al.* (1986) provide an overview of linguistic statistical analysis.

2 Pragmatics and Discourse

2.1 Introduction

This chapter examines pragmatics and discourse: that is, the way in which linguistics interactions shape linguistic structures, and how communication involves more than the words that are actually spoken. Traditionally linguists have concentrated on the formal structure and properties of what we hear as sound or see as words on a page; that is, the visible or aural aspects of language. Language and word structure are described in terms of syntax, morphology and phonology, and the field of semantics is concerned with the meaning of individual words (for details see Jeffries, 2006). Studies of variations in language use, as discussed in Chapter 1, have also concentrated on these structures, especially phonology, as well as their history and changes over time. Another dimension of the study of language is its use as a tool for communication between people in everyday settings. The desire of linguistics to define how communication, as opposed to language, works has resulted in the development of new branches of linguistics, as discussed below.

Discourse analysis and **conversation analysis** are concerned with the structure and management of discourse and conversation, whilst pragmatics is concerned with unspoken or implicit meanings in language. Another field, interactional sociolinguistics, focuses on cultural variations in the ways people use and interpret discourse. However these fields overlap in a number of ways, particularly in respect of the context in which speech occurs, how it is made meaningful and its purpose or function. Hence these fields of language analysis go beyond the study of the linguistic structure of utterances and look more closely at, for example, how the structure of a conversation can be as meaningful as its content, as well as the social force of what is said and how the assumptions and world-views of speakers are encoded or embedded in speech: in what they say or do not say. As Bonvillian (1993, p. 85) puts it: 'Understanding meaning is necessarily contextual, situating speech in interpersonal and cultural contexts. All cultures provide rules for appropriate communicative interaction, defining behaviours that *should* occur, that *may* occur and that *should not* occur in given contexts.'

In formal linguistics the term 'structure' refers to the ways in which words combine, the grammatical relations between them, and how they function within a sentence, the sentence usually being the largest unit of analysis. Pragmatics, discourse analysis, conversation analysis and interactional sociolinguistics are all concerned with much longer structures than the sentence because when people communicate there is normally a series of verbal exchanges. Indeed studies in discourse analysis, and more recently in the grammar of speech (for example Carter and McCarthy, 2006), have found that applying the term 'sentence' to speech is something of a misnomer since the ways in which we structure speech differ significantly from the ways in which we structure writing (see section 2.7.1 below). The preferred terms in pragmatics for a segment of continuous speech are therefore 'utterance' or 'speech event'.

2.2   Language, meaning and communication

As children growing up in families and/or communities, and as part of the process of socialisation, we acquire rules for appropriate communicative interaction. This is done both informally at home and in our communities and formally at school or other public settings. Learning to behave includes the proper use of language. We are told how to act and what to say – or not – in particular places, at certain times or to particular people. For example we learn to say *Thank you* when offered something, even if we do not particularly want it: *Say thank you to Aunty for offering you a biscuit*. We are also told to modify aspects of our behaviour: *Don't shout/point – it's rude! You mustn't tell your sister she looks fat in that dress, even if you think she does*. Much of what we learn comes from our own observations of people around us: interactions among our family members, peers, neighbours or strangers on the bus. In this way we learn the interactional norms that are considered appropriate in the society – or by groups within that society – in which we live. Consequently much of what we learn is implicit; that is, it is never spelt out or explained but absorbed as part and parcel of growing up in a particular community, culture and society.

Sometimes we live in more than one community or culture, or grow up in one and then move to another, and this requires knowledge of different cultural norms. For example if we happen to be the first generation of children born to immigrant parents we have to acquire the cultural norms of our parents and those of the country to which they have migrated. Similarly if we move to another country at some point in our life the process of assimilation, even if the same language is spoken, must include the acquisition and understanding of implicit norms if successful communication is to take place. If you have had experience of living in different settings, then you are probably more aware than most people of the unspoken interactional norms that govern verbal behaviour. The underlying and unstated rules of interaction, which we normally follow without thought, are usually only brought to the surface when they are violated.

For example in British culture the rules of conversation include listening to whoever is speaking before taking our turn in the conversation because it is considered rude to interrupt, and if we are interrupted because somebody cannot wait to speak, then we should stop speaking. In other cultures, such as those on the Indian subcontinent, these rules do not exist and it is acceptable for people to talk at the same time and to interrupt one another. As our communication with people in other parts of the world increases, through business travel, holidays abroad, use of the internet and so on, we shall frequently find ourselves in situations where the norms differ from the ones we grew up with (see Section 2.6 for more on this subject).

2.3   Language in context

Some sociolinguists argue that in order to identify the relevant features of communication in different contexts or situations, speech behaviour needs to be studied and analysed in its widest social and cultural context. The work of Gumperz and Hymes has been very influential in this area. Drawing on research in sociology and anthropology, Gumperz and Hymes (1986) have proposed an ethnography of communication. Ethnography – a research method associated with sociology and anthropology – is concerned with the study of human behaviour in ordinary day-to-day settings. Gumperz and Hymes' ethnography of communication extends this notion to include verbal behaviour on the ground that no verbal activity has any meaning unless it is viewed in the context of its situation. For Hymes (1974), the communicatory behaviour in a community is the starting point for ethnographic analysis. He has identified several components of communication that require description, of which the most important are (1) the setting or context, (2) the participants (a a minimum a speaker and addressee), (3) the topic(s) and attitudes, and (4) the goals.

While each of these components can be studied independently of the others, Gumperz (1982) argues that a speech event will include all of them if it is to count as a speech event, so the components are interdependent and should be studied together. The extent to which any one component dominates the others depends on the speaker's assessment of the situation in question and how things are likely to turn out. For example speech events in a formal context – such as a law court, lecture hall or seminar room – are often the preserve of designated participants and are on relatively fixed topics. At other times all four components may have a more equal share, especially in informal settings. Consider the following law court example of how the different factors interconnect (adapted from Bonvillian, 1993, pp. 85–6):

- *The setting*: a trial or hearing in a courtroom. The latter is structured in such a way as to have separate seating area for each category of participant and they are oriented in relation to one another.
- *The participants*: the judge, lawyers, defendant(s), plaintiff(s), witnesses, jurors, spectators and court officials. Each participant's behaviour, including verbal behaviour, is determined by his or her role. The judge is seated in a dominant position at the front of the courtroom, usually on a raised platform and wears special attire. The judge clearly controls the verbal behaviour of the other participants, each of whom is obliged to speak at a certain time, or not to speak at all. Indeed failure to speak or be silent when so directed are legally punishable offences (contempt of court). Only the judge, lawyers, defendant, plaintiff (if present) and witnesses may speak; all the others (jurors, officers, spectators) must remain silent. Specific discourse patterns are expected of each type of participant. Lawyers may make introductory and concluding statements and ask questions. Witnesses must restrict themselves to answering the questions. Judges have greater latitude: they can make statements, ask questions and issue commands and rulings.
- *The topics*. These are rigidly defined. The event is about a particular issue and all that is said must be relevant to that issue. The right of participants to change the topic is limited and permission to do so must be asked of and granted by the judge). When the lawyers question the witnesses the questions must be pertinent to the central issue or a logical extension of it. Similarly witnesses' answers must be restricted to the topic and relate directly to their own experience. Judges have some flexibility in the choice of topic, but they too are limited by the overall focus.
- *The goals*. The goals of the participants vary according to their role in the proceedings and their communicatory behaviour is oriented towards achieving those goals; that is, they choose their words, tones of voice, facial expressions, gestures, and so on to accomplish their purpose. For example the the judge must appear impartial, the lawyers may speak and act aggressively, the defendant portrays him- or herself as innocent, the

witnesses try to appear honest and reliable, and the jurors remain silent but convey their interest in the words and behaviour of others.

A trial in a court of law is probably the most formal of human interactions, but even in very informal settings the ways of speaking and right to speak are constrained by cultural norms. Take the example of an English family dinner:

- *The setting*: Family meals are taken in various settings, including at a table or in front of the television with a plate on the knee. If a table is used the structural design is centred on the arrangement of seats.
- *The participants*. These are the members of the family and perhaps a guest or two. Each participant's behaviour is conditioned by his or her role, including verbal behaviour. Although the setting is not as formal as a courtroom the family members usually have designated seats, with the mother, father or another adult in a position of parental authority occupying at least one of the end seats and controlling the communicatory behaviour of the other family members, encouraging talk or discouraging it as the case may be.
- *The Topics*. These are potentially limitless and can be introduced by anybody. Most typically they relate to the family members' daily experiences – at work or school, extended family members and friends, television programmes, computers or games, or current affairs that have grabbed the news headlines – for example a national election or a disaster somewhere in the world. The speech event may be about something in particular but not all verbal behaviour has to be relevant to it. The participants have the right to change the topic and permission usually does not need to be asked. The conversation may range over a number of issues, with all the members taking part in no particular order, but the overall pace and direction of the conversation may be controlled by a dominant adult.
- *The goals*. The goals of the participants may vary. For teenagers the goal may be to eat the meal as quickly as possible in order to get back to the television or computer. For adults it may be a time to talk about the day's events and perhaps plan the next day's activities. Above all, family meals are a social occasion where members catch up with one another's news.

Ethnographers of communication claim that by observing variations in speaking styles and verbal behaviour we can identify the underlying and unstated rules of interaction. One problem with this approach is that it tries to do far too much at once (see Jeffries, 2006, ch. 1). It takes into account the full complexity of grammar, personality, social structure and cultural patterns and treats them as integral to the speech activity. Although not many sociolinguists would disagree with this as an aim, it is simply too much to consider all aspects of human behaviour – social, cultural and linguistic – at the same time. In addition, because the approach is so context specific, given the apparently endless variety of situations it is difficult to generalise rules across them even when they take place in similar settings, except in the most formal of settings, such as the law court example above. While the approach lends itself well to understanding how communication occurs in particular contexts, and might lead to discovery of the underlying and unstated rules of interaction for those contexts, it is doubtful whether this discovery could then be transferred to other situations or made into a methodology. Some sociolinguists argue that an ethnography of communication is too context bound to be of much use linguistically. Nevertheless the approach is important because it highlights the central place of context in communication (see also Chapman, 2006, ch. 5).

The verbal aspects of a speech activity and the implicit rules that govern communication at all levels are what pragmatics and discourse analysis are concerned with. In the example of the court of law, verbal communication must be explicit and leave no room for ambiguity, misinterpretation or misunderstanding. Consequently identifying the implicit rules is much more straightforward than in less formal situations where the topics and goals of the participants are not as focused or explicit and there is a greater possibility of misunderstanding and misinterpretation. One question that those in the field of pragmatics frequently ask is what patterns of unquestioned meaning emerge from verbal communication? Consider the following examples:

Woman:	*What's the road number where we turn left?*
Partner:	*Oh, we've got ages to go yet.*

This conversation is between two people who live together and know one another well. The woman has asked a specific question because she wants to be prepared in good time to turn left, but her partner interprets it as indicating anxiety, so rather than answering the question he offers soothing words to calm her.

In the next example a mother and her young son are out shopping and the mother needs to go to the toilet. She goes into a cubicle and discovers too late that there is no toilet paper. She calls out to her son, *Jonny, go and see if there is any toilet paper in the men's toilets.* He does as asked, comes back and says: *Yes Mummy!* In this case the child has taken the mother's request literally and not worked out the illocutionary intent (see Section 2.4.2. below) of her sentence: *and if there is please get some for me.*

This issue of interpretation, of explaining the unspoken or implied, is a central focus of pragmatics. As the examples above illustrate, the meaning of particular utterances or exchanges between people often depends as much upon the context of the speech and the purpose of the speakers as on the literal meaning of the utterances themselves.

Consider the phrase *How're things going?* In theory this phrase is open to any number of replies but in reality they are limited by the situation, the speaker of the question and the relationship between the two participants. For example *How're things going?* is a standard opening between two acquaintances who accidentally meet in the street and have not seen one another for a long time, especially when one of them cannot quite remember when they last talked to each other. Given the situation – an unexpected exchange between acquaintance rather than close friends – the meaning potential of this utterance is limited. It cannot be interpreted as a request to walk the dog, to leap into bed or to go on holiday. There are clear social constraints on the sorts of answer that could be given, for instance, it would not be appropriate to relate minute details of relationship or health problems and so on. One option is to take the question as a purely phatic greeting, say *OK thanks* and move on, or to take it as a question about a job or a general enquiry about the family. However if one changes the context in which the question is asked, for example a relationship guidance session between a counsellor and a couple, or a consultation between a doctor and patient, then the question takes on a very different meaning. Both speaker and hearer develop topics from a range of possible utterance meanings that are appropriate to the circumstances and acceptable to all participants.

It is also the case that people do not always say what they mean. For example when saying *It's warm in here* the speaker may mean *Can you open a window?* Thus people may mean something quite different from what their words say, or even the opposite. For example a friend asks my opinion of her new hair cut I might say *It suits you* when actually I think the opposite but do not wish to hurt her feelings.

2.4 Language as action

2.4.1 Speech act theory

Our understanding of the underlying or unstated rules that govern communication owes a great deal to a particular theory of language known as **speech act theory**. Prior to the 1970s, it was presumed that spoken interactions were a relatively haphazard, chaotic way of using language that was not subject to the linguistic rules of written text. However, far from being unstructured, conversations and spoken language have unique structures of their own. In addition speech can function in a performative way; that is, speaking can be not only a way of verbalising actions but also of performing them. For example *I apologise* verbalises the remorse of the speaker but it also functions as the act of apologising itself.

Speech act theory was originated by the philosopher John Austin (1962), expanded by Searle (1969) and developed further by Grice (1975). The theory is based on the belief that language is often used to perform actions and on how meaning and action relate to language. As Austin (1962, p. 100) says, 'the words used are to some extent to be explained by the "context" in which they are designed to be or have actually been spoken in a linguistic interchange'. It is this emphasis on context that underpins speech act theory, and that has made it a far more suitable basis for linguistic method and practice than the all-encompassing ethnographic theories taken from anthropology and sociology, which attempt to cover every aspect of behaviour and interaction, as discussed above.

Austin wished to move away from traditional approaches to the study of meaning in philosophy, and particularly from the notion that the meaning of a sentence could be analysed in terms of 'truth' or 'falsity' (see: Jeffries, 2006). As humans we communicate verbally and non-verbally. Austin called verbal communication a 'speech act' and argued that speech acts performed three different acts at once: the **locutionary act**, the **perlocutionary act** and **the illocutionary act**.

- The locutionary act corresponds to the act *of* saying something. It involves uttering certain noises in a particular grammatical construction with a more or less definite sense of reference.
- The perlocutionary act is the act performed *by* saying something. It involves the effect that the speaker has on her or his listener when uttering the sentence. This effect might be upon the feelings, thoughts or actions of the hearer, even if the effect is not intended. Examples of perlocutionary acts are convincing, persuading, annoying, amusing and so on.
- The illocutionary act is the act performed *in* saying something. It reflects the speaker's intent in uttering a sentence, and it is the **illocutionary force** of an utterance that determines what illocutionary act is performed.

Austin argued that linguists should not limit themselves to the study of the literal meanings of utterances (the locutionary act) but should also concern themselves with what communicative act was intended (illocutionary act) or accomplished (perlocutionary act). We know what the sentence *I promise to be there at nine o'clock exactly* means, but how is it to be taken? As a promise? As a threat? A teacher who says to a noisy disruptive class *I'll keep you in after the lesson* is simultaneously engaging in three acts:

- Locutionary: the act of saying a sentence that means *I'll make you stay in school later than usual.*
- Illocutionary: the act of making a threat.
- Perlocutionary: the act of silencing the students (or causing a revolt!)

For Austin the illocutionary force was not part of the literal and linguistic meaning of what a speaker says. Statements can also act, as requests. *It's cold in here* can either function as a statement or be interpreted as a request to turn on some heating (see also Thomas, 1995, pp. 1, 28–54). Sometimes it is not possible to tell what is meant simply from the form of words being used. We may recognise illocutionary acts and/or the illocutionary force behind them from, our own previous experience (both linguistic and non-linguistic), from our knowledge of the speaker and from the context in question. However we can also get it wrong and we do not always interpret illocutionary acts correctly. What is important to remember is that there is no one-to-one relationship between the syntactic structure of an utterance and a particular speech act. Depending on the contrast an illocutionary act of warning could be a declarative sentence, a statement, a command, a question or any other linguistic structure. For example:

> *Your t-shirt is on fire.*
>
> *Watch out! Your t-shirt's on fire.*
>
> *Did you know your t-shirt's on fire?*
>
> *Why is your t-shirt on fire?*

After Austin's death, his work was taken up by Searle (1969). Like Austin he saw the importance of recognising that when people say something to someone, very often they are not just saying words but are also inviting or performing an action of some kind, which in some cases can be legally binding. Searle picked up from where Austin had left off and concentrated on trying to explain what speakers intend by a particular illocutionary act, and how hearers recognise such acts. He proposed that some illocutionary acts can be performed by a speaker if and only if: a linguistic item (word, phrase, clause) is uttered, this item has a determinate characteristic (for example word order, stress, intonation) and the speaker's utterance constitutes a relevant act because of specific conditions that have to be satisfied on the occasion of the utterance. So, for example, we can do things such as promising, warning and so on by using particular forms of words in particular circumstances. Searle also identified the phenomenon of **indirect speech acts**. For instance an utterance such as *Can you pass the salt please?* is syntactically a question with the illocutionary force of a request. Interpreting indirect speech acts correctly is complex in that it not only requires the identification of a set of conditions but also involves other factors such as knowledge of the participants' linguistic habits, cultural practices and present situation.

Following on from Austin and Searle, the linguistic philosopher Grice (1975) took the theory of utterances one step further by identifying the underlying rules that govern the management of conversation, as discussed below.

2.4.2   The cooperative principle

Grice's theory of conversational implicature has made a major contribution to our understanding of how conversation is managed. As a linguistic philosopher, Grice (1975) was concerned with the relationship between logic and conversation. He made a distinction between the logical meaning of given words and their broader interpretations (which he labelled 'implicatures') that arise out of the rules and principles of conversation (see Chapman, 2006, pp. 136–7). The overriding principle in all conversation, according to Grice, is the principle of cooperation or **cooperative principle** (CP). The CP assumes a tacit understanding between speakers that they will cooperate in conversation in a meaningful way. The CP is defined as:

> a rough general principle which participants will be expected (ceteris paribus) to observe, namely: make your conversational contribution such as it is required at the stage at which it occurs, by the accepted purpose or direction of the talk exchange in which you are engaged (Grice, 1975, p. 45).

This suggests that verbal interactions operate according to certain expectations. Grice proposes four principles that people tacitly assume to be the norm in conversation. He calls these 'maxims of conversation'; that is, intuitive principles that guide conversational interactions:

1. *The maxim of quantity* relates to the amount of information to be provided:
   - Make your contribution as informative as is required for the purpose of the exchange.
   - Do not make your contribution more informative than is required.
2. *The maxim of quality* relates to the truth of the contribution:
   - Do not say what you believe to be false.
   - Do not say that for which you lack adequate evidence.
3. *The maxim of relation* relates to the relevance of the contribution:
   - be relevant.

4. The maxim of **manner** relates to the manner in which the contribution is made:

- Avoid obscurity.
- Avoid ambiguity.
- Be brief (avoid unnecessary prolixity).
- Be orderly.

According to Grice, then, we have a tacit expectation that when people speak (or write) to us they will, all other things being equal, give us only the amount of information that is required, tell us the truth, be relevant, and speak in a clear, understandable manner that is not antagonistic, ambiguous and so on. The same applies when we speak to them. Adherence to these maxims is the expected norm of conversationalists, and much of our day-to-day conversation follows these maxims. Take the following example (Thomas, 1995, p. 64):

Husband: *Where are the car keys?*
Wife: *They're on the table in the hall.*

Here the wife has provided the right amount of information (quantity) and has truthfully (quality) , directly (relation) and clearly (manner) answered the question. She has said exactly what needed to be said, no more and no less, and with no implicature; that is, there was no additional level of meaning so there was no difference between what she said and what she meant. However, many conversations do in fact flout these norms and include 'conventional' or 'standard' conversational implicatures. A crucial feature of implicatures is that they must be capable of being worked out by the listener. Schiffrin (1994, p. 195) sums up Grice's description of the process as follows:

To work out that a particular conversational implicature is present, the hearer will rely on the following data:

(1) the conventional meanings of the words used, together with the identity of any references that may be involved

(2) the CP and its maxims

(3) the context, linguistic or otherwise, of the utterance

(4) other items of background knowledge

(5) the fact (or supposed fact) that all relevant items falling under the previous headings are available to both participants and both participants know or assume this to be the case.

Given this, implicatures are created by a speaker deliberately flouting one or more of the maxims, and the listener being aware of this violation of the cooperative principle. For example, there is a great deal of implicature in political language, making it hard for the listener or reader to identify – and thus to challenge – the basis of policies. Posters produced by the Conservative and Labour Parties prior to the 2005 general election carried slogans that flouted the maxim of quantity by providing almost no information: *Are you thinking what we're thinking?* (the Conservative Party) and *Are you remembering what we're remembering?* (Labour).

The Conservative slogan flouts the maxim of quantity. What the Conservatives are thinking is far from explicit, but the implication is that the country is united in its distrust of or disappointment with the Labour government. Readers are invited to identify with the slogan, even if their own thoughts on the government are different from those implied by it. It is expected that the gap in information will be 'filled in' in the reader's mind by thoughts of how the Labour government is ineffectual, lazy, arrogant and so on. The disadvantage for the Conservatives is that critical or resistant readers may fill in the gap with their own views, such as *I don't know – are you also thinking how good and socially just the Labour government has been then?*

The Labour slogan is also a direct question and relies on intertextual referencing (see Section 3.7) to build another implicature, thus again flouting the maxim of quantity. The text does not explain what it is that the Labour Party is remembering, but it hints at the years of Tory rule under Margaret Thatcher and the revelations of sleaze during John Major's years in office. Again resistant readers might sidestep the implicature and think of what they considered to be good about the time of Conservative government.

Flouting the maxim of quality can be done in several ways. One is to say something that does not reflect what the speaker thinks. For example if employers tell prospective employees that they would be happier elsewhere, this is a polite, face-saving way of saying that they do not wish to employ them. Other ways to flout the maxim of quality are to exaggerate. – *I could eat a horse* or *I'm starving* – or to use metaphors or euphemisms: *She's such a wet blanket*, or *I'm just going to wash my hands* as a euphemism for *I'm going to urinate*. The maxim can also be flouted by irony and banter. Irony expresses a positive statement whilst implying a negative one, whilst banter does the opposite. An example of irony is *I love burnt toast in the mornings*. The danger with both irony and banter is that it can offend listeners if they do not recognise the conversational implicature, and as a result take the words literally.

Flouting the maxim of relation involves uttering statements that appear to have no connection with one another and expecting listeners to work out what has not been said, thereby connecting the two utterances. For example:

John: *So what did you think of Ashley?*
Mary: *Well, his sister's a good laugh.*

By not mentioning Ashley in her reply and apparently saying something irrelevant, Mary is implying that she is not impressed by him. In technical (stylistic) terms we can argue that flouting the maxim of relation is often due to a lack of cohesion in the text (this topic is covered in Chapter 3 and in Section 7.2 of Jeffries, 2006). It should be noted that the maxims often overlap. Here John's question is not only responded to irrelevantly but also remains unanswered, which is a flouting of the maxim of quality.

Flouting the maxim of manner relates not to what is said but to how it is said. The intonation, modality, lexical connotation or other aspects of the style of a text, as well as the degree of detail, ordering of content and use of obscure language, can result in a clash between the context-appropriate style and that which is actually used. Thus the use of overly formal or complex language when talking to students or trainees may well amount to a flouting of the maxim of manner, and could either be interpreted as an attempt to demonstrate how ignorant the listeners are in comparison with their lecturer or trainer, or – in a more friendly environment and with the right intonation and body language – it could be interpreted as humorous. An example of a statement to impress first-year language students with no previous linguistic knowledge might be:

In order to explicate the precise mechanism for the articulation of utterances, we must consider the egressive pulmonary airstream mechanism and the modification of the egressive airstream as it encounters the articulatory features of the oral and nasal cavities.

Though some of the technical terms used here might indeed be introduced to students, they would normally be defined or explained and would not be accompanied by such unnecessarily formal and long-winded (prolix) language.

Grice's theory of conversational implicature has been criticised on a number of counts, including whether the cooperative principle should be interpreted as a system of social 'goal-sharing' cooperation (see for example Pratt, 1977; Kiefer, 1979; Watts, 2003) or linguistic cooperation (Leech and Thomas, 1990; Thomas, 1995). However, Grice (1975, p. 48) makes it clear that he does not intend the principle to be viewed as social cooperation as there are too many types of exchange (for example quarrelling) where social cooperation and the cooperative principle do not match or coincide. Linguistic, as opposed to social, goal sharing assumes that the only goal of a given communication is the transmission of information, and that the cooperative principle operates solely to enable the interlocutors to understand what is said or implied. It makes no claims about the intentions of the speaker, good or otherwise.

Another criticism of Grice's theory is that it applies to the management of Anglo-American English conversational exchanges, and therefore does not take account of the fact that different cultures, countries and communities have different maxims for particular situations. For example in Britain if we say to someone *I'll come and see you tomorrow* it is expected that the appointment will be kept, and if we do not turn up it will be considered a violation of the maxim of quality. In some cultures, however, this is a quite normal way of indicating lack of interest.

Nevertheless, while different conversational norms or conventions may operate in different cultural contexts, the mere fact that norms exist means that they generally need to be adhered to if effective or successful communication is to take place. Conversational norms such as the ones identified by Grice and others show how sentence meanings combine into discourse meaning and are integrated with context, in much the same way as the rules of grammar allow word meanings to be combined into sentence meaning.

A further criticism of the theories put forward by Austin (1962), Searle (1969) and Grice (1975) is that, as linguistic philosophers, they arrived at their conclusions solely by theorizing ideas about the nature of interactions and failed to examine actual language use or use real language data to inform their ideas. Despite this their work has provided linguists with a theoretical base from which to investigate the linguistic structure of naturally occurring language. Refinements, correction, elaborations or replacements of the cooperative principle continue to be published (for example Hawley, 2002; Spencer-Oatey and Jiang, 2003). Far from being unstructured and improvised, it is clear from speech act theory and the cooperative principle that what appears at first to be commonplace and trivial is on closer inspection far more complex. Speech has a performative function, and our ability to take part successfully in verbal exchanges of any kind depends on knowing how to manage and behave in conversation.

2.5 Discourse analysis

Discourse analysis is both an umbrella term for all forms of discourse analysis and the term given to a specific method of analysis. In the latter regard it relates to identifying and specifying rules to produce coherent discourse, now also called exchange structure (Cutting, 2002). It is concerned with how speakers combine utterances into broader speech units. This method of analysis was first devised by the British linguists Sinclair and Coulthard (1975) and the Birmingham school of discourse analysis. Drawing on speech act theory (see Section 2.4 above), Sinclair and Coulthard proposed a descriptive system to handle the structure of discourse within a particular setting.

2.5.1   The structure of talk

The setting in which Sinclair and Coulthard situate their work is the formal, hierarchical setting of a classroom. They show that a lesson, like any other form of verbal interaction, can be analysed sequentially as a series of turns or **exchanges**. During the course of an interaction the teacher may direct pupils to perform a particular task, elicit a verbal contribution from the pupils and then respond to that contribution. Sinclair and Coulthard identify four main types of exchange: **directive** (teacher: *The first quiz is this*), **check** (teacher: *Finished Joan?*), **informative** (teacher: *Here are some of the symbols used*) and **elicitation** (teacher: *Read us what you've written Joan*).

The structure or composition of an exchange is determined by the function of the constituent elements. In informative exchanges only the teacher's contribution is required. In the case of directives and checks, however, the pupil's response is an obligatory element. In the case of elicitiations, the structure allows for follow-up turns. Consequently the structure of the exchange can be described in terms of component **moves**, of which there are three: **initiating** (I), **responding** (R) and **follow-up** (F).

In turn moves can be divided according to function. For example when asking a question, the teacher might restrict the answer to one pupil by naming her or him; follow-up moves can be divided into accepting the response as relevant (*That's right*), evaluating the response (*That's a good answer*) or commenting on it (*That's interesting*). These functional components are called **acts** (Table 2.1).

While Sinclair and Coulthard's model of discourse analysis can be successfully applied to formal exchanges that take place in a classroom, it cannot be

Table 2.1   Examples of the functional components of the moves in an exchange

Move	Act
Teacher (I): *Read us what you've written Joan*	Elicit
Pupil (R): *The cat sat on the rug*	Reply
Teacher (F): *Yes, that's right*	Accept
Pupil: *I changed the last word*	Comment

easily transferred to other situations, particularly informal ones. A major criticism of the model is that it applies to a hierarchical, formal and ritualistic
form of discourse, with one person in a position of power over others, and it
ignores the underlying social relationships that sustain power, authority and
hierarchy.

Other criticisms of the model are as follows. First, it says nothing about the
perlocutionary force of language and the way language is used to convey
humour, irony, threats and so on. Second, it assumes that utterances have a
single function when they may in fact have more than one. Third, the categorisation of moves limits the length of an exchange to I, R and F, or subsequent variations such as R/I and F/I. Fourth it assumes that exchanges always
go according to plan and does not easily allow for disruption. Finally, centred
very much on the teacher, with the latter dominating the exchange by taking
long turns and the pupils taking short turns in response but never interrupt-
ing. Although this type of exchange might still occur, nowadays pupils often
work in pairs and groups and exchanges between them and their teacher are
generally more interactive.

Nevertheless the model is important because it was the first to show that
there is a systematically, organised structure to conversation that can be categorised and described.

Francis and Hunston (1992) have developed a revised version of the
Sinclair and Coulthard model that is designed to be more flexible and adapt-
able, and therefore able to cope with a wide variety of discourse situations.
Francis and Hunston used data from telephone conversations because these
lacked paralinguistic features such as gestures, eye-gaze and so on, and
because the interactions included rituals of greeting and leave-taking. In their
model the one-to-one correspondence between exchange and move is called
an **exchange structure**, and there are eight moves rather than four:

1. Framing: marking boundaries in a conversation.
2. Opening: initiating, (including a greeting) or closing a conversation, or
   any attempt to impose a structure on the conversation.
3. Answering: indicating a willingness to take part in conversation.
4. Eliciting: inquiring, prompting, or clarifying in order to elicit information.
5. Informing; offer information, concur, confirm or qualify.
6. Acknowledging: providing positive or negative follow-up.
7. Directing: requesting an immediate or future action.
8. Behaving: supplying or defying a direction. (See also Table 2.2.)

In order to understand the nature of conversation it would be useful to undertake an analysis of your own, applying either or both of the discourse models outlined above, especially the exchange structures, to find out the extent

Table 2.2   Examples of moves and exchange structures

	Move	Exchange structure	Exchange
B: Why I-it's not floating at all A: No, it's lying on the floor	eliciting	I	1
Like any old balloon	informing	R	
B: It's a bit strange you know	acknowledging/	F	
	Informing	I	2
A: Yeah interesting	acknowledging	R	

to which they are applicable, what they reveal about the structure of a conversation and what their limitations are (see Section 2.8.5 below).

Although Francis and Hunston's model allows for some flexibility, it is nonetheless very structural as it focuses on the nature of exchanges and the development of categories that can be applied to them. Consequently it has fallen out of vogue and attention has shifted to pragmatics and conversation analysis. In addition, in recent years studies of the relationship between language and power which have developed new analytical approaches, such as critical discourse analysis (see Chapter 4) and forensic linguistics. Nevertheless exchange structure remains an important linguistic tool in discourse analysis.

Some discourse analysts (for example Burton, 1980; Brown and Yule, (1983); Hoey, 1983) have examined written texts as well as analysing conversations. Burton has analysed dramatic dialogue with the help of descriptive frameworks that were developed originally to analyse conversational exchanges, and has produced a model that reveals the ways in which some types of modernist dramatic dialogue violate or go against discursive norms. Thus discourse analysts have widened their field of inquiry from exchange structures in a narrowly defined context such as a classroom to investigate the underlying structures of a large range of texts, both spoken and written. In general the field of pragmatics and discourse is largely concerned with speech, whilst that of stylistics (discussed in the next chapter) is predominantly concerned with writing, and especially, literary writing.

2.6   Conversation analysis

As outlined above, discourse analysis comes from the British tradition of linguistics – is concerned with the structure of conversation and how utterances fit together to make up a discourse. Conversation analysis comes from the

American tradition of sociology and is concerned with the management of conversation and how communication is achieved.

Conversation analysis also differs in its concept of conversation. It starts with the conversation itself and the data determines the structural categories, while discourse analysis starts with a linguistic theory based on a patterning of units and then fits conversation to the model, thus viewing conversation as a product. Conversation analysis is commonly applied to everyday conversations, although it has also been used to study interactions in institutions and workplaces.

According to Cutting (2002, p. 28) 'Conversation is discourse mutually constructed and negotiated in time between speakers; it is usually informal and unplanned.' Cook (1989, p. 51) defines it as follows:

1. It is not primarily necessitated by a practical task
2. Any unequal power of participants is partially suspended
3. The number of participants is small
4. Turns are quite short
5. Talk is primarily for the participants not for an outside audience

Many linguists would disagree with the first of these items – 'It is not primarily necessitated by a practical task' – citing the fact that even the most casual of conversations has an interactional function, such as chatting with a stranger at a party to ascertain whether future social interaction might be desirable, or reestablishing contact with old friends and planning future events. Other linguists (for example Fairclough, 2001) would contest the second item – 'Any unequal power of participants is partially suspended' – on the ground that to varying degrees there is unequal power in all exchanges (see also Chapter 4).

Although conversation analysis assumes that utterances have a contextual relevance to one another, not all aspects of contexts are taken as equally relevant. In practice much of the work undertaken in the field has been concerned with identifying structural features thrown up by conversation, using particular methodologies to identify how social relations are achieved by the participants. Conversation analysis focuses on the conversation as the standard domain for patterns, distributions and formation of rules that can then be applied to subsequent pieces of discourse. The overall pattern or structure of face-to-face conversation varies a great deal according to such factors as where the conversation takes place, the social relationship between the participants and the topic of conversation. Speakers construct and negotiate their conversation in real time, and as they do so the utterances or turns that emerge shape and structure the subsequent conversation.

2.6.1   Turn-taking

Turn-taking is central to the structure and management of conversation. It involves three basic strategies on the part of the speaker: taking the turn, holding the turn and yielding the turn. In Anglo-American English, if next-turn speakers are not sure when the current speaker is going to finish they will wait until the end of an utterance for a sign that the turn is complete or the speaker is willing to yield the turn. A point in a conversation where a turn of place is possible is called a transition relevance place. In British English TRPs are indicated by phonological features such as a low falling tone and syntactic ones such as the end of a main clause. When listeners do not wait for a TRP before speaking this is an interruption, whereas if they anticipate a turn being completed, miscue their entry and come in before the end, this is an overlap.

In the following exchange, between a mother and her teenage son an interruption is indicated by // and an overlap by =.

> Mother: *I want you to put // your dirty clothes in the washing basket.*
> Harry: *// I know what you're going to say.*
>   *Alright =*
> Mother: *= then why don't you do it then?*

Another aspect of turn-taking is the acceptable length of a pause between two turns. Each culture seems to have an unspoken agreement about this and participants in a conversation cannot but help to attribute meaning to a pause that is longer (or shorter) than this norm. Pauses that carry meaning are labelled 'attributable silence'. Consider the following exchange:

> Lucy: *Did you remember to buy the cheese?*
> John: [After a three-second pause] *No.*
> Lucy: *Did you forget?*
> John: *Afraid I did. Sorry.*

Lucy attributes John's three second delay in answering to his trying to remember whether or not he did remember to buy the cheese. Participants in a conversation do not usually feel comfortable when there is a pause or lull, and if it extends beyond about 10 seconds, people tend to utter fillers such as *um* or *well then* to break the silence and get the conversation going again.

2.6.2   Adjacency pairs

Turn-taking provides a basic framework for the organisation of conversation since it enables the participants to interact with one another rather than simply speaking individually in a haphazard and uncoordinated way. However turn-taking on its own is not sufficient to guarantee a purposeful and mean-ingful interaction. Take for example the following scene from the play *Equus* (Shaffer, 1975, italics added):

Dysart: *Won't you sit down?*
           Is this your full name? Alan Strang?
           And you're seventeen. Is that right? Seventeen . . . Well?
Alan: *Double your pleasure*
           Double your fun
           With Doublemint, Doublemint
           Doublemint gum
Dysart: *Now, let's see. You work in an electrical shop during the week. You*
           live with your parents and your father's a printer. What sort of
           things does he print?
Alan: *Double your pleasure*
           Double your fun
           With Doublemint, Doublemint
           Doublemint gum.

In this exchange the two parties have no problem making an orderly exchange of turns. However the content of each turn is not related to what went before. Alan's manner of speaking is intended to portray madness and he fails to provide a meaningful answer to the questions he has been asked. Mental illness leads to a suspension of the norms. As Cameron (2001, p. 95) points out, 'CA places great emphasis on the idea that conversation is "one thing after another": it is an activity that unfolds in time, and what I say now must inevitably constrain what you can meaningfully say next.' It also looks for patterns in data, so in this case conversation analysts might collect data from people in real mental health settings to see whether Shaffer has got the patterning of the turns right, or whatever 'right' means in a creative context. In the example above, Dysart's questions are a request for information, and Alan's answers seem inappropriate in response.

Thus turn-taking involves the participants in a conversation taking turns to speak, the turn-taking is structured by successive utterances and each utterance is functionally dependent on the previous one. The term **adjacency pairs** refers to a sequence of two utterances, each by a different speaker. The most obvious adjacency pairing is that of a question and answer. When we ask a question we usually expect a response, known as a **preferred response**. The following are but a few examples of preferred response adjacency pairs (Cutting, 2002, p.30):

- A question – an answer
- An offer – an acceptance

- An invitation – an acceptance
- An assessment – an agreement
- A proposal – an agreement
- A greeting – a greeting
- A complaint – an apology
- A blaming – a denial

A dispreferred response is responding to the question with another question rather than an answer, or a refusal or disagreement that can be interpreted as either meaningful or rude. For example if the response to *How are you?* is *Go away!*, whether this is meaningful or rude will depend on the circumstances and the context in which the exchange takes place. For example:

John: *Have you finished that yet?*
Paul: *No, I've just got to get an email off to John Harrap.*

John: *Oh good, well, when you've done, would you give me a hand?*
Paul: *Doing what?*

John: *Something I have to get done for Monday. It'd be great if you took a look at it.*
Paul: *Ok. Give me five minutes.*

In the first adjacency pair John asks Paul a question, to which he replies (preferred response). John then asks Paul a second question, who responds by asking a question to find out what it is that John wants (dispreferred response). John then phrases his request as a proposal, to which Paul agrees. In conversation analysis this preference system relates to the patterning of responses and not to the more usual meaning of 'preference' – that something is considered more desirable than something else. Preferred responses are prompt and short whereas dispreferred ones tend to be hesitant and elaborate. Acceptances and agreements are typically structured in one way, and refusals and disagreements in another.

Conversations also have **sequence**, of which four aspects have been identified: opening and closing, presequences and insertions (marked by (.), (1.5) and so on). Take the following example of a consultation between a doctor and patient (adapted from Montgomery, 1995, pp. 205–6):

Doctor: [Leading the patient into the consultation room] *That's only the clutter in the . . . background* (.)
Patient: *Yeah.*
Doctor: *No problem.* (.) *so* (.) *take your coat off.*

Patient: *Sure.*

[The doctor helps the patient to remove his coat]

Patient: *Thanks.*

Doctor: *Don't think Philip's got any clothes pegs in here so uh* (1.5) [Doctor hangs up coat] *I don't usually use thi . . . sit down*

Patient: *Fine*

Doctor: *I don't usually use this room, its erm* (.) *Philip's*

Patient: *Yes, of course.*

Doctor: *Anyway* (.) *going through the whole thing* (2.0) *you've changed your job* (.) *in effect* (.)

Patient: *Well* (.) *additional responsibility.*

During the first seven exchanges the doctor and patient are engaging in an **opening sequence** centred on getting settled into the consultation room. The subsequent **insertions** relate to the doctor checking the patient's file. Since consultations are time specific the exchange ends with a **closing sequence**. Cutting (2002) notes that British and North Americans often preface the closing sequence with a preclosing sequence that can be long- drawn-out. Rather than simply saying *goodbye* or *tarrah*, markers are usually given to signal that a conversation is about to end, such as A*nyway, I've got to go. It's been nice talking to you.*

The turn-taking strategies described above form an orderly system in which one person speaks at a time whilst the other waits his or her turn. However ordinary conversation does not always work like this. For example the person waiting to speak may decide to interrupt or lose concentration and/or interest and fail to respond, or the speaker may lose his or her thread, and so on.

In the normal course of events, as Montgomery (1995) notes, we expect our conversations to proceed without such difficulties because of the conversational norms we have absorbed.

Nonetheless, there is a growing body of research that has put doubt on the universality of turn-taking, and especially the 'one person speaks at a time' principle upon which it is founded. This is especially the case in relation to the way in which men and women behave in conversation. For example, Coates (1996, 1997) argues that turn-taking functions differently between women from the way it does between men. In her study of informal talk between British women friends she found that turns were more often jointly or coconstructed between these speakers than singly (Coates, 1996). She suggested that this highly cooperative kind of talk was more likely to be found among groups of all-female speakers than all-male, and this was confirmed by a similar study of men (Coates, 1997), whose patterns of conversation corresponded more closely to the 'one person at a time' form of turn-taking. Cameron (1997) supported this finding in an analysis of the talk of young men friends.

Edelsky (1981) has found that supportive simultaneous speech can also happen in institutional settings. In her analysis of talk at business meetings she distinguishes between two types of 'floor', 'F1' and 'F2'. F1 refers to the one at a time model of turn-taking, while F2 refers to more simultaneous speech. The latter, according to Edelsky, enables women to take the floor more than is the case with F1. As Cameron (2001) points out, in the one at a time model there is no obvious place for simultaneous speech that is neither a violation nor a mistake, whereas in fact, it is a normal feature of certain kinds of conversation, particularly informal ones. Studies conducted in the fields of interactional sociolinguistics and intercultural communication also show that the norms associated with turn-taking are cultural rather than linguistic, and different cultures have different turn-taking norms (see Section 2.6 below).

Shaw (2000) has examined the speech behaviour of male and female members of parliament (MPs) in debates in the House of Commons in London. The House of Commons has arcane rules that are highly codified in terms of who may speak, when, and about what. One of these rules is that contributions to a debate, can only be made by an MP who has been called to the floor, and contributions from seated, uncalled MPs are not allowed. However in practice many MPs make such contributions, and the speaker (effectively the chairperson) who is responsible for ensuring that this rule, among others, is observed, rarely censures them unless called upon to do so by the MP holding the floor. In an analysis of five debates Shaw found that male MPs were far more likely than women to make 'illegal' interventions in other people's speeches, not because women were reluctant to intervene but because they had a greater desire to play by the rules of the game. The consequence of this was that women MPs had less influence over debates than men, so were comparatively disempowered.

With regard to changes of topic in informal talk, West and Garcia (1988) have found that in discussions among men and women, men tend to make unilateral topic changes in the course of women's 'turns-in-progress': that is, they completely change a topic whilst women are still talking about the previous one. This is particularly the case when women are talking about affective (emotional) experiences.

Conversation analysts take nothing as predetermined, and view the turn-taking system and the relevance of particular actions as being governed by contingency. Contingency and probability are what conversation analysis is all about. Many conversation analysts have addressed overlap, interruption, collaborative completion, choral responses and the like. All of these practices, constitute evidence for the conversation analysis account of turn-taking, demonstrating the ways in which speakers exploit turns to influence later turns and the direction of the conversation as a whole.

2.6.3   Presupposition

One important aspect of conversation is the amount of background information shared by the participants in a conversation and their implicit understanding. For example, consider this conversation between two friends walk-
ing their dogs:

> Lucy: *How's Lawrence?*
> Pamela: *He's OK thanks. Still hobbling but getting better slowly.*
> Lucy: *When's he back at school?*
> Pamela: *Oh, next week some time.*

If Lucy were to clarify what she means by *How's Lawrence?* it might go something like this:

> *Assuming, Pamela, that you have normal hearing and sufficient knowledge of
> English. I guess that you, like me, do not want to take this walk in silence and
> wish to interact by means of a conversation. Since I know that your son has
> been in hospital recently for an operation on his knee, it seems reasonable for
> me to start a conversation by enquiring about his progress. So I am asking you
> 'How's Lawrence?' and I would appreciate it if you would say something in
> reply.*

Despite this elaboration there is still much that is implicit. It could be, for
example, that Lucy is asking for a more general update on Lawrence's well-
being beyond the matter of his knee. Complete explicitness is usually impossible in what we say and write, and language provides numerous conventional carriers of implicit meaning; that is, tools for linking explicit content
to relevant aspects of background information. One important tool is presupposition: aspects of meaning that are presupposed, understood or taken
for granted and allow an utterance to make sense. For example *How's
Lawrence?* presupposes that both Lucy and Pamela know the Lawrence being
referred to, and that he is Pamela's son. This pragmatic presupposition cannot be derived from the semantic base of the utterance; that is, the meaning
of the words. Rather it resides in the shared conventions of language use.

One factor in sentence meaning is **entailment**. Entailment is the most literal component of the meaning of a sentence, and it remains the same in
whatever context it occurs. Take for example the sentence *The cat sat on the
mat*. This sentence entails a basic proposition, *p*. Entailment also occurs in
sentences or utterances that contain more than one basic proposition. For
example the following sentence *Susan ate an apple and Peter ate a pear* entails
two propositions, expressed as *p* and *q*: *Susan ate an apple [p] and Peter ate a*

pear [*q*]. Assuming that the two claims are are true (that Susan did eat an apple and Peter a pear), then it follows that *p* and *q* must also be true (see also Section 2.3.1 above and Chapman, 2006, section 2.1). Entailment, then, can be defined more rigorously as follows: a sentence, *s*, entails a proposition, *p*, if and only if in every possible circumstance where *s* is true, *p* is true (Simpson, 1993). If someone says to you *The cat sat on the mat* or *Susan ate an apple and Peter ate a pear*, then you would expect that person to be committed to the truth of the entailment. However, as Simpson (1993) points out, the concept of truth is a complex and abstract one, and its definition has considerably exercised linguists and philosophers (see Chapman, 2006, section 2.2). A great deal of effort has gone into explaining the conditions under which a particular sentence may be true or false. These 'truth conditions' form the foundation of semantic description by specifying the components of meaning that give a sentence its overall truth value.

However the concept of entailment, while an important aspect of sentence meaning, does not provide a complete description of what utterances mean in real situations. Take the following example (Simpson, 1993, p. 124): 'Well darling . . . the dog has . . . erm . . . stopped sleeping in its kennel,' where the entailment that the dog is not sleeping in its kennel is not as important as the presupposition that it was previously doing so, triggered by the change of state verb, *stop*. Presuppositions usually fall into one of two types: existential and logical. **Existential presuppositions** state the existence of referents in the utterance and are triggered by definite noun phrases, in this case *the dog*. **Logical presuppositions** are triggered by a number of grammatical features, including **change-of-state verbs** such as *stop*, **factive verbs** such as *regret* and *realise*, whose complement is presupposed to be true, **iterative adverbs** such as *again* and *still*, which presuppose that the process has happened before, **cleft constructions** such as *It was John who let the dog out*, where the whole subordinate clause is presupposed to be true, and **comparators**, where the quality asserted is assumed also to imply in some measure to the referent, as in *This cake is richer than the last one*, where the entailment is that the first cake was rich and the presupposition is that the second one is also rich.

Further examples of grammatical triggers of logical presuppositions are: **change-of-state verbs**, Jane started swimming twice a week (She hadn't been doing so before); **factive verbs**, John realised that he had arrived too late (He had arrived too late); **cleft sentences**, it is my father that cracks all the bad jokes (My father cracks all the bad jokes); **iteratives**, you can't buy music cassettes any more (You used to be able to do so); **comparators**, Peter is as sexist as Paul (Paul is sexist).

To return to the example of *Well, darling . . . the dog has . . . erm . . . stopped sleeping in its kennel*, the additional elements *Well darling* and *erm* add meaning to the sentence. The use of an endearment such as *darling* usually indicates an intimate relationship between the speaker and addressee. This information is not relevant to the truth conditions but it forms part of the overall message. The particles *well* and *erm* also lie outside the truth conditions but have an important function as **hedges**, softening the impact of the message upon the addressee. Also to be considered is the context in which the utterance occurred, which was as part of an exchange between A and B:

A: *What are all those hairs doing on the sofa?*
B: *Well, darling . . . the dog has . . . erm . . . stopped sleeping in its kennel.*

This contextualisation of B's utterance alters its meaning from the literal one of the dog has stopped sleeping in its kennel to the inferred one that the dog is responsible for the hairs on the sofa. Inferencing is triggered by the indirectness of B's answer to A's question. The meaning that the exchange as a whole generates is a combination of B's indirectness and A's inferencing work, a process known as **conversational implicature** (see also Section 2.3.2 above).

The impossibility of being fully explicit in language lends itself to strategic exploitation. For example if asked why you missed a meeting you could answer *I didn't manage to get away.* You may not have tried to get away, but by using the word manage you give the impression that you did, a logical presupposition based on the factive verb *manage*, which presupposes trying. You have not actually said that you tried to get away, so no one can accuse you of lying. This is called presuppositional lying.

2.6.4 Politeness

Politeness in conversation refers to linguistic expressions that indicate a friendly attitude towards speakers and listeners. It lies not in the words and expressions themselves, but in their intended social meaning and function. Brown and Levinson (1987) point to the key aspect of **face** in social relationships. Face refers to self-image, and it is a universal characteristic of all cultures that speakers should take account of their listeners' feelings, respect each other's self-image and avoid **face-threatening acts** (FTAs). When FTAs are unavoidable, Brown and Levinson suggest that the threat can be lessened by **negative politeness**. Negative politeness respects the hearer's negative face, which is recognising the need to be independent, not to be imposed upon by others, to have freedom of action and generally to minimise imposition. Alternatively speakers can address the FTA by **positive politeness**. Positive politeness attends to hearer's interests, wants and needs. It respects the hearer's positive face, the need to be liked by others, to be treated as a member of a group and so on.

One way of avoiding FTAs is to speak **off record** or **on record**. Suppose you are looking for a particular product in a supermarket but there are no assistants around. You would like some help but do not wish to approach any other shopper directly because this might be taken as an FTA. You could say in a voice loud enough for other shoppers to hear, *Where have they moved the breakfast cereals to?* In this instance you would be speaking off record and using an indirect speech act (see Section 2.4 above) in the hope that a fellow shopper will hear and respond to your request for help. The illocutionary force will probably be understood by hearers, but they can choose to ignore it without losing face. Avoiding an FTA is achieved by flouting the maxim of quantity (see Section 2.4.2), since you are not saying openly that you need help and therefore are not making your utterance as informative as possible. Indirect speech acts and flouting the maxim of quantity in this way allows speakers to make requests, offers, invitations and so on without addressing them to anyone in particular and thus avoiding potential FTA.

Alternatively you have the option of approaching someone and saying *Excuse me, you couldn't tell me where they've moved the breakfast cereals to could you?* This person then has to reply unless they want to appear rude. Making a request in this direct way is called doing an FTA on record. On record FTAs are direct speech acts. In this example the speech act contains a mitigating device; that is, it is phrased in such a way as to give the listener the option of either saying *No* or giving you the help you need. If you instead said *Tell me where the breakfast cereal is*, this would be a bald on record communicative act with no mitigating device, and the hearer would have no option but to answer if she or he did not want to be thought of as uncooperative. Consequently this would be the most face-threatening mode of action. It is also possible, however, to orientate bald-on-record events to save the hearer's face. For example if you say to someone at the meal table *Have another helping* there is little risk of the hearer feeling imposed upon. The degree to which such directness is face threatening depends on how socially close we are to our hearers. The closer we are, then the more direct we are likely to be; the more distant, then the more face threatening such directness will be.

In general speakers perform on-record FTAs in ways that take account of face. Such 'face management' can be done with either negative or positive politeness. Negative politeness strategies, as defined above, pay attention to negative face. Speakers use them to avoid intruding upon a hearer's territory and also give the hearer options. For example *You couldn't tell me where the breakfast cereals are, could you?* uses negative politeness to give the hearer the opportunity to say *No*. Other strategies commonly used in negative politeness are apology and hesitation.

Positive politeness strategies aim to save positive face by appealing to friendship and demonstrating solidarity. Asking where the breakfast cereals are with on-record positive politeness, for example, would mean approaching a shopper and saying something like: *Excuse me, I'd appreciate it if you could tell me where in the store you got that packet of breakfast cereal.* One of the main types of positive politeness strategy identified by Brown and Levinson (1987) is claiming common ground. Speakers can do this by attending to hearers' wants, needs and interests. For example *I know you don't like loud music, but this concert will be fun OI. Mark and Chris'll be there and we haven't seen them for ages* uses a number of solidarity strategies, such as a nickname, knowledge of personal information and seeking agreement.

Consider the following exchange during a telephone conversation between a boyfriend and girlfriend:

(1.) Mary: *I (.) sometimes I <u>do</u>: think: I, I suppose I have (.) I (.) I have felt that maybe you =*

(2.) James: *= are cross with me?*

(3.) Mary: *<u>cross</u> with you darling*

(4.) James: *yeah: I had, = I had =*

(5.) Mary: *= I wasn't <u>cross</u> with you darling*

(6.) James: *mmm.*

(7.) Mary: *well (.) cross with you about what darling*

(8.) James: *but you know I I kind of (0.1) but you know what I'm like sort of thinking that: = I'm always*

(9.) Mary: *= right?*

Mary performs an on-record FTA in turn 1 in that she is voicing a concern about James' behaviour that he may find threatening. By turn 7 she has still failed to provide an answer to the James' question *cross with you about what?* In her responses Mary not only flouts the Gricean maxims of quantity, manner and relation but also employs negative politeness and another politeness strategy, that of extensive hedging: *but you know I, I kind of' 'I think (.) erm.* Cameron (2001) suggests that women rate FTAs more severely than men. Mary's behaviour in the above exchange bears this out, as evidenced by her difficulty in telling James of his tendency to think that he is always right.

2.6.5 Context

Much is said in pragmatics and discourse analysis about the importance of studying verbal behaviour not only as actions and their management but also in terms of its context (see Section 2.2 above and Chapman, 2006, Ch. 5). In the following example two undergraduate students, Claire and Peter, are talking about the failure of Peter's plan to visit Claire at her parents' house:

Claire: *Hello, what happened to you?*

Peter: *Well, I got the train as far as Birmingham but then there was this massive delay =*

Claire: *= What did you do? Was there another train?*

Peter: *I had to go back to Leicester because it was impossible to go on. So then I thought I'd get the coach, but when I got to Leamington I didn't have your address.*

Claire: *Oh no! why didn't you phone me?*

Peter: *my phone was out of battery, and I'd hurt my ankle when I ran for the coach. Look, its swollen like this.*

Claire: *Poor you! so what did you do?*

Peter: *Um I got the train back to Leicester.*

Claire: *Wait until I tell Debbie!*

As with presupposition the two students share a great deal of knowledge about the context of this situation. Presuppositions, though, are not really a shared background but an assumption of a background that may not in fact be shared. Typically these are contexts of:

- Situation: what the speakers know about their physical and geographical surroundings.
- Background knowledge: what the speakers know about one another and the world;
- Cotextual: what the speakers know about what they have been saying.

The situational context in the above example is Claire's room in the halls of residence at Leicester University. When Peter mentions his hurt ankle, he points to it and refers to it as *this*. This use of words such as *this* is known as **deixis** or a **deictic expressions**. Words that signal the use of deixis include personal pronouns (*I, you, we, they* and so on), demonstrative pronouns (*this, that, these, those*), the article or determiner *the* and adverbs of time and place. The more bound to a situation a conversation is, then normally the more deictic expressions are used. (see Section 3.5 for a fuller discussion of deixis and Chapman, 2006, Section 7.4).

Referring expressions and **referents** are terms used to describe the identification of something or someone and to identify the entity being referred to. For example in the phrase *I shared a car with <u>Frank</u> and <u>Michael</u>*, the first person singular pronoun *I* is a referring expression that refers to the person speaking, who is known as the referent. In the same way *Frank* and *Michael* are referring expressions which refer to two people named Frank and Michael, who are the referents.

The background knowledge speakers bring to a conversation is generally of two kinds: cultural and interpersonal. In the conversation above, Claire and Peter share a cultural knowledge of the geographical locations of particular English cities and towns and the difficulty of travelling by public transport between the ones mentioned. Claire is not overly surprised that Peter had difficulties because he was travelling on a Saturday when trains are notoriously subject to delay or cancellation without notice because of engineering works. The reference to the phone battery being dead is another instance of shared knowledge, since Peter does not have to explain what this means or why it rendered him unable to communicate with Claire. Talk with an assumption of shared knowledge of a cultural context often presupposes or shows an assumption of shared attitudes towards it. As discussed in Section 2.5.4, speakers often modify their expressions to bring them in line with those of other speakers in order to be seen as belonging to the same group. The situational context and shared knowledge is a central concern of another aspect of pragmatics and discourse, namely interactional sociolinguistics, which is discussed in more detail in Section 2.6 below.

Interpersonal knowledge is knowledge that has been acquired through previous exchanges, activities or experiences and can include personal, privileged knowledge about a speaker. In the above example both Claire and Peter know who Debbie is. Peter's interpersonal knowledge of Claire, however, does not extend to having previously visited her at her parents, and the situational context of the exchange leads one to conclude that they are contemporaries at the university and that they first met here rather than at some earlier time.

Finally, cotextual context refers to the context and the content of the text itself; that is, the actual words spoken, and the ways in which the text uses lexical and grammatical cohesion to express its meaning. This aspect of context is dealt with more fully in the next chapter.

Turn-taking, adjacency pairs, presupposition, politeness and context are major features of analysis not only in conversation analysis but also in pragmatics in general. Both discourse analysis and conversation analysis have been criticised on the grounds that their descriptive categories, descriptive such as turn-taking and adjacency pairs, are not exhaustive, and for failing to explain properly how transition relevance places (TRPs) can be recognised. Both types of analysis are qualitative in nature; that is, they analyse a finite set of fragments of conversation in detail and do not lend themselves easily to quantitative analysis of a large number of conversations. In conversation analysis, the categories emerge from the analysis of conversation itself to provide descriptions of how conversation works. Since the descriptions relate to real-time, one-off fragments of conversation, categorisation of them within any framework, conversation analysis or otherwise, can never be exhaustive as they tend to be unpredictable and new ways of interacting emerge.

Discourse analysis has also been criticised for its hierarchical structure and for the fact that its findings come from institutional settings and therefore are not applicable to naturally occurring communications. However the ideological relations underlying all discourse means that discourse analysis is inevitably hierarchical, and this has prompted the development of critical discourse analysis, which will be discussed in more detail in Chapter 4.

2.7 Language, action and interaction

Another approach to discourse analysis is interactional sociolinguistics, which focuses upon the small and subtle variations in the ways people use and interpret discourse. Gumperz (1982b) has been particularly influential in this area. Practitioners of discourse analysis and conversation analysis have tended to criticise interactional linguistics for being too broad and too context specific, as discussed in Section 2.2. However the approaches are beginning to come together.

Sociolinguistics of the kind described in Chapter 1 studies the linguistic variables in speakers' grammar, vocabulary and pronunciation to identify different ways of saying the same thing (see Sections 1.1 and 1.3). Interactional sociolinguistics goes one step further, and considers that aspects of interaction such as the rules of turn-taking, the conventions for signalling agreement or acknowledgement and the marking of utterances as particular kinds of speech act are also variables in that they are used differently in different contexts or by different kinds of speaker. The descriptive categories developed in discourse analysis and conversation analysis have enabled interactional sociolinguists to take into account both the pragmatic and the sociolinguistic aspects of interaction, including turn-taking, adjacency pairs and sequences.

Interactional sociolinguistics pays great attention to the way in which language is situated in particular circumstances in social life. It looks at situational contexts, shared knowledge, speakers' histories and purpose of speaking, as well as grammar, social structure and cultural patterns. Several scholars have documented the complex interplay of factors that shape turns and sequences in spoken interactions in a number of languages, and shown how interactional features contribute particular linguistic and communicatory outcomes. This is particularly the case with analysts who consider the relationship between grammar and social interaction within the larger sphere of human conduct and the organisation of human life (for example Ochs *et al.*, 1996).

Like discourse and conversation analysts, interactional sociolinguists acquire their data from naturally occurring interactions. Whilst discourse analysts and conversation analysts have traditionally focused on native Anglo-American speakers, many interactional sociolinguists have followed Gumperz (1982) and studied speakers from different cultural backgrounds. This field of inquiry, which is known as 'intercultural communication' or 'cross-cultural communication', tends to concentrate interactions in institutional settings such as schools and businesses. Key features of such communication – or, more often, *mis*communication – are contextualisation cues, 'crosstalk' and 'uptalk'.

Contextualisation cues are signals that convey to listeners information about how they are intended to treat the message. They include prosody (intonation, pitch and stress contrasts), paralinguistic clues (hesitation, pausing, contrasts of speed and volume, simultaneous speech) and switching to a different language, dialect style or register to signal that an utterance has a particular significance. For example, in Anglo-American English a question is signalled by a rising intonation at the end of a word. The word *Gravy?* spoken with a rising intonation indicates that the speaker is asking whether the addressee wants gravy on his or her meal. Gumperz (1982b) cites the example of a workplace in which white workers ate their lunch in a canteen staffed by Asian workers. When a customer was asked if he wanted gravy the word *gravy* was spoken not with a rising intonation but a falling one, which made it sound more like a statement – *This is gravy* – or an assertion: *I'm giving you gravy*, which was perceived as rude. But in Indian varieties of English a falling intonation has the same meaning as a rising intonation in Anglo-British varieties. Since neither group was aware of this difference misunderstanding was inevitable.

Crosstalk refers to the assumptions we all make about the norms and conventions of particular speech events, which may differ culturally. For example in an interview cited in Roberts *et al.* (1992, p. 131) a white interviewer and an Asian job applicant have the following exchange:

Interviewer: *What have you been doing since you were made redundant?*
Applicant: *Nothing.*

The interviewer's question is a veiled invitation for the interviewee to reassure the selectors that he has been doing some type of work since he was made redundant, since in the culture to which the interviewer belongs unemployment is seen as not only a misfortune but also a moral failing. However the applicant does not pick up on this hidden message and answers factually and truthfully, qualities that are considered appropriate in his culture. Such miscommunication can have serious or damaging consequences: in this example the interviewee could fail the interview by failing to pick up on hidden messages or agendas.

Uptalk refers to a rising intonation at the end of declarative sentences, for example *I went shopping today?* This is thought to have originated in Australian English, but it is also found in American English and increasingly in British English, especially among young people. Cameron (2001) reports a study of young women who used uptalk. The purpose of the study was to test the assumptions that (1) there were likely to be variations in the use of this socially and linguistically meaningful feature – that is, uptalk speakers would not use a rising intonation at the end of all declarative sentences – and (2) that the pattern of variation would be structured. The pattern revealed by the study was related to the status of the information being conveyed in an utterance: when the information was new and considered important by the speakers they would present it with a rising intonation.

2.7.1   Grammar and interaction

Most of the studies discussed so far in this chapter have focused on the way in which speech is structured and managed, and have not been as concerned with the linguistic structure of utterances. Grammars of written English almost invariably use constructed sentences to illustrate their points. However the categories designed to describe written speech do not transfer across very easily to real language data, especially data from conversations, which often contain features that are not present in written English, such as false starts, hesitations and reformulations. Carter and McCarthy (1995, 2006) and Biber *et al.*, (1999), have shown that the grammar of speech has many characteristics that are different from those found in writing. Their studies were made possible by computational techniques enabling natural language data to be processed. Computers are able to store large numbers of texts in collections known as **corpora** (the singular form is **corpus**), which can then be processed by means of specialist software. This new area of linguistic study – **corpus linguistics** – has allowed researchers to look in detail at recurring patterns of use within corpora and how they relate to the context in which they are used (see also Section 3.10).

Carter and McCarthy (1995) have studied spoken data extracted from a corpus. Their material consisted of two and a half hours of transcribed talk by male and female speakers of different ages and from different backgrounds in a variety of contexts: service encounters such as shopping and talking to a bank manager, narratives such as retelling stories, casual conversation and 'language in action'; that is, the talk that accompanies tasks such as preparing a meal, moving furniture and so on. They identified four grammatical features that were common across all types of speech: **ellipsis, left dislocation and topical information, reinforcement** and **indirect speech.**

Ellipsis is the omission of parts that would otherwise be required in a structure – was found to be a common feature across the corpus. For example at a dry-cleaner <B> is leaving a pair of trousers with A for cleaning:

> A: *Wednesday at four be okay?*
> B: *Er yeah that's fine . . . just check the pockets a minute.*

In this example, the initial *will* or *would* is missing from A' question and *I'll* is missing from the second clause in B' reply. Carter and McCarthy found that while ellipsis was common in service encounters, casual conversation and language in action it was absent from narratives. This is because the participants in and process of the story are normally separated in time and place from the moment of telling.

Left dislocation refers to the phenomenon where 'items semantically co-referential with the subject or object of the clause are positioned before the subject' (ibid.). For example: *Well Sharon, where I'm living, a friend of mine, she's got her railcard and . . .* In this example *a friend of mine* is repeated as the subject pronoun *she*. Carter and McCarthy (ibid., p. 143) argue that left-placed or fronted items of this kind are perfectly normal in conversation, and especially in narratives: 'It is apparent that speakers use the available slot to flag a variety of items of information that will be helpful to the listener in identifying participants, in linking current topics to already mentioned ones, in reactivating old topics, and generally anchoring the discourse. They use the term 'topic' to describe the slot at the front of a clause that is used to carry topic-prominent items. There is also a final slot that speakers often fill with different types of information when all other core clause constituents have been exhausted. Tags often occupy this slot (such as *you're daft, you are*), as do other noun phrases. For example:

> A: *It's lovely.*
> B: *Good winter wine that*
> C: *It's very nice that road up through Skipton to the Dales*
> D: *I can't remember the names of the places.*
> C: *Yeah.*

Indirect speech is usually in the form of 'X said that Y', where the reporting verb (for example *tell*) is in the simple past tense. However in Carter and McCarthy's corpus the reporting clause was in the past continuous. For example *Tom was saying they should have the heating on by about Wednesday.* Carter and McCarthy suggest that the past continuous seems to report the event of the uttering, whereas the past simple gives more authority to the words uttered. The use of the past continuous form of a reporting verb was found in every context but narratives, which might indicate that what people said and what words they used were considered equally important. In casual conversation the past continuous *saying* and *telling* emphasise the content of a message over its form, and entire conversations are summarised or reported rather than individual utterances.

Biber *et al.* (1999) have investigated the types of structure that characterise speech. They distinguish between the body of a speaker's message, which carries the main content, optional preceding elements or *prefaces*, and following elements or tags'. For example:

> Preface: *North and south London*
> Body: *they're two different worlds*
> Tags: *aren't they? In a way.*

Prefaces function as conversational launching devices that Biber *et al.* call **utterance launchers**; that is, they signal the beginning of a turn or an utterance. They include **fronting**, **noun phrase prefaces**, **discourse markers** and **overtures**.

Fronting is a device used for the management of information, where word order is capitalized upon to give prominence to one element in the immediate context. The grammatical structure of a clause commonly follows the subject/verb/object/predicator/adverbial word order of English (see Jeffries, 2006, ch. 6), which is the same for speech as for writing (disregarding ellipsis). The ordering object/predicator/adverbial/subject is known as topicalisation or fronting and is found in a restrictive set of conditions. It gives prominence to one element in an immediate context, and therefore its use is restricted. For example:

> A: *You always remember numbers. Don't you? Car numbers and telephone numbers and . . .*
> B: **Car numbers** *I remember more by the letters than the numbers.*

Noun phrase prefaces occur more frequently in speech, and divide clause frames into two chunks, where a pronoun corefers to a prefaced noun phrase:

> <u>This little shop</u> – *it's lovely.*
> <u>Those Marks and Spencer's bags</u>, *can you see <u>them</u> all?*
> *You know,* <u>the vase</u>; *did you see <u>it</u>?*

In sentence grammar such utterances are more usually expressed as a single clause with no coreferential pronoun, for example *This little shop is lovely.*

Discourse markers are single words or phrases that signal something is about to be said and are used to gain the listener's attention. They are a particular feature of the grammar of speech and are not normally found in writing. They comprise words such as *right, erm, well, oh, okay* and *so* and phrases such as *so anyway, you see* and *look here*, and combinations of these, for example *okay, you see* and *well, so anyway*.

Overtures are longer than discourse markers and signal a new direction in the conversation. For example *I would have thought* has the pragmatic force of signalling a point of disagreement, *there again* of adding a contrasting point to an argument and *going back to* of returning to an earlier topic.

Whilst prefaces come before the main body of an utterance, **tags** describe afterthoughts or qualify what has already been said. Biber *et al.* (1999) identify four types of tag: **retrospective comment clauses, retrospective vagueness hedges, question tags** and **noun phrase tags**.

Retrospective comment clauses are added comments that modify the preceding clause. For example, *Mm I wouldn't go into Amanda Close I don't think*. Retrospective vagueness hedges signal that the speaker has some doubt about what has just been said, for example *North and South London they're two different worlds aren't they? In a way*. Question tags have the pragmatic force of retrospectively turning a statement into a question and an interactive function of eliciting a response. For example *You had a nice trip though yeah?*.

Finally, noun phrase tags repeat and elaborate a preceding noun phrase, most commonly in order to clarify what might not at first have been clear. For example *He's had a blind up – a special blind that leads straight across the fanlight*. When there is a need to clarify retrospectively a noun phrase is linked to a preceding pronoun, for example: *Oh, I reckon they're lovely. I really do whippets*. In speech the use of a personal pronoun is common to which the speaker adds a clausal unit with a clarifying noun phrase to make the reference clear.

Carter and McCarthy (2006) identify nine basic forms of spoken grammar. Biber *et al.* (1999) 'fronting' is what they call **heads**, and retrospective comment clauses are called **tails**. The remaining categories are **discourse markers**, **ellipsis** (discussed earlier), **deixis** (*could we just move that into this corner here*), **modal expressions** (*I suppose it must be sort of difficult to phone or whatever*), **adverbials** (*you know which one I mean probably*), **spoken clause structure** (which includes the categories of topical information and re-inforcement discussed earlier) and **vague language** (A: *Do you think it is affected by your faith, like you were saying you* [B: *mm*] *have kind of moral standards or not, like hooliganising and things I mean . . .*) (See Jeffries, 2006, for explanations of grammatical terms.)

Thus Biber *et al.*, Carter and McCarthy and others have shown that speech not only has its own grammar that is distinct in many ways from that of writing, but also that it can be described and categorised into grammatical categories.

2.8   Studying speech

As the earlier sections of this chapter have shown, the focus of research in pragmatics and discourse is on: (1) identifying linguistic patterns in verbal behaviour, (2) the management of conversation and (3) the nature of interactions everyday speech, taking account of the contexts in which they occur. Conversation analysis, and indeed pragmatics in general, studies the order, organisation and orderliness of social actions, and particularly as they are located in everyday interactions. Above all it is concerned with structures and the ways in which order happens. The aims of research in pragmatics and discourse, then, are to provide analytic descriptions of the organisation of spoken interactions, to apply these to everyday speech and to analyse their implications for the linguistic system itself.

2.8.1   Selecting a topic for research

The first thing to decide when planning your own research into pragmatics and discourse is the focus of your study. For example you may wish to:

- Replicate a previous study using your own data.
- Compare talk in particular settings, such as institutional and informal.
- Compare different kinds of talk, such as between men and women, among women or men of a similar age or different ages.
- Describe something new, such as new patterns of speech arising in interactive television broadcasts or internet chat rooms.
- Compare talk amongst people from different cultural backgrounds.

We shall look at the first three of these in turn.

First, replicating a previous study using your own data is perhaps the easiest to do as the research question(s) and methods have already been established. Replication of studies is in fact an important aspect of research in pragmatics and discourse as such studies tend to be qualitative, and small in scale and have a large number of variables, which makes it difficult to draw conclusions from any one study. Reliable generalisations about the issue in question can only be made when similar results have been obtained by a number of researchers. Even then there will be differences between the results of the studies as the informants (see Chapter 1) will be different people from those in the original study, even though they may be similar in terms of age, gender, ethnicity, class and so on.

One way in which you can usefully vary your replication of a study is to ask the same questions and use the same methods, but change one or more of the nonlinguistic variables. For example the women who took part in Coates' 1996 study of talk among women friends were predominantly middle class. This study could be replicated using working-class women as informants, and the results of the two studies compared. The question here would be whether the patterns of friendly talk identified by Coates apply to women from a different social background.

Second, whereas projects that replicate earlier work have largely the same focus as the original study, if you decide to compare talk in different settings you will need to establish your own focus or research question. For example you could:

- Compare soap opera dialogue with spontaneous informal conversation to ascertain the extent to which soap opera dialogue resembles spontaneous speech.
- Compare the speech a person uses in her or his work setting with that used in a more informal and casual one to see whether context makes a difference to speech.

Third, for comparing different types of talk you will again need to establish the focus of your study or your research question. You could:

- Compare a group of elderly men or women with a group of young men or women from similar social backgrounds to see whether patterns of conversation vary with age.
- Compare a mother talking to a daughter or son with a father talking to a daughter or son, to see whether patterns of conversation vary according to gender.

Once you have chosen the focus of your project it is important to read related books and journal articles that could help you to orientate your study. By reading up on a topic you can obtain a clearer picture of the field of enquiry, including the arguments raised and the questions asked. This will help you to formulate your own question and give you an idea of the findings you might expect, and what would be unexpected. It will also provide you with ideas for data collection and methodology, such as how many informants to choose, how long the recordings should be, and perhaps even pitfalls to avoid.

It is important to take note of the date of publication of the works you consult, since the most recent ones will be up to date in developments in the field, while older works still being cited by researchers will give you an idea of the importance of these works in the field. The key to reading for the purpose of designing a research project is not to read most of what is available but to concentrate on the works that are closest to your own research question.

2.8.2   Choosing and collecting data

As with researching variation and change in English, the data you collect will usually be of naturally occurring speech. Research in pragmatics, as mentioned earlier, is qualitative in nature; that is, the data come from a small range of informants. This allows for a more detailed analysis than quantitative methods that use standardised instruments such as questionnaires (see also Section 1.4.2).

Chapter 1 described how interviews are a principle source of spoken data for research into variations in spoken English. However these are too structured in nature to be of use in discourse and pragmatics research because the aim is to find out how aspects of naturally occurring speech work in different contexts and settings. Therefore researchers are more likely to obtain their data while acting as an observer or even eavesdropping. This sounds simple as people talk all around us all the time; however capturing that talk requires a recording device and many day-to-day discussions take place in situations where it is difficult to make recordings. Since all talk is shaped by the context in which it occurs, where it is being recorded is an important part of that context. Opting for a more recording-friendly setting inevitably involves a loss of the influence that more common or usual contexts have on speech.

You could record natural conversation in a domestic or social setting. Rather than preparing questions, as you would do for an interview, you could ask your informants to discuss a particular topic, such as their views on a topical news item, or record them during a meal or some other social event. With this method of data gathering you have to ensure that background noise such as loud music will not interfere with the recording. In this regard a more institutional setting might be preferable, for example a lesson in a school or university, a discussion at a seminar, a tutorial, or a doctor's surgery or an exchange between a salesperson and a potential buyer.

Although the purposes and contexts of recording data for pragmatics and discourse studies are different from those for researching variations, the actual mechanics of the recording are very similar. These were discussed in Chapter 1. Important points to be aware of are the observer's paradox and the ethics of obtaining consent.

The term observer's paradox refers to how a researcher's presence may affect other people's speech and behaviour, which runs counter to the purpose of the exercise. One obvious way to get around this is to record people covertly, but this raises the problem of ethics. Coates (1996) describes how she secretly recorded her friends conversing at gatherings at each other's homes during the course of a year. Eventually she told them what she had been doing, and to her surprise they felt angry, exploited and betrayed, not because she had recorded them but because she had not told them. Thus recording people and informing them afterwards has to be thought about very carefully.

The current ethical thinking is that it is not acceptable to record people's voices without permission, but this raises the question of exactly how much to tell them about the purpose of your recording. If you tell them that you wish to record their accent, this will make them conscious of the way that they speak and may result in their altering their normal speech. One way to avoid this is to give a different reason for recording, such as gathering opinions on a particular issue or as part of a project of some kind. Whatever you decide you should inform them of the overall purpose of your research. Not everyone is familiar with the conventions of academic research and therefore need to be made aware of the implications of consenting to be recorded. In the case of private conversations, by analysing the data and writing it up you are effectively making that conversation publicly available. Many professional researchers have their studies published in books or journals with a large readership, and your own work, although not so widely disseminated, will be read by tutors and external examiners. For this reason it is an academic convention to use pseudonyms in the transcript and analytic comment. Your informants might feel more comfortable about taking part if they know that this convention will be adhered to in their case. It is also worth noting that informants are often interested in seeing the results, and if you offer to give them a copy of the recording or your report on the project, this might help to obtain their consent.

When it comes to the recording itself, the less obtrusive the video, tape or micro recorder the better. Section 1.5.4 explains the mechanics of recording in detail. One thing you will also have to bear in mind is that conversation and the circumstances in which it takes place can be unpredictable. You must be prepared to record more than once and for longer than you originally thought you would have to. If you are one of the participants in the recording you will have to take account of the observer's paradox.

Once you have recorded your conversation you will need to select the part to use in your analysis. This will usually be a piece of dialogue lasting from about two to five minutes, giving two to five pages of transcription. It is not usually necessary to transcribe all of the conversation, since this is very time-consuming and not necessary for the purposes of your analysis. The selections you make will be guided by the focus of your study. For example if you are investigating face-threatening acts in a conversation between a male and a female, then you should choose only extracts that feature such acts. When you have made your selections the next step is to transcribe them.

2.8.3 Conventions of transcription

Because analysing discourse is concerned with the management and order of conversation and the contexts which it occurs, speech is transcribed into ordinary orthographic script rather than the phonetic fonts of the international phonetic alphabet (see Section 1.5.5 and Jeffries, 2006, ch. 3). It is important that you transcribe what you hear, including utterances not normally found in writing such as *um*, *er* and so on, and resist the temptation to modify what you write into grammatical, punctuated English. For ease of reference it is helpful to line number the transcription down the right-hand side. There is no single set of transcription symbols that are used uniformly, but a consensus about usage has emerged. It is usual to set out the transcript like a play script; that is, with the speaker's name or initial on the left-hand side and the utterance after it (see for example Section 2.6.5). It is also usual to leave out punctuation and use the method of indicating pauses described below. Capital letters are normally either not used at all, or confined to proper nouns. They are not usually used to mark the beginning of sentences, since spoken conversation is not subject to the same rules and conventions of written language. Punctuation marks are generally used for intonation rather than for grammar. Analysing discourse is a relatively new activity and there is no standard system for transcribing talk of the kind used for transcribing accents, such as the international phonetic alphabet. However, certain conventions have been established and the most commonly used transcription notations are listed below:

- (.) – just noticeable pause
- (0.3) (2.3) – examples of exactly timed pauses, in seconds
- .hh hh – speakers' in-breath and out-breath respectively
- (h) – this is inserted in the middle of a word to denote 'laughter within that word
- word. – full stop (period) after a word denotes the falling and end of an intonation.
- word? – question mark after a word depicts a rising, questioning intonation.
- £words£ – pound signs enclose words spoken in a 'smiling voice'
- wo- – a sharp cut-off of a word or sound.
- wo:rd – a colon indicates stretching of the preceding sound.
- (word) – transcriber's guess at an unclear word or words.
- ( ) – unclear talk.
- (- - - -) – unclear word, with each syllable represented as a dash.
- A: =word – equal sign denotes the absense of a discernible pause between two speakers' turns or, when placed between two sounds in a single speaker's turn, indicates that the sounds run together.

- <u>word</u> – underlined words are those which are spoken loudly.
- WORD – capitals indicate even louder speech.
- >word word<, <word word> – inward arrows indicate faster speech, outward arrows slower speech.
- [overlap] – overlapping speech.

Transcribing accurately and faithfully is a time-consuming business since – unlike the more straightforward transcriptions used in sociolinguistics (see Chapter 1) – it involves not only the words that are spoken but also noting speech markers such as *oh*, *um* and *er*, timing the length of pauses, identifying sections of overlap and so on. Anyone who is new to transcription invariably underestimates the time it will take.

To prepare yourself for all that is involved in transcription it is worthwhile undertaking a small practice exercise with another person. Record between 10 and 15 minutes of conversation (you and your partner could be among the participants if you so wish) in an informal setting such as your home or the communal space in a shared house or flat (make sure you have permission to record before you start). Once you have recorded, you and your partner should listen to all the tape recording and then agree on the sections to transcribe. These should amount to two to three minutes in total and will provide three to five pages of transcription, which should be sufficient for the purpose of analysis. Decide which transcription conventions you are going to use, plus any additional ones that might be needed, then independently write out your transcriptions. When you have finished, compare your transcription with that by your partner. Points of comparison are: whether or not either of you have included anything other than words; whether your transcripts are identical, and if not, in which respects they are different. It is also worth taking some time to think about features of talk that were hard to capture and why.

2.8.4   Analysing data

If you have prepared yourself well by reading studies that are relevant to your work and clearly identifying the precise focus of your study, then the task of analysing your data will be straightforward. For example if you have chosen to replicate a study or changed a variant in that study, then the methods of analysis will be the same as those in the original piece of research. If you have chosen another of the topics listed in Section 2.8.1, you may decide to follow one of the approaches described in this chapter, such as Gricean pragmatics (Section 2.4), discourse analysis (Section 2.5), conversation analysis (Section 2.6) or interactional sociolinguistics (Section 2.7). Your preparatory reading will be of help here as it should give you an idea of which method of analysis best suits the data you have collected and transcribed.

The aim of your analysis will be:

- To ascertain whether the model or categories of analysis you are using can be applied to your data.
- To judge the degree to which this has been successful.
- To examine the content to which your findings accord with those in published studies in the field.

Once you have analysed your results you will need to interpret them; that is, to draw conclusions about any insights that your analysis and your comparison of it with other published research have given you.

2.8.5 Sample projects

Project 1
- Choose a study to replicate, for example Cameron (1997) or Coates (1997) which were discussed in above.

This will require you to record a conversation between participants of a similar age, gender and background to the ones in the original study. Your recording does not have to be as extensive as in the original study, but it should be long enough to enable comparison. As a rough guide, half an hour of conversation and selected sections totalling about five minutes should be sufficient. When you have finished your transcription you should analyse it according to the categories used in the original study and then compare your results with those of the original.

Project 2
- Conduct a discourse analysis or conversation analysis of talk in a particular setting, for example an institutional or informal one.

Record about half an hour of conversation in your chosen setting and transcribe segments amounting to about five minutes. Analyse your transcription according to the methods used in your chosen field of analysis. Write a discussion of your findings and conclusions that can be drawn from them, and then compare your results with those from previous research in the field. Since the focus of this study is the setting, your discussion will centre on how aspects of that setting affect verbal behaviour. You should also include an explanation as to why you have chosen either discourse analysis or conversation analysis.

Project 3

- Compare and analyse different kinds of talk, such as between men and women, among women, or among men of a similar age or different ages.

This project is very similar to Project 2 above and will follow the same procedure, except that the focus will be on the participants' verbal behaviour rather than on the effect of the setting.

Project 4

- Describe interactions on live television or internet chat rooms.

This will involve either recording from the television or printing off material from chat rooms. Recording from a television does not take as long to set up and execute as a live recording, so you could record one or two programmes, depending on their length. The chatroom material needs to be long enough to select extracts but not so long as to make the data unwieldy. For a short study, 15–20 pages should be sufficient. You should then select extracts to analyse in detail, according to the methods used in your chosen field of analysis. Finally, you should analyse your data in terms of what it reveals about the interaction and whether any conclusions can be drawn about how the context affects interaction.

Project 5

- Conduct an analysis of spoken grammar.

This will require you to record and transcribe conversation, as in Projects 1–3, but instead of using discourse analysis or conversation analysis methodologies you should analyse your data according to grammatical categories of spoken English. You should explain what these categories are, where they are found in your data and how they affect the process of interaction.

2.9 Further reading

For pragmatics and discourse see Brown and Levinson (1987), Hewings and Hewings (2005), Cutting (2002), Cameron (2001), Hutchby and Woofitt (1998), Thomas (1995), Schiffrin (1994), Leech (1983) and Watts (2003). Chapters on pragmatics and discourse also feature in general books on applied linguistics, such as Davies and Elder (2004) and Schmidt (2002).

3 Stylistics

3.1 Introduction

The linguistic fields investigated in the first two chapters of this book were concerned with spoken language. By contrast stylistics is primarily concerned with the linguistic analysis of written texts, especially but not exclusively literary ones. Early linguists concentrated on spoken language, its history, acquisition and so on. When they did study written English this was often a consideration of its formal features, as expressed through vocabulary and grammar, rather than of literary features and style. In a seminal and often quoted paper Jakobson (1960, p. 377) wrote that: 'a linguist deaf to the poetic function of language and a literary scholar indifferent to linguistic problems and unconversant with linguistic methods are equally flagrant anachronisms'. That is, just as a linguist should take account of the creativity and literariness of language, then a literary scholar should take account of the linguistic structures by which that creativity and literariness is realised.

Jakobson's statement marked the birth of the field of stylistics. Since then numerous linguistic investigations of literary texts have been conducted, often using methods borrowed from descriptive linguistics. Aspects of phonology, especially metrics and sound patterning, have also been applied to poetic texts. Linguistic analysis of literary works involves not only the identification of linguistic features, but also reflection on how these should be interpreted and the relationship between linguistic structures and the mental processing behind them. Thus in addition to the more formal properties of style there has been a parallel interest in the psychological and cognitive properties of style, particularly in respect of how readers respond to texts.

Many works on stylistics are organised around language use in particular genres, and especially in poetry, prose and plays. This chapter takes a different approach in that it is organised around key concepts or linguistic categories and the principles of language as discourse. This allows for consideration of stretches of text at the level of discourse and discussion of stylistic 'tools' across a variety of text types and genres. Sections 3.2 and 3.3 provide an overview of stylistics and the study of it. Sections 3.4–3.6 discuss major aspects of textual organisation and patterning in pieces of text. Section 3.7 explores the principles of the organisation of narrative, Section 3.8 considers representations of speech and thought in narrative, and Section 3.9 investigates the use of dialogue in drama. These sections are by no means exhaustive of all the methodological approaches in stylistics, but they cover a few in sufficient detail to give you a flavour of what is involved and get you started in in the field. Finally, Section 3.10 provides guidance and advice on research into stylistics.

3.2   What is stylistics?

At its broadest, stylistics can be defined as the study of the style of written – predominantly literary – texts, as opposed to investigation of the ideas that texts contain, which is the focus of literary criticism. However this is not to say that stylistics ignores ideas. Stylistics looks mostly at how texts are organised, whereas literary criticism focuses on what they convey. According to Wales (2001, p. 373) 'The goal of most stylistics is not simply to describe the formal features of texts for their own sake, but in order to show their functional significance for the interpretation of text; or in order to relate literary effects to linguistic "causes" where these are felt to be relevant.'

Although intuition and interpretative skills are important, in stylistic analysis the aim is to avoid vague and impressionistic judgements about the way in which formal features are used and manipulated in texts. Some literary critics take issue with what they view as an objective approach to the interpretation of literary texts. However, objectivity is an important feature of stylistics, and therefore the methods of analysis should be 'methodical, systematic, empirical, analytical, coherent, accessible, retrievable and consensual' (ibid.) Thus stylistics is concerned with identifying and examining the linguistic organisation of a text, and with how that organisation interacts with its interpretation to support a particular view or reading of the work being examined.

In recent years stylistics has also been influenced by cultural theory, which questions the assumption that an interpretation or a particular view of a text is fixed, stable and the same for all readers. Since the 1980s linguists such as Fowler (1986), Fairclough (1989) and van Dijk (1988) have added a further dimension – that is, interpretation does not happen in a vacuum or as a solely individual activity but is affected by social and cultural experiences. Consequently stylistics can be said to be made up of three distinct but inter-related strands of inquiry, any of which can independently form the primary focus of study or lend itself to combination with one or both of the others. These strands are the formal, the cognitive and the sociocultural.

The formal approach to the study of stylistics is concerned with the formal properties of a text and analyses words and other structures from a linguistic perspective. These include sounds, vocabulary, the syntax of phrases and clauses, and the textual organisation of discourse. Stylistics has a highly developed conceptual vocabulary and frames of reference. A common language or **metalanguage** has evolved; that is, a set of linguistically derived terms for describing stylistic concepts. The stylistician's 'toolbox' includes checklists of the kind offered by writers of stylistics textbooks such as Short (1988, 1996) and McRae (1997), some of which are discussed more fully in Sections 3.3 and 3.4 below.

The cognitive approach takes account of the points of contact between a text, other texts and readers. It considers the function of a text and draws on literary, cultural and psychological theories as well as linguistic theory. Thanks to research in the field of pragmatics (see chapter 2), linguists now recognise that meaning is not stable and absolute, but often depends as much on the interpretation accorded by a reader or listener as on the actual linguistic structures that are used. Stylistics also considers that the contact between the text and the reader is interactive and communicative, for example in respect of writers drawing attention to other texts and readers constructing meaning during the act of processing texts (see Sections 3.4.1 and 3.5). Thus stylisticians, like literary critics, try to understand the reception of a text.

The sociocultural approach is concerned not only with the interaction between the text and its readers but also the contexts in which reading and writing take place. Readers do not exist in isolation, but function within a wider social and cultural context. Therefore account is taken of contextual factors such as the cultural background of the reader, the circumstances in which the particular text is read and so on. The particular concerns, experiences and political views that the reader brings to bear on the text will obviously play a huge role in colouring her or his interpretation of it, and it is essential for this to be taken into account when applying objective criteria to the linguistic features contained in a text. Such an approach leaves behind the static view of a text as a self-sufficient entity and replaces it with one that is much more dynamic, cognitive, intertextual and interpersonal. Another dimension of sociocultural stylistic analysis concerns the existence of unequal relationships in society and how texts mediate authority, power and control. In this regard stylistic analysis can be embedded in a framework of critical linguistics and critical discourse analysis, where an exploration of authority, power and inequality is a central part of the analysis. This critical aspect of textual analysis is discussed fully in Chapter 4; here we shall concentrate on the formal and cognitive approaches to textual analysis and interpretation.

A further issue in stylistics is the range of texts that should be considered for analysis. Stylistics was initially restricted to literary texts, but as the notion of 'literary language' became more fluid the range of texts considered suitable for stylistic analysis broadened to include newspaper articles, advertisements and so on. Rather than focusing on instances or features of literary language, it is more appropriate to consider the concept of 'literariness', which was coined by the Russian formalists in the early twentieth century. Literariness can be a property of any text and is related to patterns of language use, irrespective of the genres. The examples presented in this chapter, then, come from a wide range of texts.

3.3 Units of language and grammar

Any utterance or written piece of language is organised into distinct units, each of which has an associated area of linguistic study (see Jeffries, 2006). These grammatical units are ranked according to size, from the largest to the smallest:

- Sentence or clause complex
- Clause
- Phrase or group
- Word
- Morpheme
- Phoneme

While these can be discussed individually in many analyses, it is central to stylistics and to our understanding of language and style that they be connected. They depend upon each other and work together, representing 'multiple and simultaneous linguistic operations in the planning and production of an utterance' (Simpson, 2004, p. 5). This is most evident in poetry. There are many textbooks on stylistics that explain this interdependence in detail (for example Wright and Hope, 1996; Short, 1996).

Phonemes, the smallest meaning-changing units in speech (see Jeffries, 2006, ch. 2), are often exploited in poetry and advertising slogans for purposes of **alliteration, repetition, assonance** and **rhyme**. Consider the following example from an old English poem:

> Over breaking billows, with belly sail,
> And foamy beak, like a flying bird
> The ship sped on.

The letter *b* is used alliteratively throughout the poem: *breaking billows, belly, beak, bird*; as are *s* (*sail* and *sped*) and *f* in (*foamy* and *flying*). Alliterative syllables are usually strongly stressed and relate to the rhythmic pattern of the rhyme, as in the following line from the medieval poem *Sir Gawain and the Green Knight*: 'The snaw snitered ful snart, that snayped the wilde' (The snow came shivering down very bitterly, so that it nipped the wild animals).

Assonance is where a vowel sound is repeated in a word with different final consonants, for example in '*Break! Break! Break! On the cold grey stones, O Sea!*' the repetition of the *o* in *cold* and *stones* as a single word, *O*, highlights the poet's anguish. Another example of assonance is the advertising slogan 'beans means Heinz' where the vowel sound /iː/ is echoed three times.

The morpheme is the smallest unit in grammar and is often also said to be the smallest unit of meaning in written language – see Jeffries, 2006, ch. 3. Certain morphemes, called **root** morphemes, are individual words in their own right, whereas **bound** morphemes, such as prefixes and suffixes, have no meaning unless they are bound onto root morphemes. For example the word *teapots* has three constituents: two root morphemes, *tea* and *pot*, plus the suffix or plural morpheme *s*. A vocabulary can be added to by creating new words. A common way of doing this is **compounding**: that is, joining two root morphemes together, such as *blackbird* or *ice-cream*. Another way is to invent completely new words, of which a famous example is Lewis Carroll's poem *Jabberwocky* (Carroll, 2001, p. 15):

> Twas brillig and the slithy toves,
> Did gyre and gimble in the wabe;
> All mimsy were the borogroves,
> And the mome raths outgrabe.
> 'Beware the Jabberwock, my son,
> The jaws that bite and claws that scratch
> Beware the jubjub bird
> And shun the frumious bandersnatch.'

Here the words *brillig*, *gyre* and *gimble* are root morphemes, whilst *toves*, *borogroves* and *mome raths* are shown by their syntactic position to be bound by the plural *s*. The word *slithy* has two morphemes, the final *y* being an adjectival one.

Thus morphemes are combined into words, which are in turn combined into **phrases** (see Jeffries, 2006, ch. 4). These can consist of a single word or a group of words and comprise the **noun phrase, verb phrase, adjective phrase** and **adverbial phrase**. To these can be added the **prepositional phrase**, which is a noun phrase with a preposition in front *The cat* is a noun phrase made up of the determiner, *the*, and the noun *cat*. *Jumped* is a verb phrase comprising the past participle of the verb *jump*, whilst *has jumped* is a verb phrase made up of two words: the auxiliary *has* and the verb *jumped*. *Over the fence* is a prepositional phrase, formed by the preposition *over* plus a noun phrase *the fence*, which is itself made up of a determiner and a noun.

Phrases combine elements of information into **clauses** (see Jeffries, 2006, ch. 5). The main difference between a phrase and a clause is that a clause contains a verb phrase in addition to other phrases. For the purposes of stylistic analysis, the clause is particularly important because it has to include a verb, thus fulfilling several important functions of language, such as providing information on tense and grammatical 'mood': that is, whether a clause is interrogative, imperative or declarative. In addition to their grammatical forms, clauses can also be categorised according to their semantic functions. The various phrase classes outlined above combine into five basic elements of clause structure:

- *Subject* (S)
- *Predicator* or *verb* (P)
- *Object* (O)
- *Complement* (C)
- *Adverbial* (A)

In English it is normal for the theme of the sentence and the process, namely the subject and the verb, to appear at the start of a sentence. Take for example this sentence from F. Scott Fitzgerald's novel *The Great Gatsby* (2000, p. 8): 'My family have been prominent, well-to-do people in this Middle-Western city for three generations.'

An SPOCA analysis of this sentence produces the following:

> *My family* (Subject)   *have been* (Predicator)   *prominent, well-to-do people* (Complement)   *in this Middle-Western city* (Adverbial)   *for three generations* (Adverbial)

The sentence consists of five phrases:

> *My family* (noun phrase)   *have been* (verb phrase)   *prominent, well-to-do people* (adjective phrase)   *in this Middle-Western city* (prepositional phrase)   *for three generations* (prepositional phrase).

The noun phrase *my family* functions as the subject of the sentence, whilst the adjective phrase *prominent, well-to-do people* functions as a complement after the verb phrase *have been*, which functions as a predicator. The predicator is the only place in a clause where form and function have one-to-one correspondence. Complements occur after certain intensive verbs, of which *be* is the most common.

Not all clauses or sentences, however, fit this standard pattern, particularly in poetry, and this can have the effect of confounding our expectations by bringing to the fore – and therefore emphasising – information that would usually come later, or putting at the end information we would normally expect at the beginning. Another important aspect is the number of clauses that a sentence contains, and whether they are independent, coordinate dominant or dependent. In the above example, there is one independent clause, but in the following extract from Wordsworth's poem *Michael* (1800, lines 10–14), the clause and sentence structures have been manipulated to serve the meaning of the poem:

> Down from the ceiling, by the chimney's edge,
> That in our ancient uncouth country style
> With huge and black projection overbrowed
> Large space beneath, as duly as the light
> Of day grew dim the Housewife hung a lamp.

Here the clauses *as duly as the light of day grew dim* and *the Housewife hung a lamp* are preceded by prepositional phrases that function as adverbials. The main clause is the last one, *the Housewife hung a lamp*. The subject of this clause is *the Housewife*, who is also the main subject of the sentence. Placing the main clause at the end delays the provision of information that is vital to the understanding of the verse, and makes the reader aware of the detail that comes before it, which might not happen if it came after the main clause. The adverbials that precede it work as a kind of camera, a filmic panning that introduces the scene, moving from the wider perspective of the gloomy, rustic country room to the housewife, who illuminates that gloom with a lamp. We may also feel a sense of frustration when awaiting the main verb, which parallels the waiting of those in the cottage as they anticipate the light illuminating the room (see Jeffries, 1993).

The above examples show how a clausal analysis of texts of this kind can tell us a great deal about how the information in them is ordered and about the effect of such ordering. Traditionally, syntactic or grammatical analysis stops with the clause as the largest element. However patterns of language can be identified across stretches of text that extend beyond the clause or sentence. Any piece of writing, if it is to make sense at all, must contain vocabulary and syntactic structures that bond the sentences together. Just as a random selection of words does not make a sentence, so too a random selection of sentences does not create a coherent text. Modern stylistics recognises that texts work as discourse; that is, discourse in the linguistic sense of a stretch of language longer than the sentence.

3.4   Stylistic methods and categories of analysis

Analysing texts that are longer than the sentence has been made possible by developments in systemic-functional grammar. In this field patterns of syntactic structure have been identified that go across sentences and beyond the text to make direct links with the situational context of the speaker or writer. Two of the most developed descriptions of such structures come under the headings of **cohesion** and **deixis** (see also Jeffries, 2006, sections 7.2 and 7.4; and Chapman, 2006, section 5.2) Cohesion refers to the ways in which syntactic, lexical and phonological features connect within and across sentences in a text, and deixis refers to the ways in which some words and phrases shift their reference, according to the speaker's position in space and time and who says or writes them. Thus cohesion performs the textual function of making explicit connections between the sentences of a text, whilst deixis, though textually based, makes direct links with the situational context of the speaker or writer and refers to the ways in which the text and the reader interact. In this section and the subsequent one attention will therefore be paid to both the formal and the cognitive aspects of textual features.

3.4.1   Cohesion

In addition to attending to the subject matter, vocabulary and the syntactic structure of individual sentences, a writer will normally make connections in and between sentences by considering the sequencing of sentences, how one thing leads to another, how certain feelings or events are implied and so on. These **cohesive ties** hold the writing together by connecting forms in the lexis and syntactic structure within and across the sentences. Jeffries (2006, ch. 7) divides cohesion into **reference, substitution, ellipsis, conjunction** and **lexical cohesion**. A further form found in poetry and advertisements is **phonological cohesion**.

References can be divided into **exophoric references** and **endophoric references**. Exophoric references refer to the immediate situational context in which the discourse is taking place. Examples of exophoric reference in the following example are *heaven, everyone, soccer, goalposts, women* (who were lumbering):

> When I first entered heaven, I thought everyone saw what I saw. That in everyone's heaven there were soccer goalposts in the distance and lumbering women throwing shot put and javelin (Sebold, (2003, p. 3).

Endophoric references refer to other parts of the text and can consist of **anaphoric references** and **cataphoric references.** Anaphoric references refer back to somebody or something that has already been mentioned, usually by using of personal or possessive pronouns. Once a referent – that is, the person or thing being referred to – has been established the noun is usually replaced by a pronoun the next time it appears, unless this would make the sense unclear and ambiguous. In the following examples from *Lady Chatterley's Lover* the two characters, Connie and Mick, are named in the first sentence. Thereafter the anaphoric referencing of *him* in the first sentence and *he* and *him* in the fourth refer back to Mick, while the *her* in the second sentence, *she* in the third and *her* in the fourth refer back to Connie:

> Connie always had a foreboding of the hopelessness of her affair with Mick, as people called *him.* Yet other men meant nothing to *her. She* was attached to Clifford. *He* wanted a good deal of *her* life and she gave it to *him* (Lawrence (2006, p. 132).

Anaphoric referencing can also have the effect of implying a previous existence for the characters in a text. Its use plunges us immediately into the world of the text, assuming that we are familiar with the person for whom a pronoun stands when this cannot possibly be the case unless we are rereading the text. The following sentence from William Golding's *The Inheritors* uses anaphora in this way: '*He* was struggling in every direction, *he* was the centre of the writhing and kicking knot of *his* own body' (Golding, 1955, italics added). Since this is the beginning of the novel we do not know who *he* refers to other than that he is a male, but the use of an anaphoric reference instead of a noun immediately draws us into the middle of a narrative and we expect to learn who he is in good time.

Cataphoric referencing is the opposite to anaphoric referencing in that it refers forward. Saying that something will appear 'below' in a text, for example, directs the reader to something that is to be encountered, such as 'in the next chapter, we shall examine this theory in more detail'. Cataphoric references delay more precise information and are important in creating an element of suspense. In the following example cataphoric referencing gradually reveals information about a particular woman before naming her: 'And slowly down the steps in *her* magnificent ballgown comes *the young woman* of the moment we have all been waiting for, *Princess Diana herself*,' (BBC/News, 6 June 1986, italics added).

Here a pronoun, *her*, is used first, followed by a noun phrase, *the young woman*, a proper noun, *Princess Diana*, and, for added emphasis, a reflexive pronoun, *herself*. Cataphonic referencing of this kind is commonly used to build up suspense in thrillers and detective fiction.

The following lines from *The Adventures of Tom Sawyer* show different kinds of referencing at work:

> 'What's gone with *that* boy, I wonder? *You* Tom!'
>   The old lady pulled *her* spectacles down and looked over them about the room; then *she* put *them* up and looked out under *them*. She looked perplexed a moment and said, not fiercely, but still loud enough for the furniture to hear, 'Well, if I get hold of you, I'll . . .' (Twain, 1986, p. 1, italics added).

Before we even know his name or what is being referred to, the cataphoric reference *that* signals that a person or thing is about to be mentioned; this is followed immediately by the noun *boy* and then the pronoun *you*. It is not until we get to the end of the second utterance that we get the proper noun, *Tom*. Just as in the Princess Diana example above, the cataphoric references delay precise information about the boy the woman is wondering about. These words are spoken by a woman who is not named, but given the exophoric reference *The old lady*. Since this is the opening of the novel there is nothing we can refer back to in order to establish who she actually is. Similarly we have nothing to refer back to in the case of *the room*. Which old lady? Which room? After the first clause mentions *The old lady* she is referenced anaphorically as *her* and *she*, and *her spectacles* as *them*. The use of anaphoric and cataphoric referencing in this extract link the world of the text to our shared reality, drawing on we already know about old ladies, rooms and young boys. In this way coherence is established between what is being described and the expectations and shared knowledge that we, as readers, bring to a text.

In addition to using pronouns to refer outwards, backwards and forwards to something or someone, referencing can include repeating a noun or noun phrase that has already been used instead of replacing it with a pronoun at the beginning of clauses, phrases or sentences. Repetition reinforces description and emotional effects in narrative; in public speeches and advertisements it is used to hammer home a point or a product:

> 'The rain fell heavily on the roof, and pattered to the ground. . . . *The rain fell, heavily*, drearily. It was a night of tears' (*Little Dorrit* Dickens, 2000, ch. 17, italics added).

'We are fighting for the rights of the little man. . . . *We are fighting,* as *we* have always *fought,* for the weak as well as the strong. *We are fighting* for great and good causes' (Margaret Thatcher, quoted in the *Guardian,* 13 October 1984, italics added).

The repetition of *the rain fell heavily* in the first example reinforces the weight of the rain and its metaphorical association with tears, whilst the repetition of *we are fighting* in the second example emphasises the point that this Conservative politician is on the side of the underdog and is meeting resistance from other political parties.

As mentioned in Chapter 2, a common feature of cohesion in spoken utterances is ellipsis: the omission of part of an utterance or a grammatical structure that can be assumed from the context. For example predicators and sometimes subsequent clause elements that have already been used are often repeated in condensed, substituted forms (generally as a form of the verb *do* or the word *so*) or are left out altogether. For example:

All trains go to the station. At least, most do.

In the second sentence the predicator *go* and the adverbial *the station* of the first sentence are left out to avoid unnecessary repetition. Similarly in the following sentence the main verb, *failed,* is left out of the verb phrase to avoid repetition:

He didn't fail. He might have done, if he'd gone later.

Because of the omission of information already given, ellipsis can help the listener or reader to focus on new or important information. It is often used when economy of words is needed, such as when note-taking and in personal newspaper advertisements *Wanted: Mother's Help. Three children, 2, 4 and 7. Must drive.* Omitting grammatical words such as determiners and auxiliaries is also common when representing an interior monologue in narratives, suggesting a quick succession of thoughts or images, as the following extract from *Ulysses* illustrates:

. . . raised his eyes and met the stare of a bilious clock. Two. Pub clock five minutes fast. Time going on. Hands moving. Two. Not yet (Joyce, 1992, p. 3).

Here Joyce uses ellipsis in a **telegraphic** way, omitting all words except for the essential *two* rather than *It was two o'clock* or *It said two o'clock,* and omitting *the* and *was* from the next sentence. The extract uses no referencing beyond *his*. Instead cohesion is achieved by cryptically describing the thoughts of one person from which we, as readers have to infer far more than we are accustomed to in order to make sense of the text.

When ellipsis is used to avoid unnecessary and tedious repetition, its use is typically anaphoric. It is extremely common in everyday conversation, which is far more context-dependent than writing. One of the most striking differences between natural, spontaneous conversation and written dialogue that aims to represent it is the use of ellipsis. Dramatic dialogue tends to be far less elliptical than natural conversation since it lacks the degree of context dependence of ordinary speech (see Section 3.9 below). In written texts that must be explicit, such as legal contracts and advertisements, there is far more repetition and explicit referencing and subsequently far less ellipsis than in other types of text.

Ellipsis can also be used in narratives and plays to signify the passing of time, speeding up the action or pace of a narrative by leaving out events that are assumed to have happened but are not described or enacted, either by leaving them out altogether or explicitly marking that they have happened.

Substitution works in a similar way to ellipsis, but rather than omitting words, one word, most commonly a pronoun, is substituted for another word, phrase or clause. Other words commonly used for substitution are:

One: *I offered her a seat. She didn't want one.*
Do: *Did Frank take that letter? He might have done.*
So/not: *Do you need a lift? If so, wait for me; if not, I'll see you there.*
Same: *He chose the roast duck, I'll have the same.*

Like ellipsis, substitution assumes that what is missing is entirely recoverable in the context in which it is used, and also like ellipsis it is a much more common feature of speech than writing. In writing its use is mainly restricted to dialogue that aims to represent spontaneous speech although, again like ellipsis, it depends on the context having been made explicit so that its use can be understood by a listener or viewer.

Conjunctions (*and*, *because*, *but* and so on) work in a different way from reference, ellipsis and substitution in that they do not search backwards or forwards for their referent; rather they signal a relationship between segments of a clause or phrase. Conjunctions join clauses within a sentence and can enable ellipsis to be used in coordinating sentences. For example *Mary walked to the car and got in (to the car)*. They also indicate that what follows in a sentence bears some relation to what has already been said, as well as grammatically joining the sentences together.

Within a text, conjunctions signal different types of relationship between sentences. In the example above, *and* connects the two parts of the sentence and marks the way that the second clause follows the first, and how the text as a whole is moving forward. Other conjunctions that perform the same function are *so, therefore* and *hence*. Jeffries (2006, section 7.2.5) notes that the signposting that conjunctions provide falls into four semantic sets:

- Additive: adding more information, as in the example above and the following one: *She's intelligent. And she's very reliable.*
- Adversative: qualifying the information already given. For example *I've lived here ten years but haven't ever heard of that pub.*
- Causal: giving a cause as to why something happened. For example *He caught a cold because he fell in the river.*
- Continuative: signals further comment, for example: *Well, he could be right.*

Consider the following extract from Thomas Harris's *Hannibal* (2000, p. 251, italics added):

> *Clarice Starling was the last to know that Dr Lecter had killed again. After she hung up the phone, she lay still for many minutes in the dark and her eyes stung for some reason she did not understand, but she did not cry. From her pillow looking up, she could see his face swarming in the dark. It was Lecter's old face, of course.*

The first conjunction, *after*, is a causal one, telling us that Clarice lay still once she had finished the phone call. The second conjunction, *and*, is additive, giving us more information, whilst the third, *but*, qualifies this information by saying that she does not give into the temptation of crying. The fourth conjunction, *of course*, is continuative, adding more comment and information to that given in the preceding sentence. Conjunctions, then, play a vital role in cohesion by logically connecting between parts of the text.

Lexical cohesion, as the term implies, describes the ways in which items of vocabulary relate to one another across clause and sentence boundaries to make a text coherent. It refers to the part played by certain semantic relations between words to create textuality; in other words, that which distinguishes sentences as a text as opposed to a random sequence of unconnected sentences. The relations between vocabulary items in texts are of two main kinds: reiteration and collocation.

Reiteration means either repeating the same word in a later section of the discourse or reasserting its meaning by exploiting **lexical relations**; that is, the stable, semantic relationships that exist between words and form the basis of descriptions or definitions in a dictionary or group of words in a thesaurus. These are of two main kinds: **synonymy** and **hyponymy** (see Jeffries, 2006, section 6.2). For example *zucchini* and *courgette*, and *bachelor* and *unmarried man* are related by synonymy: each pair of words refer to exactly the same thing or state. *Courgette* and *vegetable*, and *mosquito* and *aeroplane* are both related by hyponymy: one is a *superordinate* in the family tree of another. Consider the following example of synonymy:

> *The meeting <u>commenced</u> at six thirty. But from the moment it <u>began</u>, it was clear all was not well.*

In this example *commence* and *began* corefer to the same thing, the meeting. But this is not always the case:

> *The meeting <u>commenced</u> at six thirty; the storm <u>began</u> at eight.*

In the second example *commence* and *began* refer to separate events, although the semantic relation of synonymy between them is being exploited stylistically here to create humour or irony.

Now consider this example of hyponymy:

> *There was a fine old <u>rocking chair</u> that his father used to sit in, a <u>desk</u> where he wrote his letters, a nest of small <u>tables</u> and a dark, imposing <u>bookcase</u>. Now all this <u>furniture</u> was to be sold, and with it his own past.*

Repeating ideas by direct lexical repetition is not common, other than to achieve a particular effect such as driving home a point. Instead items tend to be varied, in this case hyponyms of *furniture*, giving variation from sentence to sentence, which taken together build a mental picture of the kinds of furniture being described. Such variation can add new dimensions and nuances to meaning, building up an increasingly complex context. Every paraphrase of an earlier word brings with it its own semantic connotations. The following newspaper report uses several types of lexical cohesion:

> *Police <u>toughened</u> up their <u>anti-protest tactics</u> at Brightlingsea yesterday and arrested 12 demonstrators who had defied their warnings against trying to block the continuing export of <u>live animals</u> from the port in Essex.*
>
> *Around 400 demonstrators, a lower turnout than the 1,000 anticipated by the organisers, failed in their attempt to turn back three <u>lorries</u> containing around 1,500 sheep. Following a clear police warning that arrests would be made if the paths of <u>vehicles</u> were blocked, the <u>lorries</u> containing the <u>sheep</u> began the final 400 yards of their journey to the quayside at Brightlingsea. A line of police riot <u>vans</u> protected the convoy, as they have through the months of protest (Independent, 19 April 1995, p. 1, italics added).*

In the first line *arrested* is used as a hyponym of *anti-protest tactics*, or as synonomous with it whilst *live animals* is reiterated as the superordinate *sheep*, which is also repeated, making it clear that it is this particular live animal that is being discussed in the article. *Lorries* and *convoy* are also used synonomously, whilst the *vans* used by the police is a reiteration to distinguish them from the *vehicles* used to transport the sheep. *Demonstrators* is repeated – a more sensationalist style of reporting might have included more lurid synonyms such as *antivivisectionists* or extended noun phrases such as *extremist animal rights protestors*.

Collocation describes the way in which certain words commonly (or sometimes uncommonly) associate with one another in a semantic way over and above their syntactic ordering (see Jeffries, 2006, section 6.5.1). For example some adjectives, are used with some nouns and not with others. The adjective *beautiful* collocates with the noun *day* more often than with *night*, as do other adjectives such as *sunny*, *warm* and *bright*. The phrase *a sunny night* is syntactically accurate but semantically rather suspect unless used in an ironic way, since *sunny* and *night* do not normally collocate. Similarly we would expect to see the adjective *shabby* applied to the nouns *clothes* and *treatment* rather than to *water* or *baby*. Some verbs regularly collocate with particular nouns, especially ones associated with animals and insects – bees *buzz*, dogs *bark* and geese *quack* – or transport: *drive* a car and *ride* a bike. The reason why some words have particular associations is not clear. We do know that some words are more likely to combine with specific items to form natural sounding combinations while others do not, even though they are possible or understandable. For example we call milk that has gone off *sour*, whereas butter that has gone off is *rancid* and eggs *rotten*. All these adjectives describe foodstuffs yet they are not interchangeable; we would think it odd for milk to be described as *rancid* and butter as *sour*, yet these words essentially describe the same process. Collocation can be exploited stylistically by collocating words that do not normally go together, particularly in poetry, as in the following lines from T. S. Eliot's poem *Morning at the window*:

> *I am aware of the damp souls of housemaids*
> *Sprouting despondently at area gates*

We do not normally collocate the adjective *damp* and the verb *sprouting* with the noun *soul*, or think of such an action as a *despondent* one. *Damp* and *sprouting* are more normally collocated with the weather and/or gardening, rather than with spirituality, which might lead us to think of a soul's growth in terms of gardening. *Despondently* also more normally describes an emotion, thereby endowing souls with feeling.

In addition to the grammatical and lexical aspects of cohesion outlined above, there is also **phonological cohesion**; that is, cohesion arising from sound. Sound patterns are particularly important when it comes to writing verse of any kind. For example in languages where stress falls on the first syllable of every word, alliteration – where the first letter of two or more words is the same – is often favoured as a poetic device.

Phonology can be a source of cohesion in a text, particularly through alliteration, assonance and rhyme, all of which involve textual patterning created by the repetition of same or similar sounds. Alliteration, assonance and rhyme are among the most obvious and easiest ways a poem can be made phonologically cohesive, and therefore are often very superficial (see for example, Short, 1996; Jeffries, 1993). When these phonological aspects form the overriding criteria for the structure of a poem, such as the use of rhyme in commercial cards for birthdays, Christmas and other seasonal events, then its meaning is often banal. A more complex kind of cohesion is that which is created through the interaction of phonological patterns with semantic ones. Even though sounds in themselves have no meaning (see Jeffries, 1998, ch. 2) and the associations between sounds and meanings in language are arbitrary and conventional, there are ways of using sound so that it complements meaning. Take for example the following passage from Alexander Pope's *Essay on Criticism*, which was written in the eighteenth century. The use of underlining in the poem is an eighteenth-century convention for emphasis, and nouns were also capitalised then.

> *True Ease in Writing comes from Art, not Chance,*
> *As those move easiest who have learn'd to dance.*
> *'Tis not enough no harshness gives Offence,*
> *The <u>Sound</u> must seem an <u>Eccho</u> to the <u>Sense.</u>*
> *<u>Soft</u> is the Strain when <u>Zephyr</u> gently blows,*
> *And the <u>smooth Stream</u> in <u>smoother</u> <u>Numbers</u> flows;*
> *But when loud Surges lash the sounding Shore,*
> *The <u>hoarse, rough Verse</u> shou'd like the <u>Torrent</u> roar.*
> *When <u>Ajax</u> strives, some Rock's vast Weight to throw,*
> *The Line too <u>labours,</u> and the Words move <u>slow;</u>*
> *Not so, when swift <u>Camilla</u> scours the Plain,*
> *Flies o'er th'unbending Corn, and skims along the Main.*
> (Pope and Churton Collins, 1896, pp. 280–1)

Pope's key advice here is that 'sound must seem an echo to the sense'. The sound, according to this advice, supports rather than creates meaning by triggering sound-symbolism associations, with the syntax contributing further to the total effect. For example the word *smooth* in the third line associates through alliteration with the *str* of *stream*, like the everflowing, stable rhythm of a stream itself. In the seventh line the word /laʊd/ cues us in to the significance of low vowels, especially the diphthong /aʊ/, which is intended to echo the roaring of the waves. Such a phenomenon is stylistically known as **iconicity**, which explores the nature of the relationship between meaning and sound.

One further form of phonological patterning is **metre**. Metre in this sense refers to patterns of stress in lines of verse. Stress is a feature of language that we internalise as we learn to speak it; metre is something that is imposed on language, in that stress patterns are made to fit a particular metre (see Jeffries, 2006, sections 2.4.3, 3.3.1). Using metre imposes a constraint on language that we do not normally use in everyday speech, particularly in a language such as English, which is time-stressed (see ibid., ch. 1). Many books on stylistics and the language of poetry (for example Hobsbaum, 1996) give thorough accounts of metrical stress in English, of which the following is a summary.

The most common metrical types in English are the iamb, the trochee, the anapest and the dactyl. An iambic foot has two syllables, of which the first is stressed less heavily than the first (as in *te-tum*). Pope's poem, quoted above, uses the iambic pentameter, which is the most common metrical line in English poetry. With this metre words are arranged in lines that make up five feet or ten syllables in alternating patterns of unstressed or weak (w) syllables and stressed or strong (s) syllables:

> *The sound | must seem | an ec | cho to | the Sense*
> (w)   (s)   (w)   (s)   (w)(s) (w)(s) (w)   (s)

The trochee reverses the unstressed/stressed or weak/strong pattern to form a stressed/unstressed strong/weak one:

> *And be| fore the |Sum mer | end ed*
> (s) (w) (s) (w) (s) (w)   (s) (w)

> *Stood the | maize in | all its |beau ty*
> (s)   (w)   (s) (w) (s)(w)   (s) (w)

The anapest has three feet, made up of two unstressed or weak syllables followed by a stressed or strong one:

> *Not a sound | hath es caped |to thy ser | vants,*
> (w)(w) (s)   (w)(w) (s)   (w)(w) (s)   (w)

> *of prayer | nor of praise*
> (w) (s)   (w)(w) (s)

The dactyl reverses the anapaest, with one stressed or strong syllable followed by two unstressed or weak ones:

> *Lulled by the | coil of his |cry stall ine | streams.*
> (s) (w)(w)   (s) (w)(w) (s) (w) (w)   (s)

As the last example illustrates, the actual number of feet or stresses in a line of poetry does not always fall precisely into ten syllables in the iambic pentameter or two strong and one weak in the dactyl. In fact the iambic pattern, especially as used by Shakespeare, can be anything from four to six iambic feet, eight to twelve syllables.

Using strict metre produces rhythm in a text, but a text does not have to be metric to be rhythmic. Free verse and prose are both discourse types that by definition do not use a fixed metrical scheme, but in both rhythm is often a source of cohesion and sound–sense connections. Virginia Woolf's prose, for example, is often very rhythmic, as the following extract from her novel *Mrs Dalloway* (1999, p. 2) shows:

> *What a lark! What a plunge! For it had always seemed to her, when, with a little squeak of the hinges, which she could hear now, she had burst open the French windows and plunged at Bourton into the open air. How fresh, how calm, stiller than this of course, the air was in the early morning; like the flap of a wave; the kiss of a wave; chill and sharp and yet (for a girl of eighteen as she then was) solemn, feeling as she did, standing there at the open window, that something awful was about to happen . . .*

Much of the rhythm in this passage comes from the repetition of similar stress patterns either within a phrase or between two consecutive phrases. The first two sentences, *What a lark! What a plunge!*, introduce repetition, the phrases being identical in syntax, syllable structure and stress and following the pattern of the anapest – two weak syllables followed by a strong one:

> *What   a   lark!   What   a   plunge!*
> (w)   (w)   (s)   (w)   (w)   (s)

The fourth sentence contains two pairs of parallel phrases: *How fresh, how calm* and *like the flap of a wave, the kiss of a wave,* in which the similarity of stress pattern accompanies virtually identical syntactic and syllabic structures. Although this is not verse, some phrases partially use the iambic pentameter; for example *and plunged at Bourton into the open air* and *that something awful was about to happen.* These alternate rhythmic patterns and mirror images of phrases strongly associate with one of the novel's main themes: life as an alteration between a joyous 'lark' and a 'plunge' into despair, and the search for an equilibrium between the two.

Taken together these various cohesive elements create what is often called the **texture** of a text; that is, they visibly hold it together as a connected entity, rather than appearing to be a random or accidental sequence of sentences. Different types of text use different kinds of cohesion to a greater or lesser extent, creating different types of cohesion and texture. For example conversations typically draw on material that is shared or taken as given, because it can be retrieved from the immediately surrounding situation, and generally use a lot of pronouns and ellipsis. Fiction such as novels and plays depend less on situational references and tend to use referring expressions to thing(s) that have already been mentioned in the text itself, rather than to anything outside it. Reports tend to use more coreference, determiners and conjunctions and less endophoric reference and ellipsis than novels. For example:

> When I first entered heaven, I thought everyone saw what I saw. That in everyone's heaven there were soccer goalposts in the distance and lumbering women throwing shot put and javelin [1] . . .
>
> After a few days in heaven, I realised that the javelin-throwers and the shot-putters and the boys who played basketball on the cracked blacktop were all in their own version of heaven [2].Theirs just fit with mine – it didn't duplicate it precisely, but had a lot of the same things going on inside [3].
>
> I met Holly, who became my roommate, on the third day [4]. She was sitting on the swing set [5]. (I didn't question that a high school had swing sets: that's what made it heaven [6]). And no flat-benched swings – only bucket seats made out of hard black rubber that cradled you and that you could bounce in a bit before swinging) [7]. Holly sat reading a book in a weird alphabet that I associated with the pork-fried rice my father brought home from the Hop Fat Kitchen, a place Buckley loved the name of, loved so much he yelled 'Hop Fat!' at the top of his lungs [8] (Sebold, 2003, p. 1).

An analysis of the stylistic range of cohesion in this passage would consider use of referencing, both exophoric (*heaven, everyone*) and endophoric: in line 1 *What I saw* points forward to *soccer goalposts in the distance and lumbering women throwing shot put and javelin*. There is repetition of *heaven* and *swings*, emphasising the importance of both. It would also consider how conjunctions such as the temporal conjunction *after* and the additive *and* in sentence 2 are used to logically connect parts of the text. If we look more closely at sentence 8 we can see that it is made up of six clauses. All of these are short and simple in structure, but are ordered in such a way as to leave the reader with interpretative work to do in order to understand what the narrator is trying to say: instead of being told that Holly is Vietnamese, we are told she is reading a book in a strange alphabet, which is then related to a Chinese takeaway the narrator knew when she was alive, which in turn leads to a reminiscence of her brother, Buckley.

3.5 Deixis and fictional worlds

Deixis refers to the ways in which words make direct links with the situational context of the speaker or writer (see also Chapman, 2006, section 7.4, Jeffries, 2006, section 7.4.1). Typically, as discussed in Chapter 2, speech often contains deixis since we rely on context a great deal in natural conversation. For example:

> Come _here_ and look at _this_ mess.
> Go over _there_ and look at _that_ mess.

These two statements point to two very different scenarios: one in which the mess is physically close to the speaker, and one where it is further away, although both are within sight. In plays or prose, as well as in poetry, deixis or deictic expressions help to create and sustain the world of the play or narrative by referring to places, people, times and events that have occurred within it. In writing, the use of deixis links the world of the narrative or the poem with that of the reader. For example in poetry deixis can be used to imply that the reader takes part in or watches a scene or events alongside the poet:

> _That_ spot with spice-blooms must need be o'erspread
> _Where such wealth to rot is run;_
> _Blossoms pale and blue and red_
> _There_ will shine full bright against the sun.
> (Hillman, 1961, lines 25–8, emphasis added).

In this example, through the shifting use of _that_ and _there_ the poet is inviting us to share his view and to read the poem as though we were standing beside him. This shifting of points of reference, known as **deictic shift**, moves the point or points of focus from one place, time, person or thing to another. In this way deixis also extends the places, times, people and things created in a text. Words that signal the use of deixis include personal pronouns (_I_, _you_, _we_, _they_ and so on), demonstrative determiners (_this_, _that_, _these_, _those_ and so on), the article or determiner _the_ and adverbs of time and place. As Stockwell

(2002) points out, understanding deixis involves mental processing that is implied or inferred rather than made explicit by the linguistic structures of the text. There are various deictic fields or categories, including **perceptual**, **spatial**, **temporal** and **textual**.

Perceptual deixis refers to participants in a text, including personal pronouns *I*, *me*, *you*, *they*, *it*, demonstrative pronouns (*these/those*), definite articles and definite references, such as *the woman*, and mental states, such as *seeing* and *believing*. Third person pronouns and names are more commonly viewed as part of reference, but Stockwell (2002, p. 46) argues that 'taking cognition seriously means that reference is to a mental representation is a socially located act and is therefore participatory and deictic'.

Spatial deixis refers to expressions that locate the deictic centre in a place, such as the adverbs *here*, *there*, *nearby* and *far away*, the demonstratives *this*, *that*, locatives such as *down the hill* and *out of Africa*, and verbs of motion such as *come* and *go*.

Temporal deixis refers to expressions that locate the deictic centre in time, such as the temporal adverbs *today*, *yesterday*, *soon* and so on, locatives such as *in my childhood* and *a week from now*, and verb tense and aspects that differentiate between the speaker, the story and the receiver.

Textual deixis refers to expressions that foreground textuality, such as chapter headings, titles, and any features that draw attention to the text itself or its production. For example take the following two paragraphs from George Eliot's *Mill on the Floss*. The first is the last paragraph in Chapter 1 of Volume 1, and the second is the beginning of the first paragraph in Chapter 2. The boundary represented by the chapter heading of Chapter 2 is an instance of textual deixis. The novel is framed at the beginning by the musings of an unnamed and unidentified narrator, who is the **deictic centre** of the narrative. The end of Chapter 1 and the beginning of Chapter 2 signal a major deictic shift from the deictic centre of the narrator to the character of Mr Tulliver:

> Ah, my arms are really benumbed. I have been pressing my elbows on the arms of my chair and dreaming that I was standing on the bridge in front of Dorlcote Mill as it looked one February afternoon many years ago. Before I dozed off, I was going to tell you what Mr and Mrs Tulliver were talking about as they sat by the bright fire in the left-hand parlour on that very afternoon I have been dreaming of.

> 'What I want, you know,' said Mr Tulliver, 'what I want, is to give Tom a good eddication: an eddication as'll be a bread to him. This was what I was thinking on when I gave notice for him to leave th' Academy at Ladyday. I mean to put him in a downright good school at Midsummer' (Eliot, 2002, p. 1).

The deictic shift to Mr Tulliver is preceded by the narrator directly addressing readers about what she or he is about to tell them. The first part is clearly deictically centred on the narrator as perceptual deixis, with first and second person pronouns appearing throughout: *I* refers to the narrator and *you* to the reader. Further spatial deixis. Mental states are also indicated in the nouns and verbs *benumbed*, *pressing*, *dreaming* and *dozing*. Spatial relations are indicated by the chair in the room in which the narrator is sitting, and beyond it by the bridge in the narrator's dream and Mr and Mrs Tulliver's parlour. Temporal relations signalled by *I was going to tell you* point to a perceptual shift in the deictic centre that occurs at the beginning of Chapter 2; a temporal shift from the narrator to Mr Tulliver in that the reported events take place at some unspecified point back in time; and a spatial shift as the narrative moves from the narrator's chair in an unspecified room to Mr Tulliver's left-hand parlour. As the novel progresses the deictic centre shifts between Mr Tulliver, his wife Mrs Tulliver, their two children Tom and Maggie, and the narrator. Viewed in this way, deixis extends categories of deictic reference from short stretches of text of two or three sentences to complete texts and beyond, providing an account of how we as readers mentally process the implied and inferred fictional or text worlds we encounter in the texts we read.

There are currently two textual meaning models based on the concept of 'worlds'. The first derives from Werth's (1999) text world theory and has been developed by Gavins (2006). This theory aims to account for the conceptual space that links narrative levels by proposing three worlds of discourse. The first is the immediate 'discourse world', inhabited by an author and a reader. The reader's understanding of this world is dependent upon his or her knowledge and experience of what is being described in the discourse world, which creates the 'text world', and requires understanding, memory and imagination as well as direct perception. Text worlds are defined deictically and referentially, anchored or fixed to the world depicted in the discourse. For example consider the opening line of David Gutterson *Our Lady of the Forest* (2003, p. 1): 'The girl's errand in the forest that day was to gather chanterelle mushrooms in a *bucket to sell in the town at dusk.*' Deictic references pick out spatial location (*in*) and temporal location (*that*) whilst referential information identifies entities present in the text world (*the girl, the forest, chanteerlle mushrooms, a bucket, a town*).

The third type of conceptual space is the 'sub-world', which occurs when a character projects thoughts and reflections to create another space inside the text world.

The second model of conceptual tracking during the course of reading a narrative is Emmott's (1997) framework of narrative comprehension. The purpose of this framework is to account for the ways in which a reader can concentrate on one context, whilst holding on to ones previously encountered. She identifies two processes: priming and binding. Priming refers to the process by which one contextual frame becomes the main focus of attention for the reader, whilst binding refers to the way episodic links between people and places are established in a text and create a context that is then monitored in the mind of the reader. Narrative strands that have been bound into the story but temporarily left alone by the narrator remain in a fictional place until they are brought back in, or 'bound out'. Text world theories such as these aim to account for or emphasise the mental processing that goes on in the act of reading, rather than giving an account of how texts represent the world. As Simpson (2004) points out, finding a balance between the two is important, as a stylistic analysis can go too far in either direction.

3.6   Similes and metaphors

The study of similes and metaphors which is traditionally associated with literary analysis, is a way of identifying patterns in language that are less to do with syntactic patterning and more to do with semantics in that unusual collocations are exploited to achieve a particular effect. Poetry and poetic language are not the only kinds of language to exploit words in this way. Considerable stylistics research has been undertaken on metaphors in recent years, most of it influenced by social psychology and building on the seminal work by Lakoff and Johnson (1980). Traditionally the study of metaphor has been restricted to literary texts, but the publication of Lakoff and Johnson's book and subsequent work in cognitive linguistics has revolutionised the way in which we think about metaphors.

Lakoff and Johnson and others working in the field of cognitive psychology have pointed out that, far from being restricted to literary and poetic language, metaphors pervade much of our everyday discourse and are therefore pervasive in all types of language, both spoken and written. For a start we are probably all aware that meaning is not stable and can change. To create new meanings, we often use existing words metaphorically. As such usage spreads it becomes commonplace and is eventually absorbed into the language. This results in what are traditionally known as 'dead metaphors', for example *foot of a bed*, *table leg*, *foot of a page*. However Lakoff and Johnson argue that far from being 'dead', they are there because metaphors permeate the whole way in which we think about the world. They argue that a metaphor is not simply a conceptual category of one aspect of language, but is fundamental to our very thoughts and actions. The concepts that govern our thoughts are not just matters of literal reason, but of allusion and analogy, which also govern our everyday functioning, down to the most mundane details. Such metaphorical concepts structure what we perceive, how we get around in the world and how we relate to other people. Our conceptual system thus plays a central part in defining our everyday realities. Since communication is based on the same conceptual system that we use when thinking and acting, language is an important source of evidence of what that system is like.

Many everyday expressions appear to have the same underlying conceptual structures that are understood and shared by groups of people. Grouped together these common expressions are called **conceptual metaphors** and are normally identified by being written in capitals. Take the following examples of the ARGUMENT IS WAR metaphor from Stockwell (2002, p. 110):

- Your claims are *indefensible.*
- He *attacked every weak point* in my argument.
- His criticisms were *right on target.*
- *I demolished* his argument.
- I've never *won* an argument with him.
- You disagree, Okay, *shoot!*
- If you use that *strategy,* he'll *wipe you out.*
- *He shot down* all of my arguments.

We do not just talk about arguments in terms of war, we win or lose them. There is no physical battle, but a verbal one, and the structure of an argument – attack, defence, counterattack and so on – mirrors the movements of war. In this sense the ARGUMENT IS WAR metaphor is one by which we live in Western culture; it structures the actions we perform when arguing. The concept is metaphorically structured and consequently the language is metaphorically structured. Far from being a dead metaphor, it has become so ingrained in thought and language that it has become the ordinary way of thinking about arguments. Metaphors are possible as linguistic expressions precisely because they are already embedded in a person's conceptual system. Conceptual metaphors such as ARGUMENT IS WAR, LIFE IS A JOURNEY, TIME IS MONEY, and so on, structure a great deal of our everyday discourse, and therefore are not confined to literature.

Researchers in the field of cognitive stylistics have built on the work of literary critics such as Richards (1925) and cognitive theorists such as Lakoff and Johnson (1980) to in propose new models for analysing metaphor. Richards divided metaphor into three constituent parts: **tenor, vehicle** and **ground**. Tenor is the subject of the metaphor, vehicle is the terms in which the subject is expressed and ground is the common properties that tenor and vehicle share. Take the example 'Juliet is the sun' from Shakespeare's *Romeo and Juliet*:

- Tenor : Juliet
- Vehicle: Sun
- Ground: warmth, beauty, life-affirmation

Those adopting a cognitive approach would argue that we can only make the inference of warmth, beauty and life-affirmation because our conceptual system perceives the sun in those terms and makes it possible to assign them to a person. We can therefore make sense of the metaphor because of how our perceptions are formed. In this approach the categories have been renamed to provide a different emphasis. Ground has been renamed **mapping**, which is defined as a process of matching the properties of the two spaces or domains that are connected by the metaphor. Similarly tenor has become **target** and vehicle has become **source**.

The cognitive approach assumes that viewing the sun in terms of warmth and life-affirmation is universal and unrelated to social and cultural background. In Europe we may well view the sun as warmth and life-affirming, but the inhabitants of the Sahara desert or the Australian bush might not. In Japan the sun is the national symbol while in seventeenth-century France it symbolised the divine right of King Louis XIV. The meaning of the word *sun* then, or more accurately the properties associated with it, vary from culture to culture and century to century. Thus mapping is culturally as well as cognitively determined.

Although the cognitive approach helps us to understand the metaphoric nature of much of our discourse and its reliance on conceptual structures being understood and shared by groups of people, it has yet to explain why particular concepts are formed or how they originate.

3.7 Narrative

A basic definition of narrative is that is a linguistic technique or techniques to report (mainly) past events. At its simplest, a narrative recounts the cause and effect of events that take place over space and time to particular people. Even the simplest narrative involves progression, with the listener or reader being steered through the course of the tale by the teller or writer. Generally we are unaware that we are being guided, and it is only when we begin to look more closely at the way in which language is structured that we begin to realise that we are.

Another important aspect of the way in which a narrative develops is how the story is narrated and how speech and thought are represented. Texts that tell a fictional story usually describe the events, characters and setting from a particular perspective – the author's, the character's (or characters') or a combination of both. While a rigorous and comprehensive model for analysing narrative has yet to be developed, there are models that can inform specific aspects of narrative.

Two basic components of a narrative are **plot** and **discourse**. Plot refers to the abstract story line of a narrative: what you would describe if asked to sum up what a narrative was about. Discourse refers to the manner in which the plot is narrated, including the use of flashbacks, repetition and prevision, which disrupt the chronology of the plot. Plots can be presented in a variety of media. For example, there have been several film versions of the novel *Frankenstein*, all using material from the plot but realised in different ways; it has also been presented as a poem by the poet Liz Lochhead. Similarly Shakespeare's play *Romeo and Juliet* is also performed as a ballet. Therefore different textual media are available for the analysis of narrative, but stylistic analysis so far restricts itself to the written medium.

Simpson (2004) identifies five other basic components of a narrative: **sociolinguistic code**; **actions and events**, **points of view**, **textual structure** and **intertextuality**. Sociolinguistic code locates a narrative in a particular place by considering the sociocultural context including the dialects and accents used in the narrative. As pointed out in Chapter 1, all speech and writing is presented in a dialect of some sort, whether it is standard or non-standard, prestigious or low status. Although many poems have been written in dialect, in narratives it is usual for the prose to be written in standard English and only the characters' speech to be presented in dialect, as in, for example, the novels of D. H. Lawrence and Elizabeth Gaskell. This representation can serve to emphasise the social class divisions between the characters and provide a flavour of the kind of society in which the characters live. One exception to the non-dialect rule in narrative is the novel *Trainspotting* by Irvine Welsh, which is written almost entirely in Scottish dialect:

> The problem wi Begbie wis . . . well, thirs that many problems wi Begbie. One ay the things thit concerned us maist wis the fact thit ye couldnae really relax in his company, especially if he'd had a bevvy. Ah always felt thit a slight shift in the cunt's perception ay ye wid be sufficient tae change yir status fae great mate intae persecuted victim (Welsh, 1993, p. 75).

Since non-standard dialects are associated with lower social class in Britain (see Chapter 1), its use by the narrator reinforces the class distinction between himself and the establishment. Later in the novel the protagonist appears before a magistrate whose speech is presented in standard English: 'You stole the books from Waterstone's bookshop, with the intention of selling them', he states. 'Sell fuckin books. Ma fuckin erse. No, ah sais' (ibid., p. 165).

Actions, events and points of view are ways of considering the intersection of narrative and character. Actions and events are described in Chapter 4 under the heading of transitivity. Points of view, as the term implies, are the particular perspectives from which narratives are told. Authors of factual texts are usually at pains to separate themselves from what they are writing, whereas in fiction the author may play a more active part in the story. This is usually done by having a **narrator**. Much has been written about the stylistics of narrators and narration, the main points of which are summarised below.

The degree to which writers make themselves known to readers as the narrator of the story depends on whether they choose to create a **personal** or an **impersonal narrator**. A further choice is about whether the narrator knows everything about the characters and events (authorial omniscience) or has a restricted narrative perspective (authorial reportage). Both of these perspectives are referred to as **authorial voice**, though the narrator might be different from the author. Taken together these factors determine the perspective or point of view from which a story is told.

A personal narrator is one who intrudes into the story to address the reader directly, by making comments, passing judgements or moralising about the characters and events, and may even speak outside the story. Such intrusion was fairly common in earlier novels such as Henry Fielding's *Tom Jones* (1749), in which Fielding interrupts the story for whole chapters at a time to pass comment on events that have just occurred. Such personal intrusions have become less and less common in narratives, so when they have reappeared in more recent novels, such as John Fowles' *The French Lieutenant's Woman*, (2004) the effect has been startling and seemingly new. First person narratives tell the story from the point of view of a character who may or may not be the author, as in autobiographical novels such as J. D. Salinger's *Catcher in the Rye* (1994) and fictional ones such as Helen Fielding's *Bridget Jones's Diary*, (1996) are more common than second person narratives – that is, written in the second person *you* – as there is less restriction on the points of view expressed. An impersonal narrator is less intrusive and simply reports the events in the story without passing comment on them. The distance of the narrator is marked by the use of the third person – that is, the personal pronouns *he*, *she* and *they* – and the absence of *you* and *I*. Some writers use both types of reporting in the same narrative. For example the nineteenth-century novelist George Eliot generally wrote as an impersonal narrator but occasionally switched style and addressed her readers directly. In the extract in Section 3.5 from *The Mill on the Floss* Eliot moves from being a personal narrator in Chapter 1 to an impersonal narrator in Chapter 2.

Telling a tale also involves deciding the extent to which details of characters are to be revealed. Writers may choose to be authorially omniscient, in which case they deliberately enter their characters' consciousness and are therefore able to tell the reader the characters' thoughts as well as their actions. The nineteenth-century writer Thomas Hardy used a generally impersonal narrative style but was authorially omniscient in revealing his characters' innermost thoughts and feelings. Alternatively, writers may choose to report events that are external to the characters and leave their thoughts alone, as in the novels by Graham Greene. In such novels what the characters think or feel has to be inferred entirely from their speech and actions.

Some writers choose to tell the tale from the perspective of a particular character, with whom the reader is invited to identify. This character may also be the chief narrator of the tale and is usually the first person to whom we are introduced in the book. Usually narratives are told from the point of view of the main character and the events described in the story are those which relate to him or her. Examples include the novels *Jane Eyre* by Charlotte Bronte, *Emma* by Jane Austen and *The Passion of New Eve* by Angela Carter. Other characters appear in relation to the protagonist, and our opinion of them tends to reflect that of the main character.

In some novels there are moves between one character's perspective and that of another or others. For example, in *Women in Love*, D. H. Lawrence moves between describing the actions, thoughts and feelings of two sisters and those of the two men with whom they form relationships. Similarly, in *Enduring Love*, Ian McEwan moves between a description of the actions, thoughts and feelings of two witnesses to a ballooning accident and the man involved in the accident. Telling the tale from more than one character's perspective enables writers to develop different narrative strands or subplots to keep the reader guessing, as in thrillers and detective fiction, as well as in fiction more generally, for example in *Little Dorrit* by Charles Dickens (1894) and *The Man Who Made Husbands Jealous* by Jilly Cooper.

Textual structure refers to the ways in which narrative units are arranged or combined in a story. There are several models of narrative structure, one of the most influential of which has been William Labov's (1972) framework of natural narrative. Labov derived the model from stories told during the course of a natural conversation. He identified six core and recurrent features or categories, each of which has a corresponding hypothetical question, a narrative function and a linguistic form:

- **Abstract**. Question: what has happened, or what is the story about? Narrative function: to signal that the story is about to begin. Linguistic form: often a one-sentence summary.
- **Orientation**. Question: who or what is involved in the story? Narrative function: to help the reader to identify, for example, when and where the

story takes place. Linguistic form: often sentences describing participants, times and places, usually characterised by use of the past continuous tense and adjuncts of time, manner and place.

- **Complicating action**. Question: what happened? Narrative function: to provide the 'what happened?' part of the story. Linguistic form: usually sentences ordered into narrative clauses with a verb in the simple past or present.
- **Resolution**. Question: and what happened in the end? Narrative function: to bring the story to its conclusion. Linguistic form: normally expressed as the last of the narrative clauses that began the complicating action.
- **Evaluation**. Question: so what? Or what else? Narrative function: to make clear the point of the story. Linguistic form: includes evaluative commentary, embedded speech, modal verbs, negatives and so on.
- **Coda**. Question: how does it all end? Or, how does it relate to the here and now? Alternatively it may relate to a moral or lesson learnt by the teller or protagonist. Narrative function: to signal the end of the story or provide a bridge to the present. Linguistic form: often a generalised, 'timeless' statement.

This model works equally well when applied to written narratives. For example the television drama *House* focuses on a cantankerous doctor of the same name. Each episode begins with a patient being admitted to hospital (abstract) for an uncomplicated procedure or diagnosis (orientation). However the illness from which the patient is suffering turns out to be far from straightforward and is medically baffling (complicating action). House and his team run through a series of options whilst the patient gets closer and closer to death (complicating action). House finally comes up with the correct diagnosis, usually at the eleventh hour (evaluation). This serves to highlight his skill as a doctor (coda), which more than makes up for his boorish and uncooperative behaviour with patients. For detailed accounts of stylistic approaches to narrative see Toolan, (1998); Simpson, (2004).

Intertextuality refers to the fact that writing does not take place in a social and historical vacuum but echoes or alludes, either implicitly or explicitly, to other works. In David Lodge's *Nice Work* (1987) which is about a female lecturer specialising in the nineteenth-century industrial novel, each chapter begins with a quotation from one such novel. Angela Carter's *The Magic Toyshop* (1981, p. 4) makes a stylistic allusion to a line by the Romantic poet Shelley in the line 'Look upon my works ye mighty and beware', where the original final word *despair* is altered but also implicit.

3.8 Representing speech and thought

One way in which a point of view can be represented or lead to a change of perspective in a narrative is by the presentation of speech and thought. Speech and thought in fictional texts are by definition imaginary, and although they may follow the rules of natural conversation, such as those discussed in Chapter 2, there is nothing natural about them here. In fictional texts they are artificial, contrived and interwoven into a wider creative structure where they do more than just represent talk, no matter how natural it may appear to be.

Real time speech is very different from speech that is written down. One important difference is that they each use different mediums of expression: speech uses sound and hearing whereas writing uses graphology and sight as the vehicle for words. Spoken speech is also interactive and usually involves a dialogue between at least two people, and depending on the situation there can be no guarantee that the topic will not change when the speakers take their turn (see Chapter 2). When speech involves little or no interaction, such as a lecture, an after-dinner speech or a parliamentary speech, then it has usually been scripted and rehearsed and takes the form of a monologue. Written dialogue or representation of speech and thought is interactive in a completely different way from spoken speech. The interaction happens on two levels: between the characters represented, and between the reader and what is read. Moreover a writer is in control of what the characters say unlike the participants in a dialogue. Consequently the frameworks and models used to analyse written speech are very different from those used to analyse actual speech, as discussed in Chapter 2. By far the most influential of these models for written speech are those developed by Leech and Short (1981), Short (1996) and Fludernik (1993).

There are five main ways in which speech or thought can be represented in a narrative: **direct**, **free direct**, **indirect**, **free indirect** and **narrative report**. Consider this example:

'Do you see her much', she said, half-concerned.

In this sentence there are two independent voices. One is a quotation of the actual words spoken and is bound by quotation marks (*Do you see her much?*). The other is a clause that reports who said it and how: (*she said, half-concerned*). This is known as a reporting clause.

Reporting speech in this way is called direct speech. The actual words spoken by a character are written, usually within a sentence that also provides information about the words and uses punctuation marks to mark the actual words spoken. The reporting verb (the word that tells us what is being done) may well tell a lot about the purpose, emotions and intentions of the utterance. It may also suggest the expression on a person's face and her or his emotional state. For example note the difference between the following:

> *'Go away!' she screamed.*
> *'Go away', she said.*

Adding an adverb or a prepositional phrase after the reporting verb, as in the following examples, is another way of conveying information about emotion:

> *'Most of them were too young', she replied.*
> *'Most of them were too young', she replied sorrowfully.*
> *'Most of them were too young', she replied with disgust.*

The reporting of direct thought is marked by the use of reporting verbs such as wondered, thought, mused and so on, as in the following example:

> *'Does she still like me?' she wondered.*

Sometimes writers use dashes instead of conventional quotation marks, or use nothing at all, depending on the particular effect they want to achieve, such as making actual speech appear to be more like free indirect speech (see below) or to distinguish it from thought. Writers have increasingly experimented with speech representation, such as presenting speech directly without the accompanying punctuation or using a reporting clause that is characteristic of direct speech. Such variations of the representation of direct speech and thought are known as free direct (speech and free direct thought). For example:

> *She said 'I want to see the elephants.'*
> *'I want to see the elephants'*

In the second sentence the reporting clause is left out but the punctuation is kept in. Representing speech in this way minimises the narrator's role and foregrounds the character and his or her speech. Consider this example:

> *She asked him whether he saw her much.*

Here there is only one voice and one point of view. The narrator is using his or her own words rather than the words that were actually used by the character. There is a reporting clause (*she asked him*) and a reported clause (*whether he saw her much*). The narrator's point of view prevails, so no quotation marks are needed. Reporting speech or thought in this way is called indirect speech or indirect thought. It has the effect of foregrounding the narrator rather than the character who has spoken.

Narrative reporting involves a narrator reporting a character's speech or thought without giving any indication of the actual words used. Unlike the explicit models given above, this form of reporting can be used to summarise long stretches of speech and thought.

The different ways in which writers represent speech and thought in writing is summarised in Table 3.1.

Table 3.1   Styles of reporting speech and thought

	Speech	Thought
Direct	*He said, 'I'll come back tomorrow.'*	*What will they say of me? she wondered.*
Free direct	*'Am I too late?'*	*'Was I too late?'*
Indirect	*He said that he would return the next day*	*She wondered what they would say of her.*
Free indirect	*He would come back tomorrow.*	*What would they say of her?*
Narrative report	*She told him about her evening.*	*She wondered about his love for her.*

Generally the narrator's role is to inform the reader of what is going on and/or to evaluate a particular situation for the benefit of the reader. The characters' role is usually to make claims, express doubts and desires, display various emotions and evaluate themselves and/or others and/or a particular situation from their own point of view. Consider the following example from Virginia Woolf's *Night and Day*:

Denham's one wish was to leave the house as soon as he could; but the elderly ladies had risen, and were proposing to visit Mrs Hilbery in her bedroom, so that any move on his part was impossible. At the same time, he wished to say something, but he knew not what, to Katherine alone. She took her aunts upstairs, and returned, coming towards him once more with an air of innocence and friendliness that amazed him (Woolf, 1978, p. 140).

This passage reports Denham's free indirect thought and places the reader in the privileged position of reading Denham's mind and his reaction to the news he has just heard: that Katherine is to marry somebody else.

We might ask, why we should have speech represented in narrative at all? It is perfectly possible to recount a tale without using speech, but its use has become a common feature of fiction and is expected by the reader. Including speech and thought representation in writing does three things:

- It interrupts the general flow of the narrative, slowing it down and concentrating attention on a particular character, event, relationship and so on. In the above extract, the flow of the narrative is interrupted to focus on Denham and his thoughts.
- It develops and brings out relationships between characters; their personalities may be revealed by what they say, their reaction to what is said, or what others say about them. In the above extract, aspects of Denham's personality are revealed by his thoughts.
- It provides a sense of social background by conveying personal mannerisms, concerns, choice of subject matter and so on. In the above extract, the setting not only places the story in a particular place and time in history but also situates Denham in a social class.

3.9   Dialogue in drama

Most scripted speech, especially dialogue, aims to reproduce spontaneous, natural, everyday speech. However there are several important differences between actual spoken speech and the written speech that is intended to imitate it, and these make it difficult or inappropriate to apply spoken discourse models to analyse it. First, someone else has usually written the words are spoken, unlike in normal conversation where the speakers are the authors of their own words. Second, in conversations we can take an active part, whereas with scripted speech we are onlookers who see and hear but do not engage directly with the speakers, although we may be appealed to in a way that invites response. Scripted speech implies an audience in much the same way as any other form of written language, and this has implications for the pace at which something is spoken, its phrasing and degree of implication. Third, scripted speech is written in advance of being spoken and can be edited, unlike everyday conversation.

On the page scripted speech may look like spoken language, but if you compare it with a transcript of a normal conversation you will immediately notice many differences. In conversation, while we usually take it in turns to speak often we interrupt before someone has finished their turn, whereas in scripted speech this does not normally happen. Moreover, scripted speech cannot assume a shared understanding on the part of the listeners. For example in the scripts of long-running soap operas or series such as *Coronation Street*, *Neighbours*, *Friends* and *The Simpsons* the characters nearly always refer to one another by name and explain details of events so that viewers new to the programme or who have not watched it for a while can pick up the thread of the story. In spontaneous conversation names and details are usually taken for granted. Scripted speech also tends to be more organised as it operates within a narrative structure. It is usually about one particular thing, event or person at a time, whereas spontaneous speech can hop from one topic to another and back again in a seemingly haphazard way. Finally, scripted speech rarely has the normal features of spontaneous conversation, such as repetition, restructuring and fillers.

The writers of scripted speech normally have control over both the content of what they write and how it is to be spoken. The people who speak the words can add meaning to them through tone of voice, expressions, gestures and so on, but they do not create the words. Scripted speech therefore has two audiences: the actors or people who are to do the talking, and the people who are watching them.

Scripted dialogue has to convey to the viewer or listener all the things that are normally provided by the narrative in writing. All the information about characters' personalities, behaviour and actions comes from the words the actors say, how they say them and the emotions they convey. When analysing a script, then, we need to look very closely at the words spoken by the characters and the stage directions for clues to the context, the characters' personalities and the reasons for their actions.

The notion of **context** can be divided into three main categories – **physical**, **personal** and **cognitive** – to which can be added **interactive** and **imaginary** in the case of drama (see also Sections 2.3 and 2.6.5). Physical context refers to the actual setting. Personal context refers to the social and personal relationships of the participants, including social networks and group networks as well as the social status of and the distance between the participants. Cognitive context refers to the background knowledge shared by the participants, their world view, cultural knowledge and past experiences. These three aspects of context can be applied to any face-to-face interaction, dramatic as well as natural. However with drama there is also an interactive context; that is, what we as the audience make of the unfolding dialogue and the extent to which it accords with our world views, cultural knowledge and past experiences. There is also an imaginary or creative aspect, where the actors on the stage and the audience engage in the creation of a shared world. This requires us to move beyond what we can see in front of us – a stage with people on it – and be drawn into a world that is entirely imaginary (see Jeffries, 2006, section 7.31; Chapman, 2006, section 5.2).

Deixis (see Section 3.5 above) plays an important part here, since it serves not only to bind the text together but also to incorporate elements of the world beyond the stage that do not actually exist but we are invited to believe in as they have a direct bearing on the action being played out on stage. For example at the beginning of Shakespeare's play *The Merchant of Venice* the merchant Antonio talks about the ships he has at sea. His friend Bassanio wants to marry Portia, an heiress, but he is in debt and needs money to set himself up as a nobleman. Antonio tells Bassanio that his money is tied up at sea but he will borrow money on his behalf. Thus although we do not actually see the ships (or the sea) the success of their voyage is an integral part of the plot.

Like natural conversation, dramatic dialogue consists of exchanges. Therefore a structural analysis of dialogue can be conducted, based on exchanges such as questions and answers, statements and acknowledgements, commands and requests and so on. In her seminal work on the structure of dialogue Burton (1980) has uses a variety of models from conversation analysis and speech act theory (see Chapter 2) to uncover patterns of dialogue that serve to delineate characters in the text of plays. In the case of Pinter's *The Dumb Waiter* she concludes that the unequal status of the characters is reflected in the dialogue. There is a conversation (quoted in Burton, 1980, pp. 161–2 between Gus and Ben in which, in saying *I want to ask you something* Gus is attempting to initiate an exchange. The fact that Ben ignores him and fails to provide the anticipated second half of the exchange – *Do you?*, *What is it?* or suchlike – immediately places Gus in a subordinate position to Ben. Ben then asks his own questions, to which Gus responds, further reinforcing the inequality between the two characters.

More recently Culpeper (2001) has applied stylistic and pragmatic models of discourse to Shakespeare's plays, among others. Culpeper uses models drawn from social psychology and ideas from cognitive linguistics to argue his case. He points out that inferring someone's character from dialogue, or indeed any text, relies in part on the cognitive structures and inferential mechanisms that the audience or reader has already developed for real-life people. Consequently the measure of success of a characterisation is not how life-like it is but how closely it resembles our own understanding of the particular character being portrayed.

Strategic analysis considers the ways in which speaker's communicative strategies are sensitive to context, employing utterances that range from direct to indirect and from polite to impolite. Dialogue that is designed to violate our understanding of such strategies, such as that in the Theatre of the Absurd, for example, is often made deviant, antirealist or simply absurd in order to reinforce the play's central concern: the futility of human existence. In some plays, however, violation is used to provide contrast between the world of the sane and the insane. Consider the following exchange in Peter Shaffer's play *Equus* (1975, 1:3).

> Dysart: *So: did you have a good journey? I hope they gave you lunch at least. Not that there's much to choose between a British Rail meal and one here.*
> *Won't you sit down?*
> *Is this your full name? Alan Strang?*
> *And you're seventeen. Is that right? Seventeen . . . Well?*

> Alan: *Double your pleasure*
> *Double your fun*
> *With Doublemint, Doublemint*
> *Doublemint gum*

Here Dysart, a doctor, is talking to Alan, who has been brought in for a consultation by his parents. Alan's madness is signalled by his refusal to answer Dysart's questions directly as a well-behaved and sane patient might, thereby flouting the Gricean maxim of relevance (see Section 2.4.2) and choosing instead to sing an advertising jingle. In the lines that follow this extract, Dysart continues to observe the communicative strategies of consultation even though Alan persists in singing.

3.10 Studying stylistics

Before conducting a stylistic textual analysis it is necessary to formulate the research question, select texts to analyse, and choose tools and a framework for the analysis. Research in stylistics, just as in dialectology and pragmatics, should be reliable, replicable and rigorous. In theory any of the analytical models or frameworks outlined above can be used for the stylistic analysis of any text. However some methodologies lend themselves more readily to certain kinds of text than others, as discussed below.

3.10.1 Selecting a topic for study

The first thing to decide when beginning your own research is the focus of your study. The form of data used in stylistic analysis, unlike that used in variations in English or pragmatics, is written texts. It may be that the text to be analysed will be given to you, together with the focus of your analysis. If however you have the option of choosing your own text or texts to analyse, either for an essay or for a larger piece of work, then your choice will depend on which aspects of stylistic analysis you are most interested in investigating. Conversely you could choose a text and then decide which aspects of it to analyse. It is no good, for example, choosing poetic texts or instruction booklets to undertake an analysis of dramatic dialogue, since you will find few if any examples. Equally, investigating speech and thought representation is best achieved through an analysis of prose rather than poetry or drama, because examples of such representation are found more often in prose than in any other genre. Some aspects of stylistics, such as narrative, can be found in a variety of written genres, such as newspaper reports, prose fiction and spoken discourse, so it is not essential to restrict yourself to one genre. Your research could be into one of the following:

- Vocabulary and word structure in writing for children.
- Aspects of cohesion and coherence in poetry or a prose extract.
- Deixis and metaphor in poetry or an extract of prose fiction.
- Narrative structure in detective fiction or an other type of genre fiction.
- Point of view and authorial voice in prose fiction.
- The use of free direct and indirect speech and thought in Modernist novels.
- The structure of dialogue in plays.

Your methodology will to a certain degree be determined by the type of text(s) you choose and the specific focus of your investigation. As emphasised throughout this chapter, stylistics is eclectic in nature and draws on methodologies used in a number of areas of linguistic investigation including grammatical theory, literary theory, narrative theory, pragmatic theory and social psychological theory. For example if you decide to look at vocabulary and word structure in texts written for children, then you will draw on methodologies used in the fields of phonology and grammar. If you wish to investigate differences and similarities in the narrative structure of detective fiction or any other kind of genre fiction, then you will draw on methodologies associated with discourse grammar and narratology. Or if you wish to investigate the structure of dialogue in drama, then you will draw upon methodologies used in pragmatics. Conducting stylistics research is a very practical activity, and your success will rest on demonstrating your understanding of your chosen methodology by applying it successfully to your analysis.

Once you have chosen the focus of your research you should read reports in books and journals of previous research in the field. This will give you a clearer picture of the field of enquiry, the arguments raised in it, the questions asked, the findings you might expect and what unexpected findings might arise. Another important aspect of such reading is that it will give you an idea of the number of texts to choose and the length of the extracts to be analysed. As noted in Section 2.8.1, the important thing when reading for the purpose of designing a research project is not the amount of reading you do but identifying and concentrating on works that come closest to your own research question. The more recently published ones will be most up to date with new developments.

3.10.2 Choosing and collecting data

The most pressing question here is how many texts to choose, how many extracts to take from them and the length. Much of the work undertaken in stylistics is qualitative; that is, it analyses a few texts in detail to demonstrate how a particular stylistic method works. Therefore the texts you choose have to be sufficiently lengthy to allow for a detailed analysis, but not so long that you cannot complete the analysis or exceed the designated word limit.

If you wish to investigate, say, vocabulary and word structure in books for children, for a short study of essay length you could choose a complete story of about 200 words or extracts from two or three stories of about 75 words each. These extracts could be from stories by the same author or from stories by two or more authors to add a contrastive dimension to your study. For a longer study, as a rough guide you would double these numbers. If you decide to study aspects of cohesion and coherence or deixis and metaphor in poetry or a prose extract, then the length and number of texts will depend on whether you choose poetry or prose. In the case of poetry, three poems of about 20–30 lines each would be sufficient, or one 100-line poem or an extract from a longer one. For prose, irrespective of whether you choose to focus on one extract from one text, or one or more extracts from the same text or different ones, a total of about 600-800 will be sufficient for an essay-length study.

If you decide to focus on aspects of narrative such as narrative structure and/or point of view and authorial voice, then the texts will have to be longer, perhaps complete texts. If you concentrate solely on narrative structure you could choose four or five complete novels for an essay-length piece of research. There may be some need for sampling, depending on the detail of the analysis.

If you choose to examine narrative structure and point of view and authorial voice, then two novels plus short extracts of 20–100 words from each would suffice. For a study that is longer than essay length more novels will be necessary, and either longer or a greater number of extracts. The same applies if you are investigating the use of free direct and indirect speech and thought in novels of a particular period. Depending on the range of the data you choose, it should be possible to generalise your findings.

An investigation of the structure of dialogue in plays will require one play for a short study and two or more for a longer one. From these you will need to select extracts for more detailed analysis or worked examples. The length of these will depend on the point you wish to make, and can be 4–5 lines or as many as 20–25.

It is also possible to conduct a quantitative analysis by collecting texts into corpora. Qualitative analyses of the types described above are based on a small sample or range of texts, from which generalisations are made and theories or models proposed. A corpus-based approach allows for that range to be extended. The two main approaches in corpus linguistics are corpus annotation and the analysis of collocation.

With corpus annotation a particular linguistic feature is investigated by constructing a corpus of texts and conducting a thorough analysis of its appearance in those texts. The results of the analysis are normally inserted into an electronic version of the text as tags or annotations. Because this type of analysis covers a wide range of texts it is arguably a more empirically sound procedure for identifying linguistic phenomena than choosing examples from which to make generalisations, and it also allows for a statistical analysis of frequency, distribution and so on. Once annotated a corpus is then available to researchers who wish to replicate or further the study. This approach, for example, was adopted by Semino and Short (2004) in their study of speech representation, which built on Leech and Short's (1981) system of classifying speech presentation in novels. A corpus of modern British English narrative texts was categorised, annotated and analysed in order to test the researchers' theoretical model against real data. They not only found that the the model would have to be adapted in the light of their analysis, but also identified new categories.

The second approach to corpus stylistics is to study literary effects in texts against the background of linguistic norms in a reference corpus, to establish the extent of any perceived deviance. A corpus can provide information what is normal and expected in texts and therefore enable identification of deviations from the norms of language use. For example if a particular word or phrase is thought to be exclusively literary, then it can be searched for in a corpus of non-literary texts to test this hypothesis. Following on from the work of Firth (1957) and Sinclair (2004), Louw (1993, 2006) has developed a methodology for analysing literary effects through the study of collocation. This is based on the idea that certain words, phrases or constructions become associated with certain types of meaning because of their regular co-occurrence. For example Sinclair (1988) discovered that the subjects of the phrasal verb *set in* are usually unpleasant things, such as *rigor mortis has set in* and *the rain had set in for the day.* This allows for unpleasantness to be evoked without using evaluative words or phrases other than the phrasal verb. Louw argues that such a phenomenon can only be revealed computationally and is not generally accessible to our intuition. Only collocation, he argues, can reveal the covert meanings of literary worlds and the feelings and attitudes of those who create and inhabit them, unfettered by the overt meanings related to levels of language, as outlined in Section 3.3 above.

Hoey's (2005) theory of lexical priming adds a cognitive dimension to collocation and can also be used to account for creativity in language. This theory proposes that speakers and hearers associate meanings with words not only because of their intrinsic meaning but also because of the linguistic contexts in which they are accustomed to speaking and hearing them. In this way words are primed for certain uses and meanings. For example *set in* has an intrinsic or primary meaning of a process having started and continuing, but also a primed meaning of unpleasantness. Corpora have made it possible to study the ways in which primings are created and the cognitive aspects of language.

3.10.3 Analysing data

The methods you use to analyse your data will depend on the particular stylistic features you wish to identify in your chosen text. Corpus methods notwithstanding, it is still most common for stylistic analysis to be carried out on a small sample of texts.

If you wish to undertake a stylistic analysis of poems you should investigate the following:

- The general patterns of grammar in the poems, including their general clause structure.
- Sequences that are different from the basic grammatical pattern.
- The sound and rhythm of the poems including the dominant metrical pattern or the use of free verse.
- The way in which the words are set out on the page and the impact this may have on the other levels of language.
- Vocabulary and word structure, including whether there are any words or word structures that deviate from the norm, and if so the ways in which they intersect with other levels of language, such as sound and metre.
- The use of similes or metaphors and the effect they have on the poems.

For a short study you could choose two poems by the same poet or two poems by different authors and examine the above aspects of each of them to identify what is similar or different about them. Alternatively you could compare a poem from, say, the seventeenth or eighteenth century with a late twentieth/early twenty-first century one to examine whether changes in structure and form have occurred between the two periods. For a longer study you will need more poems, say four or five of 100–150 lines in total.

If you decide to analyse prose fiction or narrative reporting you will need to investigate one or more of the following:

- The authorial voice; that is, whether the narrative is written in the first, second or third person or switches from one to the other, and whether or not this changes, narration is omniscient or otherwise.
- Aspects of cohesion and deixis, for example the way in which deixis and cohesion are used in the text, how it coheres, and if similes and metaphors are used, how they contribute to the fictional world of the text.
- The point of view or perspective(s) from which the narrative is written and the ways in which the characters are presented.
- The representation of speech and thought; that is, the ways in which speech and thought are used in the narrative and the part they play in constructing characters and furthering the action.
- The narrative structure. This involves identifying features from the model of narrative structure to see the extent to which the narrative you are analysing accords with or differs from what is expected.

For a short study you might wish to restrict yourself to applying one to three of the aspects listed above to two novels or examples of narrative reporting, either by the same author or by two different ones. For a longer study you could either include all five aspects or examine more novels or narrative reporting.

If you choose to study dramatic texts you should investigate one or more of the following:

- The context: is it physical, personal, cognitive, interactive or imaginary? How is deixis used?
- The structure: what is the pattern of dialogue, and how is it structured in terms of exchanges?
- The strategy: what conversational strategies are employed or violated?
- The characterisation: how are the context, structure and strategy interrelated or interwoven to produce characterisation?

Again, the number of plays you choose and the length of extracts will depend on the length of your study. For a short study extracts from one or two plays, either by the same playwright or different ones, will be sufficient and you might wish to restrict your analysis to one to three of the aspects listed above. For a longer study, you could include all four aspects or analyse more plays.

3.10.4   Sample projects

Project 1
- Conduct a stylistic analysis of a poem.

You should look at its clause structure, sound and rhythm, graphology, vocabulary and word structure, cohesion and deixis and use of similes and metaphors. For a longer study you could compare and contrast two poems from different periods of time, two by poets of the same age, or several by the same poet in a particular period.

Project 2
- Conduct a stylistic analysis of a prose extract.

Here you should look at clause structure, authorial voice, cohesion and deixis, point of view, representation of speech and thought, narrative structure, and the use of similes and metaphors and how they help to create the fictional world of the text. For a more in-depth or longer study you could analyse a particular genre, such as detective or romantic fiction, in order to identify any one or more of these categories which stylistic features may account for the distinctiveness of a particular author's style.

Project 3
- Conduct a stylistic analysis of a scene from a play.

Here you should pay particular attention to the creation of contexts, the structure of the dialogue, the conversational strategies, and how all these interrelate or interweave to produce characterisation. For a longer or more in-depth study you could analyse more than one scene one play, or scenes from different plays by the same playwright.

Project 4
- Conduct a corpus-based study.

Here you could test the application of a stylistic model against real data, such as the deictic categories outlined in Section 3.5 above, in a corpus of prose texts.

3.11   Further reading

For books on stylistics see Carter and Nash (1990), Short (1996), Jeffries (1993), Werth (1999), Wales (2001), Semino and Culpeper (2002), Simpson

(1993, 2004), Stockwell (2002), Semino and Short (2004) and Watson and Zyngier (2006). Chapters on stylistics also feature in general books on and encyclopedias of applied linguistics, such as the one by Clark and McRae in Davies and Elder (2004).

Critical Discourse Analysis　4

▌ 4.1　Introduction

Critical discourse analysis (CDA) investigates the structures of power that underlie all acts of speech and writing, and is therefore concerned with the politics of language. It analyses the ways in which speech and writing and the practices associated with them construct and shape reality and the world in which we live. It is 'critical' in the sense that it encourages readers to question assumptions and not to take anything for granted, to analyse social issues as they are constructed in discourse and how discourse contributes to the construction of society. It draws on sociological and critical theory as well as linguistic theory when considering power relations, including those of gender, ethnicity and social class. CDA also differs from the other fields of applied linguistics discussed in this book in that its approaches and analytical methods allow for the study of both spoken and written language in all genres.

The precise relationship between language and reality is a matter of much debate (see Chapman, 2006, ch. 4). That the two are closely connected and in many ways inseparable is undeniable, but how they act upon each other is unclear. During the twentieth century, linguists (most notably the French linguist Ferdinand de Saussure, 1916 and the Russian linguist Mikail Bakhtin, 1981), anthropologists (such as the Americans Edward Sapir, 1921, and Benjamin Whorf, 1956), philosophers (for example the German philosopher Ludwig Wittgenstein, 1951) and cultural theorists (for instance the French theorist Michel Foucault, 1972), showed that language plays an important part not only in structuring but also in creating reality (for more about this see: Chapman, 2006, section 6.4). If it is indeed the case that language structures and creates rather than reflects reality, then the source of power and

137

control – of who has the authority to determine what is said, when and by whom – shifts in a seismic way. The authority to construct reality shifts from some god-like authority who exists outside of and independently of society, to a community of language users. Linguistic structures, as well as being described and analysed, can therefore be studied in terms of the underlying structures of authority and control, ideology and power. It is this dimension of linguistic analysis that CDA adds to the study of language in action.

Sections 1–4 of this chapter discuss the major studies of the relationship between language, power and ideology that have influenced the development of CDA. Section 5 describes the principal methodological tools used in CDA, namely transitivity and nominalisation. Section 6 discusses CDA as it is understood today; that is, as both a theory and a methodology for research and analysis. Section 7 provides students with advice on conducting their own research.

4.2   Language, society and ideology

Ideology is commonly defined as a set of fundamental beliefs and ideas; that is, the values and attitudes held by any society or community that govern behaviour and social interaction. Much of our understanding of ideology comes from sociological theory. In sociology, there are two slightly different definitions of the term ideology. The first comes from Marxism and the work of the German writers Karl Marx and Friedrich Engels, and the second from neo-Marxists such as Louis Althusser.

Both Marxists and neo-Marxists define ideology as the system of beliefs, ideas, speech and cultural practices of a particular social group. This system disguises or distorts the social, economic and political relations between the dominated and dominant classes. For Marxists the fundamental differences of interest between social groups give rise to conflict, and therefore conflict is a common and persistent feature of society, rather than a temporary disorder after which things will return to normal. Marx (1976) claimed that the basis of all human organisation is economic and consists of two levels: the base (or infrastructure) and a superstructure. The base is made up of the forces of production and the social relations of production. The forces of production include raw materials, technology and workers, and the social relations of production refers to the relations between those involved in the production of goods, such as managers, workers, and the owners of the means of production. The superstructure comprises political, legal and educational institutions. These are not independent of the base, rather they are shaped by it. In Marxist theory, ideology is the set of dominant ideas promulgated by the ruling class that controls the superstructural institutions. These ideas are used to justify the power and privilege of the ruling class, and to hide from all other members of society the fact that they are being exploited and oppressed.

One example of this comes from feudal Europe, when the dominant concepts were honour and loyalty. These were held up as the natural order and were celebrated in literature and implicit in superstructural institutions such as law courts and educational establishments. In the capitalist age exploitation is disguised by the ideology of equality and freedom. Marxists argue that this ideology conceals the fact that capitalism inherently involves unequal relationships since workers have to work in order to survive, and their only freedom is to exchange one form of wage subordination for another. Marx believed that many modern societies contain basic contradictions that prevent them from being sustainable. These contradictions are based on the exploitation of one group by another, for example the exploitation by landlords of serfs or peasants in feudal times, and they have to be resolved as a social system containing such contradictions cannot survive unless it changes.

For Marxists, ideology is part of the superstructure rather than the economic base. However neo-Marxists view it as something more fundamental. Althusser (1971) argued that ideology works by putting people into 'subject positions', in that all social relations, including what Marx called the base or infrastructure, are subject or subordinate to some power (for example 'the Queen's subjects'). Ideological processes take place in what Althusser called ideological state apparatuses: the church, the legal system, the family and most of all the education system. Nicos Poulantzas (1976) went further and divided the state system into (1) the ideological apparatus of church, political parties, unions, schools, the mass media and the family, all concerned with the promotion and naturalisation of certain values and beliefs, and (2) a repressive apparatus of army, police, tribunals and sometimes even the government and its administration, all concerned with enforcing values and beliefs.

Thus Marxists and neo-Marxists have concentrated on the ways in which society is structured, and particularly on how social inequalities are developed and maintained. What none of them has taken into account is the part that language or discourse has played in the construction of ideology.

4.3 Language, linguistics and ideology

A major influence on how the relationship between language and society is perceived has been the shift in thinking on how language functions in society, and particularly how the meaning of words is determined (this is discussed in detail in Chapman, 2006). Very briefly, prior to the twentieth century it was assumed that the meanings of words were stable and fixed. This view had a long history, dating back to the work of the Ancient Greek philosopher Plato and continued in the writings in the Bible. According to Chapter 2 of the Book of Genesis, God took the living creatures he had created to Adam and commanded him to give names to 'all the cattle, and to the fowl of the air, and to every beast in the field'. Names then, are treated as vocables; that is, sounds, that stand in a consistent relationship to the things (persons, beasts, plants and so on) which they name. This assumes that the meaning of a word exists independently of the thing it names.

4.3.1   Words and meaning

The relationship between words and their meaning has preoccupied many philosophers, initially with regard to how a word, for instance *gold*, related to the object it named; that is, its **referent** 'gold'. They considered matters such as the relationship between a word and what it stood for, whether or not the relationship depended on a natural connection of some kind; and whether the word represented something that existed independently in the world or was merely an idea in the mind. When linguistics came into being as a discipline, linguists joined philosophers in subscribing to this view of language. Neither philosophers nor linguists questioned the assumption that words and their meaning existed independently of each other. It was assumed that the individual words of a language named objects, that sentences were combinations of such names, that every word had a meaning and that the meaning correlated to the referent or the word.

This notion of language and its relationship with meaning was increasingly challenged during the twentieth century, most notably by Saussure (1916; see also Jeffries, 2006, section 7.7; Chapman, 2006, section 5.4). Saussure took issue with the notion that a language, reduced to its essentials, was a nomenclature: that is, a list of terms corresponding to a list of things – a 'picture-dictionary'. He thought that asking about the relationship between words and objects was irrelevant because this would assume that ideas existed independently of words. Furthermore the prevailing view of the nature of meaning did not make clear whether a name was a vocal entity (that is, made up of sounds) or a mental one (that is, something imagined). He argued that it was both. Together the vocal and mental entities made up the linguistic sign. A linguistic sign was not a link between a thing and a name, but between a concept – the signified – and a sound pattern, the signifier (See also: Chapman, 2006, section 5.2; Jeffries, 2006, section 7.7.3). Saussure explained that the relationship between the signifier and signified was not, as had been traditionally thought, logical or necessary but arbitrary (see Jeffries section

7.5.1). That is, the concept 'tree' and the sounds /triː/ were not intrinsically bound together in any way but were a matter of convention.

Saussure's theory of signs, known as semiotics, has revolutionised the way in which the relationship between words and meaning is perceived because it has shifted the allocation of meaning from an external, godlike figure to humanity itself and a process of social negotiation. In practice, then, meaning in language is not natural but conventional. The relationship between a sound or symbol and what it represents is fundamentally arbitrary in that any sound or letter can be used to represent any concept. Meaning results from a shared understanding amongst a community of users as much as from anything else.

Take, for example, the ways in which the definitions in dictionaries were constructed. As discussed in Chapter 1, when Samuel Johnson wrote the first dictionary of English he was explicit about the assumptions and prejudices upon which he based his selections and definitions. Since that time lexicographers (dictionary compliers) have endeavoured to make their definitions much more objective and neutral. However, given that dictionary definitions are based on examples of actual language usage, no matter how neutral dictionaries try to be they inevitably not only reflect bias but also help to perpetuate it. For example Hoey (1996) has analysed definitions containing *man* and *woman* in the *Collins COBUILD English Language Dictionary*. These were constructed from examples taken from an extensive corpus of contemporary English as one of its fundamental principles was that all definitions should be based on how words were actually being used. Another of its principles was that there should be no reinforcement of sexist attitudes in and towards language. However Hoey found that such reinforcement was noticeably present. Take definition 1.2 of *man*: 'A man is . . . a human being of either sex' (quoted in Hoey, 1996, p. 158). As Hoey points out, if this definition were strictly accurate it would not specify 'of either sex'. Moreover *man* would be synonymous with *human being* and it would be possible to reverse the two noun phrases without making them nonsensical, which is not the case: *A human being is a man of either sex.*

Hence the definition implies that male human beings are viewed as the only human beings by the users of the language, and female human beings are a subclass of male human beings. Two other definitions make the same assumptions:

> *The man in the street* is an ordinary person who is not especially rich or educated or famous, and who is therefore considered to be a typical representative of public taste and opinion.

> *Modern man*, primitive *man*, etc means all modern people, primitive people, and so on considered as a group (ibid.)

As Hoey says, 'It is worth noting the democratic implications of the phrase *the man in the street* are replaced by sexual ones in the closely parallel phrase *a woman in the street*. It would appear that men can in the English language go about in the street and be regarded as normal, but that women go about the street at the peril of their reputations'(ibid.)

Hoey's analysis shows that no matter how hard lexicographers try not to reinforce sexism in language, or indeed or any other kind of prejudice or bias, no corpus of real language use is value-free or neutral, but inevitably reflects and embodies bias. The explanation Hoey gives for the bias he found is that the corpus chosen for the dictionary predominantly consisted of published texts by male writers, and therefore strongly reflected the value system of the male-orientated establishment.

Returning to Saussure, in addition to redefining the nature of the relationship between words and meaning, he made a distinction between two axes of time in linguistic study: the diachronic axis – the time line of the past, present and future; and the synchronic axis – language as it is used in the present. The fact that language was subject to change had proved something of a headache to linguists. By distinguishing between the two axes, Saussure suggested that the description of a language could be based on how it was used at a particular time, thereby ignoring its history. This resulted in subsequent linguistic endeavours focusing on the synchronic, present-day aspects of language and setting aside its diachronic, developmental aspects.

During the passage of time meaning is determined by what suits the needs of a society, usually the needs of the dominant, privileged groups. As Fowler (1986, p. 31) notes: 'These dominant groups control the means of legitimating the preferred systems of meanings – schools, libraries, the media. Language thus becomes a part of social practice, a tool for preserving the prevailing order. It does this not only through propaganda, but also by inertia, the settlement towards stability and resistance to change.' One example of legitimating a preferred system of meaning has been the change in the meaning of the word *gay*. Until the 1960s this word was synonymous with *happy* or *glad*. It began to be applied to homosexual men as a derogatory term, but with sexual liberation in Anglo-American society from the mid 1960s, the homosexual community appropriated the term for itself, thereby legitimating its use as their own status in mainstream society altered. Nowadays the term gay is rarely used to mean happy, except by the older generation, and its use as a synonym for homosexuality has none of the derogatory overtones it once had. Thus language is not only a tool for preserving the social order but also a means of acknowledging change within it.

4.3.2   Language and reality

A further influence on the change in linguistic thinking on the nature of the relationship between language and society was the study conducted by the American anthropologist Edward Sapir (1884–1939) and his student Benjamin Whorf (1897–1941). Sapir and Whorf made a record of American Indian languages and then compared the grammatical features of these languages with those of the standard average European (SAE) languages, including English, French and German. In his comparison of the Hopi language and SAE Whorf (1956) found that the way in which Hopi Indians expressed verb tenses was radically different from their expression in SAE and reflected the specifities of the Hopi culture, particularly when time and space were being talked about. In Western culture we mark our verbs to indicate whether we are talking about the past, present or future, for example *I wrote this chapter, I am writing this chapter* and *I will write this chapter*. Time, then, is separated into three distinct periods – past, present and future – that succeed each other linearly. In the Hopi culture time is expressed very differently. Rather than being linear it is viewed as cyclical. It is expressed through the stages of the human life cycle: from birth to through childhood, adolescence, adulthood, maturity and death. Although each of these stages is defined it flows seamlessly into the next one. At each point an individual is the same person, although aspects of that individual may change, such as appearance and certain characteristics. Consequently expressions such as *next week* and *seven days*, which reflect a belief that each day is different, is not possible in Hopi. Instead the 'return of the day [is] felt as the return of the same person, a little older but with all the impresses of yesterday' (ibid., p. 156). As a consequence the Hopi language has no tenses.

Since Europeans and American Indians have evolved in different circumstances and with different influences (geographical and historical), their experience of reality has been different. Their world-views inform all aspects of their lives and their language, culture and behaviour are constantly influencing and reinforcing each other. Sapir (see Lucy, 1992) claimed that once the language habits of a group have been fixed, then its speakers are at their mercy, in the sense that they cannot but help acquire these habits as part of acquiring language. This has been taken to mean that we are passive victims of our language, and that the language we speak determines our world-view; a kind of linguistic determinism. In other words, our world-view is so encoded that we cannot think beyond it. However, what has become known as the Sapir–Whorf hypothesis in fact claims that perceptions and concepts are encoded in language systems and are reinforced by constant and unquestioned use by their speakers, but this does not necessarily mean that no questioning of or alternative to that system is ever possible. According to Sapir, as our awareness of language grows, so too must our questioning of it and how it is used. The Sapir–Whorf hypothesis suggests that language use is not only determined by sociocultural factors but it also, and more importantly, determines our very ways of thinking. This hypothesis has led to the theory of **linguistic relativism**, and it is this which underlies CDA.

4.4 Language as discourse

The term **discourse** has several meanings in linguistics. In traditional descriptive linguistics, discourse is used to describe manifestations of speech and the term text to describe manifestations of writing. In discourse analysis the former is used to describe the physical, aural and visual manifestations of both speech and writing and the study of their management in relation to structure and grammar, taking account of the interaction between speaker and listener and writer and reader, as discussed in Chapters 2 and 3. There is, however, a further meaning of the word, derived from social and cultural theory and particularly from the work of the French social theorist and philosopher Michel Foucault (1972). For Foucault the term discourse applies not only to what is said and written but also to the invisible structures and forces through which the ideas – the ideology – of a society are shaped. These ideas are subject to change, and alter over time.

Discourse therefore has two dimensions: a tangible dimension, that is, speech and writing produced from the structures of the language in question; and an intangible one that consists of the underlying assumptions and practices that govern the production of language. Any discourse at any given time is structured as much by the assumptions about what constitutes it as a discourse as by the boundaries of language itself. As an example Foucault cites institutional practices associated with education. He points out that 'Every educational system is a political means of maintaining or modifying the appropriateness of discourses with the knowledge and power they bring with them' (ibid., p. 46).

For Foucault, discourses are to do with the ways in which sets of statements are systematically organised in order to give expression to the meanings and values of an institution or a society. In this sense discourses define and delimit what it is possible to say or do and what it is not possible to say or do, depending on the interests of particular institutions or societies. To quote O'Halloran (2003, p. 12), 'different religions have their own discourses which delimit explanation of natural behaviour. Catholicism now accepts that the universe began with the "Big Bang" (scientific discourse) but believes that the Christian God initiated it (a mixture of scientific and religious discourse).'

Social and cultural theories of discourse such as those by Foucault have given rise in linguistics, and especially in CDA, to different interpretations of the terms discourse and text. So far the term discourse has been used to describe either the manifestation of speech and its organisation (discourse and conversation analysis), or the invisible structures that shape what is said (social and cultural theory). A text is anything that is actually produced by a language, both spoken and written. In cultural and social theory this notion has been taken further and the term text is used to describe any manifestation of human communication. As the cultural theorist Fornas (1995) puts it, texts are 'signifying practices [that] combine meaningful signs into complexly structured and ordered symbolic units. These are referred to as texts, whether they consist of spoken or written words, images, sculptural or architectural forms, musical sounds, body movements or any combination of these or other symbolic entities.'

Hence the term text can be extended beyond the written word to include any visual manifestation in the material world: images, the way we furnish our houses, the clothes we wear, even our bodies, can all be read as texts. As CDA is primarily concerned with linguistic analysis, the texts it examines are those produced by speech and writing. Unlike traditional discourse analysis, however, CDA does not differentiate between speech and writing, and manifestations of both are called texts. In CDA, then, discourse (or discursive practices) refers to the underlying structures that shape what is said: pedagogic discourse, religious discourse, political discourse and so on, and text refers to a manifestation or realization of that discourse: a lesson, a sermon, a speech and so on.

These uses of the terms text and discourse have been applied to the analysis of language by writers from two linguistic traditions: the critical linguists Fowler *et al.* (1979) and Hodge and Kress (1993), and later the critical discourse analysts Fairclough (1989), Caldas-Coulthard and Coulthard (1996), Fairclough and Wodak (1997), Chouliaraki and Fairclough (1999) and van Dijk (2001), among others.

4.5 Critical linguistics

The field of critical linguistics arose from two seminal books: *Language and Control* (Fowler *et al.*, 1979) and *Language as Ideology* (Hodge and Kress, 1979). Drawing on sociological and critical theory see section 3 above), critical linguists took issue with the purely objective model of linguistic criticism, which claimed that the meaning and value of a text could be determined solely by its linguistic construction; that is, the words on a page or the sounds made by speech. Fowler (1986, p. 169) argued that although linguistic structures were themselves objective, 'their significances in discourse cannot be read off automatically from the text: a semiotic assessment in relation to cultural factors is required'. That is, communication results not only from what is said or heard, or written and read, but also from an understanding or 'reading' of the cultural and social norms associated with the acts of speaking, listening, reading and writing (see also Chapter 2). Consequently Fowler (1991, p. 70 describes the central concerns of critical linguistics as 'the ordering of experience and with the mediation of social relationships and values'.

Critical linguistics draws on cultural theory to extend the term 'text' to every kind of writing – newspapers, advertisements, leaflets as well as novels, plays and poetry – and also to spoken speech. Thus unlike pragmatics, which focuses mainly on spoken speech used in context, or stylistics, which focuses mainly on written literary texts, critical linguistics (and CDA) includes the whole spectrum of texts that speech and writing make possible. This necessitates a specific model of linguistics, and one has been drawn from systemic functional linguistics (see Halliday, 1971, 1973). Systemic functional linguistics is concerned with how language is used in real life and the way in which linguistic structure is related to communicative function and social value. At its heart is the notion of **function**, a concept used in a general, global sense. All language performs three functions at the same time: the **ideational**, the **interpersonal** and the **textual** (see also Jeffries, 2006, section 7.3.2).

The ideational function is concerned with the content of language, as it is used to express our experience of the external world the inner world of our own consciousness. The interpersonal function is to do with language's role as a mediator: as it is used to express our personalities and personal feelings during our interactions with others. The textual function is concerned with language in operation as opposed to or as distinct from strings of words or isolated sentences and clauses: 'It is this component that enables the speaker to organise what he is saying in such a way that makes sense in the context and fulfils its function as a message' (Halliday, 1973, p. 66).

As Halliday (1978) makes clear, the ideational, interpersonal and textual functions are, constrained by social and cultural practices, rather than being a matter of personal choice. The three functions provide a way of classifying linguistic structures according to their communicatory roles, so syntax, vocabulary and so on are examined in terms not only of their formal structure but also the particular jobs or functions they perform. This requires linguistic tools that go beyond those normally associated with grammatical analysis. These include transitivity, syntactic transformations of the clause, lexical structure and modality. While details of tools can be found in various works (for example Fowler, 1991; Simpson, 1993), it is worth considering transitivity and modality here as they exemplify the concept of functionality in language.

4.5.1   Transitivity

The ideational function of language – that is, the content of what is said or written and the writer's or speaker's experience that the content embodies – is best illustrated by semantically categorising clauses that reveal speakers' or writers' experience or point of view. A clause is essentially a basic unit of syntax that determines the position and sequence of elements (words and phrases), rather than being concerned with propositional meanings and functions. Nevertheless meanings are encoded in clauses because of the way in which processes are represented in language. There are three components of processes:

- The process itself, typically realised grammatically as the verb phrase, for example *hit, sees, broke.*
- The participant(s) associated with the process, typically realised grammatically by the noun phrase, for example *John, she, the vase.*
- The circumstances associated with the process, typically realised grammatically by the prepositional and adverbial phrases, for example *in the room, at breakfast, over the wall.*

Simpson (2004) identifies six types of process: material, mental, behavioural, verbal, relational and existential.

Material processes are concerned with doing, and they happen in the physical world. In this process there is always an actor or actors, and usually, though not always, a goal. For example:

> *John* (actor) *hit* (process) *the ball* (goal).
>
> *The vase* (actor) *broke* (process).

Mental processes are concerned with sensing and consciousness, involving cognition (encoded in words such as *understanding*), reaction (such as *despising*) and perception (such as *tasting*).

> *Lucy* (sensor) *puzzled over* (process) *the problem* (cognition).
>
> *Harry* (sensor) *can't stand* (process) *fish* (reaction).
>
> *Cathie* (sensor) *saw* (process) *the dress* (perception).

Behavioural processes embody physiological actions, for example *breathe* and *sneeze.* They can also be expressed as states of consciousness, as in *cry* and *laugh*, or forms of behaviour, such as *dream*, and *worry*. The participant in a behavioural process is the 'behavor', the conscious entity who is behaving:

She (behavor) *gasped* (process) *at the sight* (circumstance).

Joan (behavor) *laughed* (process) *at the clown* (circumstance).

The dog (behavor) *barked* (process).

Verbal processes are processes of saying. The roles associated with this are the 'sayer' (the producer of speech), the 'receiver' (the entity to which the speech is addressed) and the 'verbiage' (what is said). For example:

John (sayer) *told* (process) *a joke* (verbiage) *to his friends* (receivers).

The Judge (sayer) *announced* (process) *the sentence* (verbiage) *to the court* (receivers).

Verbiage can apply to the content of what is said, as in *the joke* above, or the name of what is said, such as *the sentence*.

Relational processes are to do with 'being', in the specific sense of establishing a relationship between two entities. The process is almost always taken from forms of the verb *be* (or a very small number of similar verbs, such as *seem* or *become*), and the participants' roles are the 'identifier' and the 'identified'. For example:

The show (identified) *is* (process) *on all evening* (identifier).

Catherine's car (identified) *is* (process) *a Volvo* (identifier).

Harry's dog (identified) *was* (process) *in the park* (identifier).

Finally, **existential processes** assert that something exists or happens. Typically they include the word *there* as a dummy subject, as in *There has been a theft* or *Has there been a fight?* They normally contain only one participant role, realised in examples such as *a theft* and *a fight*. Existential processes are similar to material ones in that both can answer a question for instance *What happened?* In a material process an actor and a goal will be identified, with the participant role being replaced by a process. Thus *There has been a theft* would be replaced by something like *John stole*. In the existential version the actor and goal disappear, to be replaced by the 'existent' which is a nominalised element.

Applying the transitivity model to media texts such as newspaper headlines and articles, can be very revealing of ideology. Trew (1979, pp. 94–116) has analysed the news coverage of an incidence of civil disorder in pre-independent Zimbabwe. The headlines and opening sentences of articles in two British newspapers read as follows:

POLICE SHOOT 11 DEAD IN SALISBURY RIOT

Riot police shot and killed 11 African demonstrators (*The Guardian*, 2 June 1975, p. 1).

RIOTING BLACKS SHOT DEAD BY POLICE

Eleven Africans were shot dead and 15 wounded when Rhodesian police opened fire on a rioting crowd (*The Times*, 2 June 1975, p. 1).

In the *Guardian* headline and first sentence there is an active construction, a standard SVO pattern, with the actor, 'police', appearing as the first element in the clause and the goal, the '11 dead' and 'African demonstrators', appearing at the end. This places considerable emphasis on the agents involved in the process. By contrast *The Times* employs a passive construction, inverting subject and object, actor and goal, thereby placing the goal, 'Rioting blacks' and 'Eleven Africans', at the start of the construction, and therefore in a position of prominence. The actor element is placed in a less prominent position at the end. Furthermore in *The Times'* first sentence, agency is deleted from the first clause, 'Eleven Africans were shot dead and wounded', and can only be inferred from the second. Trew contends that the effect of the passivity and agency deletion in *The Times* is to shift attention away from who did the shooting and onto the victims. In other words the two messages, whilst reporting accurately, are slanted in different directions. This slanting can be said to correspond with the political orientation of the two newspapers: the *Guardian* reflecting the political left and *The Times* the political right. An analysis and interpretation of this kind, extrapolating from textual analysis to questions of political bias, essentially summarises the critical linguistic method.

Take a further example: the shooting of a suspected terrorist following the July 2005 terrorist bombings in London, as reported by the BBC and the *Guardian*. The BBC purports to take a politically neutral stance and the *Guardian*, as noted above, is associated with the political left:

POLICE SHOT BRAZILIAN EIGHT TIMES

The man mistaken for a suicide bomber by police was shot eight times, an inquest into his death has heard (BBC News On-Line, 25 July 2005).

b) SHOT MAN WAS NOT BOMBER – POLICE

The man shot dead in Stockwell tube station yesterday was not connected to the attempted bombings of London on July 21, police said tonight (The *Guardian On-Line*, 23 July 2005).

The lexical choices of the two texts are different and clearly significant: the 'Brazilian' of the BBC becomes 'Shot Man' in the *Guardian*. These lexical differences are accompanied by differences in the transitivity structures of the two reports:

> POLICE [actor] SHOT [process] BRAZILIAN [goal] EIGHT TIMES
>
> The man mistaken for a suicide bomber [goal] by police [actor] was shot eight times [process], an inquest [receiver] into his death [verbiage] has heard [process].

Although the headline uses an active SVO construction, the lexical choice and foregrounding of the dead man's nationality as 'not British' is offered as something of an explanation for the shooting. The London bombers were at first assumed to be foreign terrorists, and marking the shot man as 'foreign' can therefore be interpreted as a justification for the shooting. However, stating the number of times the man was shot implies excess on the part of the police, since it does not usually take that number of bullets to kill someone. The headline is followed by a passive construction, inverting subject and object, actor and goal, thereby placing the goal, which is further elaborated as 'The man mistaken for a suicide bomber', in a prominent position. The fact that he was shot eight times is repeated, again reinforcing the suggestion that excessive force was used. This report appeared a day after the shooting, by which time it had become evident that the shot man was not in fact a suicide bomber, as had first been claimed by the police. Placing the first clause construction of goal–actor–process before the reporting clause emphasises not only that the police used excessive force, but also that any force was unjustifiable, since the man was not after all a suicide bomber.

The *Guardian*'s headline does not mention nationality and instead focuses on the shooting:

> SHOT MAN WAS NOT BOMBER [verbiage] – POLICE [sayer]
>
> The man shot dead in Stockwell tube station yesterday was not connected to the attempted bombings of London on July 21 [verbiage], police said tonight [sayer].

The *Guardian*'s headline and first sentence summarises the admission by the police that they had made a mistake. Actual admission of the mistake is implied, not stated. The *Guardian* headline does not offer the excuse of mistaken nationality, as in the BBC example, but focuses instead on the fact that the shooting was an error and the result of, at best, overreaction and, at worst, panic. Both, however, are unequivocal in their condemnation of the action. The *Guardian* uses allows the words of the police themselves to condemn the attack, while the BBC takes a more ambivalent stance, highlighting or offering 'foreignness' as a possible excuse for the shooting, but immediately condemning the excessive firing of bullets.

4.5.2   Modality

Whereas transitivity serves an ideational function, modality serves as an interpersonal one; that is, to express comments, attitudes and evaluations. Modality is to do with the way in which speakers and writers use language to comment on or express attitudes and beliefs and present their own point of view. It is a grammar of explicit comment, and it signals the varying degrees of certainty we have about what we say or write, and the sort or degree of commitment and obligation we express. Grammatically, it is most commonly realised through modal auxiliary verbs, but lexical verbs, adverbs, adjectives, intonation and even body language can also be modal.

Fowler (1986) identifies four aspects of modality: truth, obligation, desirability and permission. Truth implies a commitment to the truth of any proposition uttered, or a prediction of the likelihood of an event taking place. Modality appears when the speaker or writer is expressing an opinion on what will, might, could or should happen. Truth modality ranges from absolute confidence, signalled by *will*, to uncertainty, signalled by *could*. It can also be indicated by adverbs such as *certainly* and modal adjectives such as *likely* and *unlikely*. An example of absolute confidence is:

> Strikes end but airport misery *will* last for days (*The Times*, 13 August 2005, italics added).

An example of uncertainty and lesser confidence is:

> He said the issue *could* only be resolved by the courts and he predicated that passengers *would* bring a case against BA (*The Times*, 13 August 2005, italics added)

Obligation is where speakers and writers express an opinion on what ought to or should happen:

> Although the frustrated holiday makers marooned west of London *will* find it difficult to do so, there *should* be sympathy with the workers' cause (*Guardian*, 13 August 2005, italics added).

It is important to note that in English, unlike in other languages that have future tenses, there is only a modal way of talking about the future; that is, with *will*. This means that all future statements are modal, whilst statements about the present or past can be categorical.

Desirability is where the speaker or writer shows approval or disapproval of the state of affairs that is being communicated. This use of modality is widely used in the press, particularly in editorials and especially in tabloids and broadsheets with right-wing leanings. Modality of this kind can be expressed through a range of evaluative adjectives and adverbs as well as some lexical verbs (for example *wish* and *want*). For instance:

> To be sacked by megaphone is *callous*, even for a part of the service sector well known for low pay, insecure job tenure and poor career prospects (*Guardian*, 13 August 2005, italics added).

Permission is where the speaker or writer gives permission to do something, signalled by *may, can* and *shall*. Here the auxiliaries *may* and *can* indicate a degree of cautiousness or hedging, as opposed to *shall*, which is more definite, as illustrated by the fairy godmother's statement to Cinderella: 'You *shall* go to the ball!'

Modality is also an important feature in the study of narrative. Simpson (2004) points out that the degree of modality expressed by the writer or reader can be categorised as degrees of shading, ranging from positive, through neutral to negative.

Positive shading is where the writer, narrator or speaker tell you what she or he thinks and believes by foregrounding expressions, beliefs, opinions and obligations. Modality that expresses desire and obligation is known as **deontic modality**: for example *I ought to visit my Gran* or *I need* a drink. This is the most common use of modality, and it underpins many first and third person narratives as well as newspaper editorials, commentaries and analyses.

Negative shading is where the writer or narrator is uncertain about events and other characters' motivations and is often expressed through grammatical structures based on perception: *as if, it seemed, it appeared to be* and so on. This kind of shading is marked by **epistemic modality**, which foregrounds a narrator's, writer's or speaker's effort to interpret and make sense of what is read or heard, and is often characteristic of Gothic or existentialist styles of narrative fiction. For example *Maybe the sound came from…*, or *his horse must have thrown her off*.

Neutral shading is where the writer or narrator gives no evaluation or interpretation and hence there is a complete absence of either deontic or **epistemic modality**. Rather it is typified by categorical assertions such as *My name is Bill* and *Bus hits 10 cyclists*. This kind of modality is rare in narrative but is often found in news reporting that aims to be factual and neutral.

Transitivity and modality show how linguistic structures encode both ideational and interpersonal functions. Tools such as these, together with those which perform a textual function, such as discourse and conversation anlaysis in pragmatics (see Sections 2.5 and 2.6) and cohesion and deixis in stylistics (see Section 3.4) are all drawn upon by CDA to describe and interpret both spoken and written texts. Where CDA differs from other methods or frameworks for the analysis of spoken and written discourse is its emphasis on the underlying ideologies of the social and cultural context within which description and interpretation occur, and which, it is argued, also shape that description and interpretation.

4.6   A Framework for Critical Discourse Analysis

In combination, sociological and cultural theory (Section 4.2), changes in theories of language (Sections 4.3 and 4.4) and developments in functional grammar (Section 4.5), have facilitated insights into the ways in which language functions in society. They show how points of view, world-views and beliefs are not only socially constructed but also grammatically encoded in language in ways that often reveal unequal relationships based on authority and power. Critical linguistics and the grammatical tools associated with it (Section 4.5) have furthered the analysis of spoken and written texts, as outlined in Chapters 2 and 3, and extended the range of texts studied to non-literary ones such as newspaper articles and advertisements. They also take account of the social element of how language represents the world. In CDA this aspect of analysis is taken further. It is argued that language, as well as playing a part in constructing (or misrepresenting) reality, is also the primary medium of social control and power, and is therefore fundamentally ideological. For practitioners of CDA, ideology is all-pervasive in language, and consequently it is with revealing the ideological nature of language that they are most concerned.

CDA integrates linguistic analysis of the kind described above, and in other chapters of this book, with social and cultural theories in order to expose the ideological assumptions and relations at play in language, which are essentially to do with power. Although critical linguistics recognises that texts are essentially a form of social practice, the methods of analysis associated with it are grounded in the text, as the previous section has shown. Critical discourse analysis takes matters one step further by arguing that the text is itself part of the wider discourse practice within which it is situated. This discourse practice is in turn located within wider sociocultural practices. Consequently the interactions between all three layers – text, discourse practice and sociocultural practice (that is, between all aspects of the social use of language) – became the subject of analysis. Figure 4.1 illustrates this model of discourse. CDA, then, acts as both a theory and a method of analysis. As Fairclough (2001, p.19) argues:

> It is not uncommon for textbooks on language to have sections on the relationship 'between' language and society, as if these were two independent entities which just happen to come into contact occasionally. My view is that there is not an external relationship 'between' language and society, but an internal and dialectical relationship. Language is a part of society; linguistic phenomena *are* social phenomena of a special sort, and social phenomena *are* (in part) linguistic phenomena.

Corresponding to the three dimensions of discourse, Fairclough distinguishes three dimensions or stages of CDA:

1. Description is the stage which is concerned with formal properties of the text.
2. Interpretation is concerned with the relationship between text and interaction – with seeing the text as the product of a process of production, and as a resource in the process of interpretation; notice that I use the term *interpretation* for both the interactional process and a stage of analysis.
3. Explanation is concerned with the relationship between interaction and social context – with the social determination of the processes of production and interpretation, and their social effects (ibid., p. 21).

Linguists working in CDA consider language to be an important tool in the production, maintenance and change of social relations of power. Their aim is to increase language users' consciousness of how language contributes to the domination and control of some people by others. It is a means of 'helping people to see the extent to which their language does rest upon common-sense assumptions and the ways in which these common sense assumptions can be ideologically shaped by relations of power' (ibid., p. 22). For description and interpretation CDA uses linguistic tools developed for other traditions, such as pragmatics and discourse analysis, stylistics and critical linguistics. Where CDA differs from these traditions is that it embeds the descriptive and interpretative dimensions within the evaluative one. (It is this interface between linguistic interactions, the social contexts in which they occur and the underlying ideologies of those contexts that is the most controversial aspect of CDA – see Widdowson, 2004.)

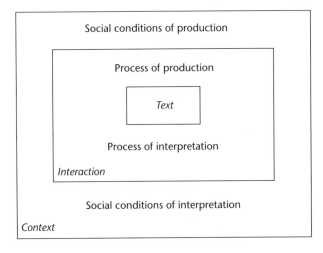

Figure 4.1   Discourse as text, interaction and context

Source: Fairclough (2001, p. 21).

For example common sense assumptions are evident in the conventions for traditional consultations between doctors and patients, where authority and hierarchy are treated as natural and this is embedded in the style of language used. Another example is in the relationship between the police and witnesses. Consider the following extract from an interview in a police station of a witness to a burglary. The policeman is filling out a form and his questions follow the order in which they appear on the form:

Policeman: *You say you saw them as they left the shop?*
Witness: *Yeah, I saw their faces. There were two of them. I think they were . . .*
Policeman: *What age would you say they were?*
Witness: *Dunno. One was younger than the other. Twenties I guess. Mid twenties. The other . . . Fortyish? I think one of them was carrying . . .*
Policeman: *Height?*
Witness: *Medium, I'd say. About six foot, maybe less. One was slightly shorter than the other . . .*
Policeman: *Six foot. Five foot ten. Did you notice the colour of their hair?*
Witness: *I think the shorter one had fair hair. Look, how long's this going to take? I've got to . . .*
Policeman: *Not much longer, no. What about the other one?*
Witness: *Can't say, I'm sorry.*
Policeman: *Short? Long?*

Witness: *Short.*
Policeman: *What about their clothes?*
Witness: *One was wearing a dark, heavy jacket...*
Policeman: *Like a donkey jacket?*
Witness: *Yeah.*

A discourse or conversation analysis of this exchange would emphasise the verbal utterances that make up the questions and answers and the structure of the interaction, focusing for example, on turn-taking, adjacency pairs, pre-supposition and politeness (see Section 2.6). A critical discourse analysis would consider what the conversation reveals about the relationship between the participants and the social conditions that determine the properties of the discourse. The interviewer – the policeman – is in control of the process and reduced questions such as *Height?* are typical of someone filling out a form. The witness is forthcoming with information but the policeman will only deal with each piece as it is determined by the order on the form, not in the order given by the witness. The witness signals her frustration by asking *how long's this going to take?* The policeman, though, has his task to perform and the witness, as a law-abiding citizen, complies with the requirement of that task even if it means being late for an appointment. It could also be argued that the sensitive nature of the situation is contained or framed by the norms of form filling. Filling in the form structures the questions the police-man asks, and he ignores any information volunteered by the witness that is not relevant to the particular question on the form, even if it is relevant to the incident as a whole.

When looked at this way, it is clear that the relationship between the police-man and the witness is unequal. The way in which the interview is carried out follows social conventions based on the nature of the relationship between the police and members of the public. In this regard it can be said that social conditions have determined the properties of the discourse. Looking beyond the text itself, we can consider the way in which we produce and interpret texts and investigate how these processes are socially shaped and relative to social conventions. For example there is no acknowledgement by the police-man when the witness gives information. In a conversation between friends this would not be acceptable, whereas in this case it generally is.

In terms of the three-dimensional model in Figure 4.1 the interaction between the policeman and the witness can be analysed as follows:

- Text: a linguistic analysis of the actual speech exchange and its charac-teristics in terms of conversational properties, politeness phenomena, narrative or argument structure, characteristics of grammar and accent and so on.

- Processes of production and interpretation: consideration of the type of discourse produced in the interaction – argument, small talk, political discussion and so on. Identification of the ways in which the exchange fits in with genres or speech events.
- Social conditions of production and interpretation: consideration of whether the exchange derives from, reinforces or challenges expected relations between the police and the public and law enforcement as an institution.

As mentioned above, analyses of actual speech exchanges or written texts within a CDA framework draw on tools used in other fields of linguistics. For the remaining two dimensions – the processes of production and reception and the social conditions within which they occur – new frameworks or categories have been developed.

4.6.1   Schema theory and members' resources

In recent years the processes of production and interpretation have been the focus of much linguistic study (see also Chapter 3). Interpretation is generally arrived at through a combination of what is present in any given text and what is 'in' the interpreter. One influential theory in accounting for the relationship between the two is **schema theory**, which has been derived from cognitive linguistic theory, as proposed by Schank and Abselon (1977) and developed by Sperber and Wilson (1995). A schema (or in the plural, schemata) is a mental representation of a particular type of activity according models of social behaviour. Frames represent the entities that occur in the natural and social world. A frame is a representation of the topic, subject matter or referent of an activity. Scripts refer to 'a predetermined, stereotyped sequence of actions that defines a well-known situation' (Schank and Abselon, 1977, p. 41). Although scripts relate to what we already know, they are subject to modification and change as our experience of situations, well-known or otherwise, grows. A script-based framework of the kind proposed by schema theory is a way of understanding texts without everything in them being made explicit linguistically.

Going back to the example of the policeman and witness, the schema in this case is a police activity and the frame is the questioning of a witness. Scripts relate to the subjects involved in the activity – the policeman and the witness – and their relationship with one another. Scripts typify the ways in which specific classes of subject behave in particular situations, and in this example explain why the witness accepts the absence of acknowledgement in this schema when she might not in another; she is behaving according to the script set out for how a police interview should be conducted, based on her previous experience – real, imagined or hearsay.

Fairclough (2001) expands upon schema theory in his notion of **members' resources** (MRs). Like schemas, MRs are the interpretative processes that take place in any communicative act. '[F]rom the point of view of the interpreter of a text, formal features are "cues" which activate elements of interpreters' MR, and . . . interpretations are generated through the dialectical interplay of cues and MR' (ibid., p. 118). That is, interpretation results from an interaction between the structural content of the text and the textual activation of the reader's or listener's store of interpretative procedures. Fairclough shies away from using the term 'background knowledge' to describe MRs, on the grounds that it is too restrictive and that it misses the point that many of the assumptions we make in interpretation are ideological, thus making 'knowledge' a misleading term. MRs are the representation each of us has stored in our long-term memory of, for example, the shapes of words, grammatical forms of sentences, typical narrative structures, the expected sequence of events in a particular situation and so on. We draw on this both to produce and to interpret texts. MRs are cognitive in the sense that they are in people's heads but they are also social in that they have social origins, being dependent upon social relations and the struggles that have generated them. Fairclough (ibid., pp. 119–20) identifies four levels of textual interpretation: **surface of utterance**, **meaning of utterance**, **local coherence** and **text structure and point**. Surface of utterance refers to the processes by which we convert strings of sound or marks on a page into recognisable words, phrases, sentences and utterances. The aspect of MRs we draw on when doing this is commonly known as 'knowledge of the language'; that is, its phonology, vocabulary and grammar. Meaning of utterance refers to semantic aspects such as representation of the meaning of words, including implicit ones. It also draws on pragmatic conventions associated with speech acts. Local coherence refers to the ways in which MRs infer connections or cohesive relations between utterances in a particular part of a text. This is possible even when formal cohesive cues are absent, when we make implicit assumptions that are often of an ideological nature.

Finally, text structure involves matching the text with one of a repertoire of *schemata* or representations of characteristic patterns of organisation associated with different types of discourse' (ibid., p. 120). For example when we take part in a telephone conversation we can expect the conversation to follow a particular structure of greeting, establishing a topic, changing the topic, closing the conversation and saying goodbye. The 'point' of a text is its primary purpose. For example a telephone conversation may include an exchange on the participants' well-being, recent activities and so on, but the overall point of the conversation is an invitation to go out. It is this point that is stored in the long-term memory and is available for recall.

Fairclough's MR categorisation is more specific than that of schema theory, as it incorporates linguistic processing into the process of interpretation, in addition to pragmatic and schematic processing. To return to the example of the policeman and witness, the two participants interpret what is being said in terms of phonology, semantics and the surface and meaning of the utterances; they make sense of what is implied by means of local coherence; and they manage the exchange through text structure and 'point'. This is all in addition to interpreting aspects of the context in which the exchange is taking place.

To the four levels of interpretation Fairclough adds contextual aspects of interpretation; that is, situational context and intertextual context. Situational context refers both to the physical cues the environment in which an exchange takes place – its situation, what has previously been said and so on – and to the ways in which MRs interpret these cues. 'How participants interpret the situation determines which discourse types are drawn upon, and this in turn affects the nature of the interpretative procedures which are drawn upon in textual interpretation' (ibid., p. 121). Intertextual context refers to the ways in which the participants in an exchange make assumptions about it based on their experience of previous exchanges to which the present one is connected. This is similar to scripts in schema theory. These assumptions determine what can be taken as given and do not need to be restated as they are part of common experience, what can be alluded to, what disagreed with and so on. Situational and intertextual contexts thus correspond closely with the schemas, frames and scripts of schema theory, whilst the four levels of textual interpretation add a further dimension. When interpretation takes place, all six levels of the interpretative process interact with one another in what are clearly complex, and dynamic, ways.

Fairclough offers a further diagrammatic example of how people arrive at interpretations of the situational context, and the way in which this determines decisions about which discourse type is the appropriate one to draw upon.

On the left hand side of the lower half of the figure, are four questions that relate to four dimensions of the situation: what is going on, who is involved, what the relationships are and the role of language in the situation. On the right-hand side are the four discourse types, in the CDA sense of a set of underlying conventions belonging to a particular order of discourse. Taking again the example of the policeman and witness we can ask the following questions:

- *What is going on?* The activity type here is the interviewing of a witness, and the purpose is to elicit and document information on a crime.
- *Who is involved?* Subject positions are multidimensional and alter according to the situation; in this case the subject positions are those of inter-

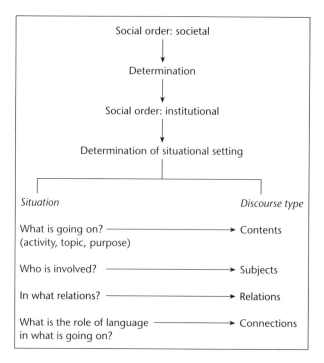

Fig 4.2   Situational context and discourse type

Source: Fairclough (2001, p. 122).

viewer and interviewee. A second dimension is that the institution ascribes social identities to the subjects who function within it, here a policeman and a member of the public who is also a witness and a likely victim. A third dimension is that different situations have different speaking and listening positions associated with them: speaker, addressee, hearer, spokesperson and so on. In this example the roles of speaker and addressee roles alternate between the policeman and the witness.

- *In what relations?* Here subject positions are looked at more dynamically in terms of power, social distance and so on. In this case the focus is on the nature of the relationship between the police and the public, with the policeman anxious to get his form completed, and the member of the public in a hurry to get away and back to schedule.

- *What is the role of language?* Language in this case is being used in an instrumental way as part of a wider institutional and bureaucratic objective. Language determines the genre – an interview – and its channel as spoken or written. Here the form is being filled out by the policeman, who is in full charge of the course of the interview, and this is indicative of the degree of control the police exercise over all aspects of the case. The information given by the witness is mediated and checked by the police and only then is it valid.

The first three discourse dimensions listed on the right-hand side of the figure are conventionally associated with a particular type of situation. The fourth dimension, connections, relates to the ways in which texts connect and are tied to situational contexts, and to the ways in which connections are made between parts of a text, both of which can vary among discourse types. When making judgements about these connections, we draw upon elements of MRs that are particular to a discourse type. A CDA approach to analysis involves consideration of the social conditions of production and interpretation, which are again divided into three levels: the level of the social situation (the immediate environment), the level of the social institution, and the level of society as a whole. Fairclough suggests that these social conditions shape both the MRs we bring to production and interpretation and the way in which texts are produced and interpreted. The determination of social order in terms of society and institution is also a matter of interpretation. Observable features of the physical situation and the text that has already been created – that is, the interview between the policeman and the witness – do not of themselves determine the situational context. They are clues that help the interpreter to interpret it, read in the light of and in conjunction with the interpreter's MRs.

In CDA the relationships between all three levels or dimensions of texts, processes and their social conditions are analysed, both the immediate conditions of the situational context and the more remote conditions of institutional and social structures, as shown in the example above. In addition discourses are viewed as hierarchical, so there are different orders of discourse. Discourse is determined by underlying conventions and these conventions are clustered in sets called orders of discourse, which are more general than specific types of discourse. For example in the the policeman and witness example the discourse type is associated with policing as a social institution, in contrast with the discourses of making an arrest, charging a suspect and so on. It also differs from the discourse of interviewing a witness to tease out a story. It is the prerogative of the more powerful participant to determine which discourse type is appropriate. In our example the witness is placed in a determinate position in the order of discourse and the social order of police work. The policeman and witness are positioned to operate in terms of one of a number of possible procedures for dealing with cases of crime: for example information gathering is usually followed by interrogation, then perhaps by a charge being laid and so on.

The way in which orders of discourse are structured and the ideologies that are embedded within them are determined by relationships of power in particular institutions and society as a whole. Thus it is social structures that determine discourse, which in turn has an effect on social structures and contributes to social continuity or social change. Take for example 'subject' positions in schools. In schools there are a number of situations in which discourse occurs (for example class, assembly, playtime, meetings), a set of recognised roles for the participants in discourse (headteacher, teacher, pupil, friend, peer) and approved purposes for discourse for example learning, teaching, examining, maintaining social control. Occupying a subject position is a matter of doing certain things and reproducing conventions. Teachers and pupils know (or learn) what they are allowed to say or not to say in particular discourse situations. Therefore discourse reproduces social structures. Such reproduction can be conservative, in the sense of maintaining continuity by replication, or transformative, in terms of effecting change. Since much of this goes unquestioned and is implicit in people's relations with one another, the aim of CDA is to make people conscious of the power relations that exist within and are propagated by discourse. This it is argued, makes it possible to bring about change.

4.6.2 CDA, written discourse analysis and stylistics

As we have seen, CDA is a broad and complex method of analysing texts, both spoken and written, within a three-dimensional framework of the text, the interaction between the text and its processors, and the social and institutional contexts in which the text and interaction occur. The corresponding categories of description, evaluation and interpretation provide frameworks for categories of analysis to be generated and replicated. As a theory it draws on sociological theory, cultural theory ad linguistic theory, though the ways in which all three aspects of its framework interrelate have yet to be fully developed into a methodology. Its attraction as a theory and method is its focus on exposing the underlying ideologies of a text, and its underlying assumption that every discourse is based on internal relations of language and power. The strength of this critical approach is that it can also be used in the field of stylistics when analysing written texts to discover underlying ideological assumptions (see Simpson, 1993; Clark and Zyngier 1998). Transitivity analysis can reveal much about the various roles played by the characters in question and the relationships between them. For example a transitivity analysis of passages from romantic novels or fairy tales will usually reveal that women and girls are 'acted upon' and that men or boys take charge of the action.

Mills (1995, p. 199–202) has provided a framework for stylistic analysis from a feminist perspective, of which the following is an adaptation:

- Context (CDA dimension of explanation): this involves asking questions such as what sort of text is it? To which genre does it belong (novel, advertisement, newspaper article and so on)? Is there a tendency for women or men to be associated with this type of text? What is its status, history and the reason for analysing it?
- Gender, reading and writing (CDA dimension of interpretation): this involves asking questions such as what assumptions have to be made about the voice of the author? Is the latter female or male? Does knowing this serve any purpose? Does the text address (1) you as male or female, or (2) a universal audience? Does the text address you directly in other ways? Does the background knowledge draw on stereotypical assumptions about men and women?
- Gender vocabulary, the clause and discourse (CDA dimension of description): this involves asking questions such as how are males and females named and/or referred to in the text? Do any of the terms used have sexual connotations or taboos associated with them? Is 'he' used as a generic pronoun? Who acts in the text? Why is the text using humour? What are the transitivity choices, and are they the same for men and for women? From whose point of view does the text emanate? What elements are associated with male and female?

Consider the following text of a car advertisement that appeared in *The Times Magazine* (29 April 2006). The text was positioned in the bottom half of a left-hand page and there was a picture of the car on the opposite page.

THE TOPLESS MODEL YOU CAN TAKE SERIOUSLY.
CHRYSLER

Inspiration comes as standard   The New PT Cruiser Cabrio

Context. Although the magazine aims to appeal to both men and women, with a mixture of gender-specific and general articles, this particular advertisement is aimed at men. The purposes of analysis is to demonstrate the underlying assumption about men's superior purchasing power and the persistence of stereotypical portrayals of females in car advertisements.

Gender, reading and writing. The voice of the author is male and is speaking to male readers. Positioning the text on the left-hand page and the picture on the right means that attention is drawn to the text first. Although the pronoun *you* is generic, in this instance it addresses men, not women. The background knowledge draws on stereotypical assumptions, particularly that men are voyeuristic and that it is men, not women, who buy cars.

Gender vocabulary, the clause and discourse.   The most obvious naming in the text from the point of view **of** gender is *The topless model*, which is used as a pun for an open-topped car but the full sentence casts doubt on the intelligence of women who work as topless models. The transitivity process of the sentence *The topless model you can take seriously* is a verbal one, with some unknown male addressing the male reader through the deictic use of *you*. The modal *can* is an example of truth modality and positive shading, thereby portraying open-topped cars in a positive light and topless models in a negative one. The larger typeface used for this sentence is intended to attract attention, whilst the factual information about the car is placed in a subordinate position.

The use of sexual connotations to sell cars is nothing new, and this advertisement illustrates that gender stereotyping and sexual inequality is still ideologically ingrained in sections of Western society. Women are still portrayed as sexual objects and men as those with the purchasing power to buy cars, and, by implication, women.

However, unlike in CDA, uncovering underlying ideological assumptions is not the main focus of all stylistics analyses as stylistics also considers other factors: cognitive, descriptive and so on. Nevertheless, ideology is still encoded and embedded in literary texts just as much as those of any other kind, just as ideology can affect a reader in a literary work as it can in any other.

CDA has been criticised on a number of theoretical and methodological counts. The method of data selection, the lack of a clear and complete set of tools and a subjective political bias have been the basis of these criticisms. (Widdowson, 1995, 2004; Toolan, 1997). However, CDA has been the first attempt so far to formalise a methodology which seeks to articulate the relationship between a text, the context in which it is produced and its processes of production, reception and interpretation and it is still developing. One recent development arising from CDA has been forensic linguistics, which examines the relationship between language and the law. This field of inquiry not only has a theoretical dimension, but also an applied one in working with the police and lawyers on actual cases such as appeals in order to bring a linguistic dimension to them.

4.7   Studying CDA

The aim of all CDA analysis is to expose the ideology embedded in language. Your task, then, will be to investigate the ways in which inequalities are expressed through language and the effect this has on the reader. For example if a newspaper may continually demonise Muslims, this not only illustrates their relative powerlessness but might also affect the readers' view of Muslims. The focus of research in CDA is the ways in which language structures (and conceals) issues of power and equality. The aim of research in CDA then, is to uncover issues of power, authority and control through not only analytic descriptions of the organization of spoken and written interaction but also by analysing the underlying social, cultural and institutional structures through which the interaction occurs.

4.7.1 Selecting a topic for study

The first thing to do is to determine the focus of your study. You may wish to do one of the following:

- Compare different newspaper reports of the same event.
- Analyse a speech or speeches.
- Analyse an advertisement or contrast two advertisements.
- Analyse a spoken exchange in a particular setting, for example between a teacher and a pupil, between a policeman and a witness, or between a mother or father and a child.
- Compare coversations between men and women, or among women or men of a similar age or different ages.

Once you have determined the focus of your study, as with the other fields of enquiry considered in this book you should spend time on background reading (see Section 3.10.1 for hints).

4.7.2 Choosing and collecting data

Since CDA is concerned with both spoken and written texts, your data will come from naturally occurring speech or written texts. Research in CDA, as with that in pragmatics, is usually qualitative in nature; that is, detailed analysis of a small range of data. For a more quantitative study you could compare like studies with like, and the more studies that have been conducted in a particular area, such as parliamentary speeches, the larger the research database will be.

Your choice of data will be largely determined by the topic of your research. If you decide to analyse newspaper coverage of a particular story, such as a shooting, a large robbery, a political scandal or some other equally newsworthy event, you should choose two or three newspapers published on the same day but with different political orientations, for example the *Mirror* and the *Daily Telegraph* or the *Daily Mail* and the *Guardian*. If you choose to analyse advertisements with a view to exposing ideological assumptions about gender, then you should select advertisements in which such assumptions are likely to be present, for example those for household appliances or cars, rather than furniture or music.

In the case of spoken data you can choose between collecting your own or obtaining transcripts from sources such as the internet. Transcripts of trials by jury in the United States are available on the internet and the television programme *Court TV* broadcasts live trials. Alternatively you could record television news reports of a particular event.

How much data to collect will again depend upon the topic of your study. The CDA framework presented in the next section allows for a very detailed analysis so a great deal can be written about a small amount of data. For example, for a comparison of newspaper reports of the same event two articles of 200–300 words each will be sufficient. For speeches a total of 600 words should be enough. The data required for an analysis of an advertisement or a contrastive analysis of two advertisements is more difficult to quantify, but between 50 and 100 words per advertisement might suffice.

4.7.3   Analysing data

Having chosen your text or texts, you are now ready to apply the three dimensions of CDA: description, interpretation and evaluation.

First, description involves analysing one or more of the formal linguistic properties of the text:

1. Subject positioning through transitivity and modality.
2. The relational values between the subjects; that is, how pronouns and forms of address are used and the implications of such use.
3. Pragmatic analysis for example, turn-taking.
4. Negative and positive sentences that indicate a struggle between the producer of a text and its audience. This is especially evident in political texts such as speeches.

If you are comparing newspaper reports of the same event or analysing advertisements your analysis should include numbers 1 and 2 above plus the use of reported speech or metaphorical language in constructing relations between subjects. If you are analysing a speech or speeches you should include number 4 in your analysis. For spoken exchanges of any kind, number 3 would be more relevant. When transcribing your data you should follow the conventions described in Section 2.8.3.

Second, interpretation involves examining your descriptive analysis for the following discourse types (see also Figure 4.2 above):

- Contents: the type of activity going on, its topic and purpose.
- Subjects: the subjects involved.
- Relations: the relations between the subjects.
- Connections: the role of language in what is going on.

For example, if you were interested in looking at the newspaper reporting of particular political events, such as the so-called 'War on terror', you would wish to establish what particular events or processes were being reported; who was involved and the relations between them; the role of language both within the news story and in relating it to the wider public. In doing so, you would need to consider what kinds of members' resources (MR) the producer of the text has available, and the extent to which this may be matched by the MR of the typical – or any actual – reader. Assumptions about shared MR will differ according to the nature of the news being reported, so that a local political scandal will assume more shared knowledge than one concerning a far flung part of the world.

Third, evaluation requires an analysis of the discourse in terms of the institutional and social conditions of production and interpretation, and includes consideration of:

- The institutional process (e.g. law or news reporting) to which the discourse belongs and how they are determined ideologically, particularly if there is an underlying institutional ideology, such as a capitalist or socialist outlook.
- The social processes that influence the discourse (e.g. family or religious pressures), and their ideological effects, including any caused by particular ideologies relating to race, gender, class, etc.

For example, a television advertisement for a car will form part of the economic discourse in a society with an underlying capitalist ideology, though it may also involve 'characters' in a story who represent the social institution of the family and are likely to display certain ideological characteristics in relation to the ideology of the family, such as the importance of the nuclear family with two parents, or the relationship between the genders and their control over, and aspirations for material or technological goods.

Undertaking a CDA analysis involves the researcher in identifying and describing not only the linguistic features of a text, but also setting this analysis into a wider social and political context with the aim of discovering the ideological basis of the text under analysis. What makes this a critical, rather than simply a stylistic analysis is the critique of the ideologies that may be being naturalised by their presence in the background of a text's meaning.

4.7.4   Sample projects

- Critically analyse one or more recent news reports for evidence of ideology. You could concentrate on just one newspaper, television or radio report or contrast reports of a single event in two or more sources.
- Critically analyse one or more advertisements for evidence of ideology in the text.
- Critically analyse a spoken exchange between (1) a teacher and a pupil, (2) a policeman and a witness, or (3) a mother or father and a child, and explain the underlying ideologies of the exchange.
- Critically analyse a spoken exchange between (1) men and women or (2) among women or men of a similar age, for evidence of underlying ideologies.

 4.8   **Further reading**

Fairclough (1995, 2001), Wodak and Meyer (2002), Caldas-Coulthard and Coulthard (1996), Van Dijk (1997) and Toolan (2002) provide an overview of CDA, whilst Meinhof and Richardson (1994) investigate particular aspects of social life from a CDA perspective. Widdowson (2004) offers a comprehensive critique of the approach, and Wodak and Chilton (2005) chart recent developments. Chilton (2004) provides an account of political discourse and Lazar (2005) contains a collection of feminist approaches to CDA.

Bibliography

Aitchison, J. (2001) *Language Change: Progress or Decay?* (Cambridge: Cambridge University Press).

Althusser, L. (1971)' Ideology and ideological state apparatuses', in L. Althusser, *Lenin and Philosophy and other Essays* (London: New Left Books).

Austin, J. L. (1962) *How to do Things with Words* (Oxford: Oxford University Press).

Bakhtin, M. (1981) *The Dialogic Imagination* (Austin, Tex.: University of Texas Press).

Baugh, A. C. and Cable, T. (2002) *A History of the English Language*, 4th edn. (Harlow: Pearson).

Beal, J. (2006) *Language and Region* (London: Routledge).

Biber, D., Finegan, E. and Leech, G. (1999) *The Longman Grammar of Spoken and Written English* (Harlow: Pearson).

Biddulph, J. (1986) *A Short Grammar of Black Country English* (Pontypridd: Languages Information Centre).

Bonvillian, N. (1993) *Language, Culture and Communication: The Meaning of Messages* (Englewood Cliffs, NJ: Prentice-Hall).

Brontë, Charlotte (1994) *Jane Eyre* (London: Penguin).

Brown, G. and Yule, G. (1983) *Discourse Analysis* (Cambridge: Cambridge University Press).

Brown, P. and Levinson, S. (1987) *Politeness* (Cambridge: Cambridge University Press).

Burrow, J. W. (ed.) (1982) *Sir Gawain and the Green Knight* (London: Penguin).

Burton, D, (1980) *Dialogue and Discourse: A Sociolinguistic Approach to Modern Drama Dialogue and Naturally Occurring Conversation* (London: Routledge & Kegan Paul).

Caldas-Coulthard, C. R. and Coulthard, M. (1996) *Texts and Practices: Readings in Critical Discourse Analysis* (London: Routledge).

Cameron, D. (1997) 'Performing gender: young men's talk and the construction of heterosexual masculinity', in S. Johnson and U. Meinhof (eds), *Language and Masculinity* (Oxford: Blackwell), pp. 47–64.

Cameron, D. (2001) *Working With Spoken Discourse* (London: Sage).

Carrol, L. (2001) *Jabberwocky and other Poems* (London: Dover Publications).

Carter, A. (1977) *The Passion of New Eve* (London: Virago).

Carter, A. (1981) *The Majic Toyshop* (London: Virago).

Carter, R. and McCarthy, M. (1995) Grammar and the spoken language, *Applied Linguistics*, 16(2), pp. 141–58.

Carter, R. and McCarthy, M. (2006) *The Cambridge Grammar of English* (Cambridge: Cambridge University Press).

Carter, R. and Nash, W. (1990) *Seeing Through Language: A Guide to Styles of English Writing* (Oxford: Basil Blackwell).

Chambers, J. K and Trudgill, P. (1980) *Dialectology* (London: Cambridge University Press).

Chapman, S. (2006) *Thinking about Language: Theories of English* (Basingstoke: Palgrave).

Cheshire, J. (ed.) (1991) *English Around the World: Sociolinguistic Perspectives* (Cambridge: Cambridge University Press).

Cheshire, J. (1993) *Real English: The Grammar of Written Dialects in the British Isles* (Harlow: Longman).

Chilton, P. (2004) *Analysing Political Discourse: Theory and Practice* (London: Routledge).

Chouliaraki L. and Fairclough, N. (1999) *Discourse in Late Modernity: Rethinking Critical Discourse Analysis* (Edinburgh: Edinburgh University Press).

Clark, U. (2001) *War Words: Language, History and the Disciplining of English* (Oxford: Elsevier).

Clark, U. (2004) 'The Phonology of the English West Midlands', in B. Kortmann and E. W. Schneider (eds), *A Handbook of Varieties of English*, vol. 1 (Berlin and New York: Mouton de Gruyter), pp. 260–88.

Clark, U. with McRae, J. (2004) 'Stylistics' in A. Davies and C. Elder (eds), *A Handbook of Applied Linguistics* (Oxford: Blackwell).

Clark, U. and Zyngier, S. (1998) 'Women beware Women: Detective Fiction and Critical Discourse Stylistics', in *Language and Literature*, 7(2), pp. 141–58.

Coates, J. (1996) *Women Talk* (Oxford: Basil Blackwell).

Coates, J. (1997) 'One-at-a-time: the organization of men's talk', in S. Johnson and U. H. Meinhof (eds), *Language and Masculinity* (Oxford: Blackwell).

Coates, J. and Cameron, D. (eds) (1986) *Women in Their Speech Communities* (Harlow: Longman).

Cook, G. (1989) *Discourse* (Oxford: Oxford University Press).

Cooper, J. (2003) *The Man Who Made Husbands Jealous* (London: Corgi Books).

Coulthard, M. (1977) *An Introduction to Discourse Analysis* (London: Longman).

Coulthard, M. and Montgomery, M. (eds) (1981) *Studies in Discourse Analysis* (London: Routledge & Kegan Paul).

Crowley, T. (1991) *Proper English: Readings in Language, History and Cultural Identity* (London: Routledge).

Crowley, T. (1996) *Language in History: Theories and Texts* (London: Routledge).

Cruse, A. (2000) *Meaning in Language: An Introduction to Semantics and Pragmatics* (Oxford: Oxford University Press).

Crystal, D. (1995) *The Cambridge Encyclopedia of English Language* (Cambridge: Cambridge University Press).

Culpeper, J. (2001) *Language and Characterisation* (London: Longman).

Cutting, J. (2002) *Pragmatics and Discourse: A Resource Book for Students* (London: Routledge).

Davies, A. and Elder, C. (2004) *A Handbook of Applied Linguistics* (Oxford: Blackwell).

Dickens, C. (1994) *Little Dorrit* (Harmondsworth: Penguin).

Dickens, C. (2000) *American Notes* (London: Penguin).

Dillard, J. L. (1976) *American Talk* (New York: Random House).

Eckert, P. (1988) 'Adolescent social structure and the spread of linguistic change', *Language in Society*, 17, pp. 183–207.

Eckert, P. (1989) *Jocks and Burnouts: Social Categories and Identity in the High School* (New York and London: Teachers College Press).

Edelsky, C. (1981) 'Who's got the floor?', *Language and Society*, 10, pp. 383–421.

Eliot, T. S (2002) *Collected Poems: 1909–62* (London: Faber & Faber).

Eliot, G. (2002) *Mill on the Floss* (London: Penguin).

Emmott, C. (1997) *Narrative Comprehension: A Discourse Perspective* (Oxford: Oxford University Press).

Fairclough, N. (1995) *Critical Discourse Analysis* (London: Longman).

Fairclough, N. (2001) *Language and Power* (Harlow: Longman).

Fairclough, N. and Wodak, R. (1997) 'Critical Discourse Analysis', in T. van Dijk (ed.), *Discourse as Social Interaction* (London: Sage).

Fielding, H. (1996) *Bridget Jones's Diary* (London: Picador).

Fielding, H. (1998) *Tom Jones* (London: Orion).

Firth, J. R. (1957) *Papers in Linguistics 1934–1951* (London: Oxford University Press).

Fitzgerald, F. Scott (2000) *The Great Gatsby* (Harmondsworth: Penguin).

Fludernik, M. (1993) *The Fictions of Language and the Language of Fiction: The Linguistic Representation of Speech and Consciousness* (London: Routledge).

Fornas, J. (1995) *Cultural Theory and Late Modernity* (London: Sage).

Foucault, M. (1972) *The Archaeology of Knowledge* (London: Tavistock).

Fowler, R. (1991) *Language in the News* (London: Routledge).

Fowler, R. (1996) *Linguistic Criticism* (Oxford: Oxford University Press).

Fowler, R., Hodge, R., Kress, G. and Trew, T. (1979) *Language and Control* (London: Routledge).

Fowles, J. (2004) *The French Lieutenant's Woman* (London: Vintage).

Francis, G. and Hunston, S. (1992) 'Analysing everyday conversation', in M. Coutlhard (ed.), *Advances in Spoken Discourse Analysis* (London: Routledge).

Garfinkel, H. (1967) *Studies in Ethnomethodology* (Englewood Cliff, NJ: Prentice-Hall).

Gavins, J. (2006) *Text World Theory: An Introduction* (Edinburgh: Edinburgh University Press).

Golding, W. (1955) *The Inheritors* (London: Faber).

Grice, P. (1975) 'Logic and Conversation', in P. Cole and J. Morgan (eds), *Speech Acts (Syntax and Semantics Vol 3)* (New York: Academic Press), pp. 113–28.

Gumperz, J. J. (ed.) (1982a) *Language and Social Identity* (Cambridge: Cambridge University Press).

Gumperz, J. J. (ed) (1982b) *Discourse Strategies* (Cambridge: Cambridge University Press).

Gumperz, J. J. and Hymes, D. (eds) (1986) *Directions in Sociolinguistics: The Ethnography of Communication* (New York and Oxford: Basil Blackwell).

Gutterson, D. (2003) *Our Lady of the Forest* (London: Bloomsbury).

Halliday, M. A. K. (1971) 'Linguistic Structures and Literary Style: An Inquiry into the Language of William Golding's *The Inheritors*', in S. Chatman (ed.), *Literary Style: A Symposium* (New York and London: Oxford University Press), pp. 332–4.

Halliday, M. A. K. (1973) *Explorations in the Function of Language* (London: Edward Arnold).

Halliday, M. A. K. (1978) *Language as a Social Semiotic: The Social Interpretation of Language and Meaning* (London: Edward Arnold).

Harris, T. (2000) *Hannibal* (London: Arrow).

Haugen, E. (1972) 'Dialect, Language, Nation', in J. B. Pride and J. Holmes (eds), *Sociolinguistics* (Harmondsworth: Penguin) pp. 97–111.

Hawley, P. (2002) 'What is said', *Journal of Pragmatics*, 34 pp. 969–91.

Hewings, A. and Hewings, M. (2005) *Grammar and Context* (London: Routledge).

Hillman, M. V. (1961) *The Pearl* (Notre Dame and London: University of Notre Dame Press).

Hobsbaum, P. (1996) *Metre, Rhythm and Verse Form* (London and New York: Routledge).

Hodge, R. and Kress, G. (1993) *Language as Ideology* (London: Routledge).

Hoey, M. (1983) *On the Surface of Discourse* (London: Allen & Unwin).

Hoey, M. (1996) 'A Clause-Relational Analysis of Selected Diary Entries: Contrast and Compatability in the Definitions of "Man" and "Woman"', in R. Caldas-Coulthard and M. Coulthard (eds), *Texts and Practices: Readings in Critical Discourse Analysis* (London: Routledge).

Hoey, M. (2005) *Lexical Priming: A New Theory of Words and Language* (London; Routledge).

Honey, J. (1989) *Does Accent Matter?* (London: Faber & Faber).

Hughes, A., Trudgill, P. and Watt, D. (2005) *English Accents and Dialects: An Introduction to Social and Regional Varieties of English in the British Isles* (London: Hodder Arnold).

Hutchby, I. and Wooffitt, R. (1998) *Conversation Analysis: An Introduction* (Cambridge: Polity Press).

Hymes, D. (1972) 'Models of the Interaction of Language and Social Life', in J. Gumperz and D. Hymes, *Foundations in Sociolinguistics* (Philadelphia, PA: University of Pennsylvania Press).

Jakobson, R. (1960) 'Linguistics and Poetics', in T. Seboek (ed.) *Style in Language* (Cambridge, Mass: Massachusetts Institute of Technology Press).

Jeffries, L. (1993) *The Language of Twentieth Century Poetry* (Basingstoke: Palgrave).

Jeffries, L. (1998) *Meaning in English* (Basingstoke: Palgrave Macmillan).

Jeffries, L. (2006) *Discovering Language: Describing English* (Basingstoke: Palgrave).

Johnson, S. (1755) *A Dictionary of the English Language* (London).

Joyce, J. (1992) *Ulysses* (Harmondsworth: Penguin).

Joyce, P. (1991) 'The People's English: Language and Class in Nineteenth Century England' in P. Burke and R. Porter (eds), *Language, Self and Society* (Cambridge: Polity Press), pp. 154–91.

Kerswill, P. (2004) 'Social dialectology/Sozialdialektologie', in K. Mattheier, U. Ammon and P. Trudgill (eds), *Sociolinguistics/Soziolinguistik. An international handbook of the science of language and society*, 2nd edn., vol 1. (Berlin: De Gruyter), pp. 22–33.

Kerswill, P. and Williams, A. (2000) 'Creating a new town koine: children and language change in Milton Keynes', *Language in Society*, 29 (1), pp. 65–115.

Kerswill, P. and Williams, A. (2002) 'Dialect Recognition and Speech Community Focusing in New and Old Towns in England: The Effects of Dialect Levelling, Demography and Social Networks', in D. Long and D. S. Preston (eds), *A Handbook of Perceptual Dialectology*, vol 2 (Amsterdam: Benjamins).

Kiefer, F. (1979) 'What do the conversational maxims explain?', in *Linguisticae Investigationes*, 3 (1), pp. 57–74.

Labov, W. (1966) *The Social Stratification of English in New York City* (Washington, DC: Center for Applied Linguistics).

Labov, W. (1972a) *Sociolinguistic Patterns* (Philadelphia: University of Pennsylvania Press).

Labov, W. (1972b) 'The study of language in its social context', in P. P. Giglioli (ed.), *Language and Social Context* (Harmondsworth: Penguin), pp. 283–307.

Labov, W. (ed.) (1978) *Sociolinguistic Patterns* (Oxford: Blackwell).

Labov, W. (1979) 'The logic of non-standard English', in *Language in the Inner City: Studies in the Black English Vernacular* (Philadelphia: University of Pennsylvania Press).

Labov, W. (1997) 'Sociolinguistic Patterns', in Christina Bratt Paulston and G. Richard Tucker (eds), *The Early Days of Sociolinguistics: Memories and Reflections*, 147–50. Publications in Sociolinguistics, 2 (Dallas: Summer Institute of Linguistics).

Labov, W. and Fanshel, D. (1977) *Therapeutic Discourse* (New York: Academic Press).

Lakoff, G. and Johnson, M. (1980) *Metaphor We Live By* (Chigago, Ill: University of Chicago Press).

Lawrence, D. H. (1996) *Women in Love* (London: Penguin).

Lawrence, D. H. (2006) *Lady Chatterley's Lover* (London: Penguin).

Lazar, M. (ed.) (2005) *Feminist Critical Discourse Analysis: Gender, Power and ideology in Discourse* (London: Palgrave).

Leech, G. (1983) *Principles of Pragmatics* (London: Longman).

Leech, G. N. and Short, M. H. (1981) *Style in Fiction* (London: Longman).

Leech, G. N. and Thomas, J. (1990) 'Language, Meaning and Context: Pragmatics', in N. E. Collinge (ed.), *An Encyclopedia of Language* (London: Routledge), pp. 173–206.

Leith, D. (1997) *A Social History of English* (London: Routledge & Kegan Paul).

Levinson, S. (1983) *Pragmatics* (Cambridge: Cambridge University Press).

Lodge, D. (1987) *Nice Work* (London: Penguin).

Louw, B. (1993) 'Irony in the Text or Insecurity in the Writer? The Diagnostic Potential of Semantic Prosodies', in M. Baker, G. Francis and E. Tognini-Bonnelli (eds), *Text and Technology* (Philadelphia/Amsterdam: John Betjamins).

Louw, B. (2006) 'Collocation as the Determinant in Verbal Art', in Donna R. Miller and Monica Turci (eds), *Language and Verbal Art Revisited* (London: Equinox).

Lucy, J. A. (1992) *Language Diversity and Thought: A Reformulation of the Linguistic Relativity Hypothesis* (Cambridge: Cambridge University Press).

Marx, K. (1976) *Capital*, vol 1 (Harmondsworth: Penguin).

McRae, J. (1997) *Literature with a Small 'l'* (London: Macmillan/Prentice-Hall).

Meinhof, Ulrike and Richardson, Kay (1994) *Text, Discourse and Context: Representations of Poverty in Britain* (London and New York; Longman).

Mencken, H. L. (1921) *The American Language: An Inquiry into the Development of English in the United States)*, 2nd edn (London).

Mills, S. (1995) *Feminist Stylistics* (London: Routledge).

Milroy, J. (1992) *Linguistic Variation and Change* (Oxford: Blackwell).

Milroy, J. and Milroy, L. (1993) *Real English: The Grammar of English Dialects in the British Isles* (London: Longman).

Milroy, L. (1987) *Observing and Analysing Natural Language: A Critical Account of Sociolinguistic Method* (Oxford: Blackwell).

Milroy, L. and Gordon, M. (2003) *Sociolinguistics: Method and Interpretation* (Oxford: Blackwell.).

Montgomery, M. (1995) *An Introduction to Language and Society* (London and New York: Routledge).

Muller, M. (1862) *Lectures on the Science of Language* (London: Royal Institute of Great Britain).

Murray, J. (1888–1928) *A New English Dictionary Based on Historic Principles* (Oxford: Clarendon Press).

Ochs, E., Schegloff, E. A. and Thompson, S. A. (1996) *Interaction and Grammar* (Cambridge: Cambridge University Press).

O'Halloran, K. (2003) *Critical Discourse Analysis and Language Cognition* (Edinburgh: Edinburgh University Press).

Orton, H. (1962) *Survey of English Dialects: Introduction* (Leeds: Arnold).

Pope, A. and Churton Collins, J. (1896) *Essays on Criticism* (London: Macmillan).

Poulantzas, N. (1976) *Classes in Contemporary Capitalism* (London: New Left Books).

Pratt, M. L. (1977) *Towards a Speech Act Theory of Literary Discourse* (Bloomington, IA: Indiana University Press).

Richards, I. A. (1925) *Principles of Literary Criticism* (London: Kegan Paul).

Roberts, C., Davies, E. and Jupp, T. (1992) *Language and Discrimination: A Study of Multiethnic Workplaces* (London: Longman).

Sacks, H., Schegloff, E. and Jefferson, G. (1974) 'A simplest systematics for the organization of turn-taking in conversation', *Language*, 50 (4), pp. 696–735.

Salinger, J. D. (1994) *The Catcher in the Rye* (Harmondsworth: Penguin).

Sapir, E. (1921) *Language: An Introduction to the Study of Speech* (New York: Harcourt, Brace and World).

Saussure, F. de (1916) *Course in General Linguistics* (London: Duckworth).

Schank, R. C. and Abselon, R. P. (1977) *Scripts, Plans, Goals and Understanding* (Hillside, NJ: Lawrence Erlbaum).

Schiffrin, D. (1994) *Approaches to Discourse* (Oxford: Blackwell).

Schmidt, N. (2002) *An Introduction to Applied Linguistics* (London: Edward Arnold).

Schneider, W., Burridge, K., Kortmann, B., Mesthrie, R. and Upton, C. (2004) *A Handbook of Varieties of English Vol. 1* (Berlin and New York: Mouton de Gruyter).

Searle, J. R. (1969) *Speech Acts: An Essay in the Philosophy of Language* (Cambridge: Cambridge University Press).

Sebold, A. (2003) *Lovely Bones* (London: Picador).

Semino, E. and Culpeper, J. (eds) (2002) *Cognitive Stylistics: Language and Cognition in Text Analysis* (Amsterdam: John Benjamins).

Semino, E. and Short, M. (2004) *Corpus Stylistics: Speech, Writing and Thought Presentation in a Corpus of English Narratives* (London: Routledge).

Shaffer, P. (1975) *Equus* (London: Penguin).

Shaw, S. (2000) 'Language, gender and floor appointment in political debates', *Discourse and Society*, 11 (3), pp. 401–18.

Short, M. (ed.) (1988) *Reading, Analysing and Teaching Literature* (Harlow: Longman).

Short, M. (1995) 'Discourse Analysis and Power Relationships in *The Ebony Tower* by John Fowles' in P. Verdonk and J.-J. Weber (eds), *Twentieth Century Fiction: From Text to Context* (London: Routledge), pp. 45–62.

Short, M. (1996) *Exploring the Language of Poems, Plays and Prose* (London: Addison Wesley Longman).

Simpson, D. (1986) *The Politics of American English 1776–1850* (New York and London: Oxford University Press).

Simpson, P. (1993) *Language, Ideology and Point of View* (London: Routledge).

Simpson, P. (2004) *Stylistics* (London: Routledge).

Sinclair, J. M. (1988) 'Collocation: A Progress Report' in R. Steele and T. Threadgold (eds) *Language Topics* (Amsterdam: John Benjamins), pp. 319–31.

Sinclair, J. M. (2004) *Trust the Text: Language, Corpus and Discourse* (London: Routledge).

Sinclair, J. and Coulthard, M. (1975) *Towards an Analysis of Discourse: The English Used by Teachers and Pupils* (London: Oxford University Press).

Smith, O. (1984) *The Politics of Language* (Oxford: Clarendon Press).

Spencer-Oatey, H. and Wenying, J. (2003) 'Explaining cross-cultural pragmatic findings: moving from politeness maxims to sociopragmatic interactional principles', *Journal of Pragmatics*, 35, pp. 1633–50.

Sperber, D. and Wilson, D. (1995) *Relevance: Communication and Cognition* (Oxford: Blackwell).

Stockwell, P. (2002) *Cognitive Poetics: An Introduction* (London: Routledge).

Stubbs, M. (1986) *Educational Linguistics* (London: Blackwell).

Swift, J. (1712) *Proposal for Correcting, Improving, and Ascertaining the English Tongue* (www.books.mirror.org/gb.swift.html).

Tatalovich, R. (1995) *Nativism Reborn? The Official English Language Movement and the American States* (Lexington, Ken.: University of Kentucky Press).

Thomas, J. (1995) *Meaning in Interaction: An Introduction to Pragmatics* (London: Longman).

Toolan, M. (1997) 'What is Critical Discourse Analysis and Why are People Saying Such Terrible Things About It?', *Language and Literature*, 6 (2), pp. 83–103.

Toolan, M. (1998) *Language in Literature: An Introduction to Stylistics* (London: Hodder).

Toolan, M. (2001) *Narrative: A Critical Linguistic Introduction* (London: Routledge).

Toolan, M. (2002) *Critical Discourse Analysis: Critical Concepts* (London: Routledge).

Trew, T. (1979) 'Theory and Ideology at Work', in R. Fowler, B. Hodge, G. Kress and T. Trew (eds) *Language and Control* (London: Routledge & Kegan Paul), pp. 94–116.

Trudgill, P. (1974) *The Social Differentiation of English in Norwich* (Cambridge: Cambridge University Press).

Trudgill, P. (ed.) (1978) *Sociolinguistic Patterns in British English* (London: Edward Arnold).

Trudgill, P. (1983) *On Dialect: Social and Geographical Perspectives* (Oxford; Blackwell).

Trudgill, P. (1999) 'Standard English: What it isn't', in T. Bex and R. J. Watts (eds), *Standard English: The Widening Debate* (London: Routledge).

Trudgill, P. (2002) *Sociolinguistic Variation and Change* (Edinburgh: Edinburgh University Press).

Twain, M. (1986) *The Adventures of Tom Sawyer* (London: Penguin).

Van Dijk, T. (ed.) (1997) *Discourse as Structure and Process. Discourse Studies: A Multidisciplinary Introduction*, vol 1 (London: Sage).

Van Dijk, T. (2001) 'Critical Discourse Analysis', in D. Shiffrin, D. Tannen and H. Hamilton (eds), *The Handbook of Discourse Analysis* (Oxford: Blackwell).

Van Leeuwen, T. (1996) 'The Representation of Social Actors', in C. R. Caldas-Coulthard and M. Coulthard (eds), *Texts and Practices: Readings in Critical Discourse Analysis* (London: Routledge), pp. 32–70.

Verdonk, P. and Weber, J.-J. (eds) (1995) *Twentieth Century Fiction: From Text to Context* (London: Longman).

Wardhaugh, R. (2006) *An Introduction to Sociolinguistics* (Oxford: Blackwell).

Wales, K. (2001) *A Dictionary of Stylistics*, 2nd edn (Harlow: Longman).

Wareing, S. and Thornborrow, J. (1998) *Patterns of Language: Stylistics for Students of Language and Literature* (London: Routledge).

Watson, G. and Zyngier, S. (eds) (2006) *Literary Education: A Critical Reader* (Basingstoke: Palgrave).

Watts, R. J. (2003) *Politeness* (Cambridge: Cambridge University Press).

Wells, J. C. (1999) *Accents of English* (Cambridge: Cambridge University Press).

Welsh, I. (1993) *Trainspotting* (London: Vintage).

Werth, P. (1999) *Text Worlds: Representing Conceptual Space in Discourse* (Harlow: Longman).

West, C. and Garcia, A. (1988) 'Conversational Shift-work: A Study of Topical Transitions', *Social Problems*, Y2h 35 (5), pp. 551–75.

Whorf, B. L. (1956) 'The Relation of Habitual Thought and Behaviour to Language', in J. B. Carroll (ed.), *Language, Thought and Reality* (Cambridge, Mass.: MIT Press).

Widdowson, H. G. (1995) 'Discourse Analysis: A Critical View', in *Language and Literature*, 43, pp 157–72.

Widdowson, H. G. (2004) *Text, Context, Pretext: Critical Issues in Discourse Analysis* (Oxford: Blackwell).

Widdowson, J. D. A. and Upton, C. (2006) *An Atlas of English Dialects* (London: Routledge).

Whitman, W. (2005) *Leaves of Grass* (London: Penguin).

Wittgenstein, L. (1951) *Philosophical Investigations* (Oxford: Blackwell).

Wodak, R. and Chilton, P. (eds) (2005) *A New Agenda in (Critical) Discourse Analysis* (Amsterdam: Benjamins).

Wodak, R. and Meyer, M. (eds) (2002) *Methods of Critical Discourse Analysis* (London: Sage).

Wolfram, W. and Schilling-Estes, N. (2006) *American English*, 2nd edn (Oxford: Blackwell).

Woods A., Fletcher, P., Hughes, A. and Anderson, S. R. (1986) *Statistics in Language Studies* (Cambridge: Cambridge University Press).

Woolf, V. (1978) *Night and Day* (London: Granada).

Woolf, V. (1999) *Mrs Dalloway* (London: Penguin).

Wright, L. and Hope, J. (1996) *Stylistics: A Practical Coursebook* (London: Routledge).

Wyld, H. C. (1927) *A Short History of English with a Bibliography of Recent Books on the Subject*, 3rd edn (London: Murray).

Index